MW00975394

ADVENTURE ATHLETES

Cyclists

How the world's most daring riders train and compete

Steven Boga

STACKPOLE
BOOKS

Copyright © 1992 by Stackpole Books

Published by
STACKPOLE BOOKS
Cameron and Kelker Streets
P.O. Box 1831
Harrisburg, PA 17105

Printed in the United States of America

Cover design by Caroline Miller

First Edition

10 9 8 7 6 5 4 3 2 1

Library of Congress Cataloging-in-Publication Data

Boga, Steve, 1947–
   Cyclists : how the world's most daring riders train and compete /
Steve Boga. – 1st ed.
     p.   cm. – (Adventure Athletes)
   Includes bibliographical references (p.).
   ISBN 0-8117-2413-1 : $14.95
   1. Cyclists – Biography I. Title. II. Series.
GV1051.A1B64   1992
796.6'2'0922 – dc20
   [B]   91-40307
                                                   CIP

For Madeleine and Karen

When faced with two alternate
courses of action, each of equal merit,
choose the bolder course.
——Field Marshal Lord Slim

Best wishes!

Bogo

Steve

Contents

Preface

I only use my body to carry my brain.

——Thomas Edison

Why do we play the sports we do? For me, as for most kids, it began in school. It was there that I learned to play the Big Three — baseball, basketball, and football. As a child, I harbored the archetypal dream of playing major league baseball; later, as a teen mugged by puberty, I had to abandon that dream. Yet I remained devoted to team sports. As an adult, I continued to play on teams. I was a good teammate — solicitous, supportive, quick with the congratulatory handshake and pat on the back.

Then one day it was all over. Realizing that I was no longer capable of "taking one for the team," I began to run and ride my bike and intensify my backpacking and mountain scrambling. My passion became individual, often solitary, pursuits. After half a lifetime of being a teammate, it was now gratifying and fun to rely completely on myself.

I wasn't the only one enjoying self-reliance. The 1970s and 1980s saw an explosion of interest in individual sports like biking, running, hang gliding, rock climbing, and triathloning. The baby boomers, it seemed, were drawn to calculated risks, perhaps as a counter to the decreasing risks in our society. Though I personally had not become involved in most adventure sports, I maintained an undiminished admiration for those who did.

Then one rainy Sunday afternoon, while viewing the movie *Heart Like a Wheel*, the story of world-champion drag racer Shirley "Cha Cha" Muldowney, my involvement with adventure sports deepened.

As I watched Muldowny's car explode from the starting line in one of the fastest sports on earth, two questions gnawed at me: Why does someone go into such an offbeat sport, and what skills are needed to become great?

It occurred to me that others, too, might be curious about the answers to those questions. The idea became a project. Armed with little more than those two questions, I set out to interview a world-class athlete in an unsung sport and, well, sing out about him or her. But I wanted to explore more than just the risk of losing; I required, vicariously, the risk of dying, or at least of suffering a serious injury.

Cyclists is the first book in the Adventure Athletes series. Although many people don't regard bicycling as a risk sport, it's at the top of almost every demographic injury list. Riders contend with such hazards as unforgiving road surfaces, cars, and other cyclists. Mountain bikers face roots and rocks, and endurance riders add fatigue, dehydration, hyperthermia, and hallucinations to their list of dangers.

On the other hand, one of bicycling's greatest appeals is that it offers something for nearly everyone. It need not be a sport at all. It can be a languid activity – the two-wheeled equivalent of a stroll in the park or a kids' game of follow the leader. The bike itself is an efficient, relatively inexpensive, environment-friendly form of transportation. Tooling down the open road or along an abandoned trail with the wind whistling around your helmet offers a freedom rare in today's world. Bicycling's wide appeal is irrespective of gender, class, age, or conviviality and fitness levels; there are now more than ninety million bikes in the United States.

However, it is not the masses but the elite athletes who compel. For them bicycling demands maximum performance from muscles, heart and lungs. Studies have shown big-time endurance cyclists to be the fittest of all athletes. The cyclists in this volume are not only fit, they are pioneers, transcenders of limits; they have taken their sport countless revolutions further than most competitive cyclists. From Martha Kennedy, who biked in the wintry wilds of Alaska, to Greg LeMond, whose stage races require the cardiovascular system of Robogoat, these bikers pedal not only long and hard but perilously close to the edge.

For the men and women who push the limits, the question is not so much "Why?" as "Why not?" They see with their own special vision the physical and psychological benefits derived from their sports and can only wonder why everyone isn't out racing ships to Alaska or pursuing the land-speed record. One reason, of course, is that such activities run counter to modern society's drive to eliminate risk from nearly every facet of life. The element of rebellion inherent in risk sports is clearly one of their great attractions.

In his book *The Ultimate Athlete* (New York: Viking, 1975), George Leonard discusses the research of Dr. Sol Roy Rosenthal of the University of Illinois. Convinced of the salutary effects of calculated risk, Rosenthal divides sports into two camps: RE (risk exercise), such as skiing, climbing, and many types of bicycling, and non-RE, such as tennis and golf. His research has shown that RE sports tend to exhilarate and non-RE sports tend to exhaust. There seem to be at least two reasons for this: First, tennis players and golfers are often maniacal about winning, but adventure athletes are able to enjoy their sports for the sports' sake. Second, the tension created where great skill meets risky adventure produces the healthiest kind of focus. According to Rosenthal, regular participation in RE sports makes men and women more productive, efficient, and creative. It even enhances their sex lives.

I have interviewed more than twenty world-class adventure types, many of them bicyclists. It is a rare privilege to be allowed into the lives of people who have scaled the dizzying heights of athletic success. Although my questions have remained essentially the same over the years, each athlete's story has been different.

Nevertheless, I am frequently asked what common attributes can be found among the truly excellent. It's a fair question with another lurking just beneath the surface: "Is there something – one thing, preferably a simple thing – that *I* can do to achieve excellence?"

To the unspoken question I say no; there is no single characteristic that assures excellence. No matter how easy Greg LeMond may make it look, no matter how steady and relaxed Elaine Mariolle may appear pedaling coast to coast, their successes are due to a complex mix of many intangibles. Mostly, though, it's a head-on collision of talent and dedication.

Besides those necessities, successful adventure athletes share another notable quality: a remarkable kind of physical genius I call "body smarts." It can be seen in the way they move, with their exquisite balance and grace. Even bicyclists, who participate in one of the few land sports not dependent on running, have a unique lightness to their step. Though I ran no tests, I'm sure all the athletes are impressive kinesthetic learners with immense muscle memories. I believe athletes like Dave Scott and Eric Heiden are to the body as Einstein and Edison were to the mind. And college-educated Scott and Heiden are not just dumb jocks, either. They're intelligent, reflective types who are no doubt better with an idea than Einstein and Edison were with a bicycle.

Still, the question persists: Why be an extremist? Why do these athletes put it all on the line when it's so much easier not to? Because they have to, because they want to, because they love to. Perhaps it's just to get high. Most adventurers admit that physical risk can produce an intense rush of euphoria. A climber once described his sport in a manner that applies just as well to bicycling or bungee jumping: "You've roared and cried and grunted your way up that impossible wall, then that last little scramble gets you to the top and you stand there yodeling."

Seems to me that we could all use a little more yodeling in our lives.

Acknowledgments

I am especially grateful for the steady aid, counsel, friendship, and editorial advice of Bruce Maxwell; also for editorial help in the resource section, especially the glossary, from Tom Makris; for the map work of Jeff Doran and Scott Geiger; for historical photos from the Seaver Center for Western History Research, Natural History Museum of LA County; for the generous photo assistance of Jan Cavecche of California Bicyclist, Doug Gaynor of UNIPRO, Bill Glazier of the American Lung Association; for the quality work of photographers Dave Nelson, Larry Lebiecki, Budd Symes, Barbara Hanscome, and Carol Shanks; for the incalculable help of my wife, Karen, in all sorts of areas; and most of all for the cyclists themselves.

PROFILES

JOHN HOWARD

Pedal Pusher

It is not death that a man
should fear, but he should
fear never beginning to
live.

—Marcus Aurelius

John Howard recalls exactly when and where the seeds of his competitive cycling career were first planted: "In the fifth grade in Springfield, Missouri, where I grew up—I was the dodge ball champ." He is sitting at the dining room table in his southern California home, looking lean and fit and tough. With his receding curls of dirty-blond, flyaway hair and his coarse, weathered skin, he looks every bit as old as his forty-two years. "It was then I learned that I had not just athletic ability but also the will to win."

Howard's comfortable two-story townhouse, twenty-five miles north of San Diego, is a monument to a man with not only the will but the talent to win. It is the home of a bicycle magnate. The dining room walls are festooned with dozens of plaques and awards, most the result of first-place cycling finishes. The garage is a clutter of bicycles, perhaps a dozen, most of them expensive, state-of-the-art models that were designed by or for Howard himself. In the living room on an exercise stand sits the *Outlaw*, a sleek black racing bike that is Howard's latest design achievement.

He goes to the bike and looks upon it fondly, like a painter regarding his chef-d'oeuvre. "This is the culmination of some real technological achievements," he says proudly. "We're the first to use a drop-head tube. See how it slopes down in front." Indeed, the front tire appears tiny, almost fragile. "A twenty-seven-inch tire in the rear, a twenty-

John Howard celebrates his victory in the 1971 Pan American Games 200-kilometer individual road race. Howard's father, once skeptical of bicycling, rushes into the street to congratulate his son. (Courtesy of John Howard)

four-inch in the front," he points out. "Air resistance is the single most detrimental thing in cycling; eliminate air resistance and you'll go faster."

Since he was a kid growing up in the Ozarks, John Howard has wanted to go faster, and further, than anybody. He received a bike in the first grade, but it was a clunker, a big heavy three-gear Schwinn that was built for neither speed nor distance. When John and his brother were in junior high, they started their own business (landscaping in good weather, selling firewood in bad), then poured their first profits into a pair of the new ten-speed touring bikes that had hit the market.

Although Howard continued to run track—the mile—and play football and baseball, his love affair with the bicycle had begun. "Springfield in the fifties was right out of a Norman Rockwell painting," he says. "In high school, riding my bicycle everywhere instead of driving a pickup truck got me branded a weirdo." He smiles. "I never minded that too much. I've always kind of thrived on it. I like playing the crazy."

It wasn't only Howard's peers who looked askance at his obsession with pedaling. His track coach ranted at him for—what else?—riding

John Howard's three power foods for setting an endurance cycling record

1. Power bars
2. "Exceed" – an energy drink
3. Chinese herbs – "Sold as 'Elan Herbal Energy,' these herbs keep you awake, and just as important, they maintain your energy at a steady level. They were used by the Sansu warriors before they went into battle twenty-five hundred years ago."

Howard plans to maintain this diet when he attempts to aqua-cycle two hundred miles across the Bermuda Triangle in the summer of 1991.

---

his bicycle. "Coach thought I was riding my bike too much, so he gave me a choice: biking or running the mile. I chose biking."

Then one day he quit football – just walked off the field during practice, got on his bicycle, and rode off, never to return. He was off the team, and his father was angry. A former football player himself, his father lived vicariously through John and his athletic endeavors. He wanted a football player, not a kid on a bike.

"Looking back," says John, "I realize that what he really wanted was success. When he saw that I was a success in bicycling, he became – and still is – my biggest fan."

Upon graduation from high school in 1966, Howard set his sights on the 1968 Olympics in Mexico City. He began to train hard, riding 400 to 500 miles a week, exploring the frontiers of his mental and physical capabilities. "I made cycling a total commitment," he says. In his first competition – a 102-mile road race – he finished second. Commitment approached obsession.

During the summer of 1968 Howard left home and traveled to southern California for the Olympic cycling qualifiers. In order to make the team, a rider had to finish in the top four in either of two one-hundred-plus-mile road races. In the first race, a twenty-year-old, inexperienced John Howard finished back in the pack, out of the glory.

In the second race, a still young but no longer inexperienced Howard came from behind to finish second and make the team.

Two days later he won the U.S. Cycling Federation National Championship.

Thus began Howard's reign as America's number-one cyclist. For the next decade he dominated the sport as no American has before or since: participating in three Olympics; winning countless races, including seven national championships; winning – as no other American has ever done – a gold medal in individual cycling at the Pan Am games.

In 1979 he was selected Competitive Cycling's Rider of the Decade. As the senior member and number-one rider on the U.S. Olympic team, he was in top form. He seemed to have it all – but still he wasn't satisfied. There were the losses, of course, particularly the disappointing performances in the Olympics (as the team's top rider, he is quick to explain, he had to ride both the road race and the team trials and consequently was unable to concentrate fully on either). But it was more than that.

Then one day it struck him: It was the whole "team" thing all over again. As a kid, he'd rejected football and baseball because they were group sports, requiring the support and cooperation of others. He'd left all that to be on his own in the supposedly solitary sport of cycling. But as a member of the U.S. Olympic team, he was still expected to be a team player.

Being a team player didn't come naturally. He recalled one time in particular, in the world championships in England, when the U.S. team was composed of Howard, a second rider who was nearly his equal, and two who were definitely slower. Although the American team started eight minutes ahead of the Soviets, Howard knew they couldn't hold it. Eventually the two weaker riders began to lag, and the American team steadily lost time to the Soviets. But the team members, drafting off each other, stayed together. When the Soviets went by in their snappy red uniforms, their chains singing in perfect harmony, it occurred to Howard that they were his equals. "Sure, I wanted the U.S. team to do well, but I also wanted to join that Russian team. With them I could've ridden at my full potential."

Howard's innate lack of esprit de corps did not go unnoticed. It was no doubt a factor when the U.S. cycling coach kicked him off the team. "I pointed out that I was his best rider," Howard says. "But he told me he was going with a younger team."

So Howard was once again "off the team." His feelings were hurt, but he consoled himself with the words his father often spoke: "Eventually you outgrow everything."

That was fine as far as it went. But what of the competitive urges that still seethed within him? His marriage had gone sour, which seemed to make him all the more fiery. A nine-to-five job was unthinkable. He needed more – damn it, he needed adventure! Clearly, it was going to take extraordinary mortar to fill the gaps of his life.

Then *Sports Illustrated* ran an article about a new sport: the Hawaiian Ironman Triathlon – a grueling combination of a 2.4-mile swim, a 110-mile bike ride, and a 26.2-mile run. When Howard had finished reading the article, he was a triathlete.

"I just decided to do it," he says. "Without knowing anything about it, I was sure I could take an hour off the winning time."

To his weekly four hundred miles of cycling, he added sixty to eighty miles of running. His training routine broadened into a holistic, multisport regimen that eventually included calisthenics, mountain biking, swimming, running, kayaking, weight lifting, and backpacking. He began to study sports psychology, physiology, yoga, and deep breathing for pain control.

Three weeks after starting, he completed a respectable 3:10 marathon but developed shin splints and stress fractures. So he turned to swimming, which had never been more than an occasional activity for him. "I put some time in the pool," he says, "but I didn't bother to get a coach. As a result, I was just flogging the water, reinforcing my bad form. I have never really connected with what it takes to be a good swimmer."

Nevertheless, in the next five years Howard completed thirty triathlons, including the Hawaiian Ironman four times. He won it in 1981 and finished in the top ten in 1980 and 1984. In 1982, however, someone dumped thousands of tacks on the road, and he went down during the bike phase with two flat tires.

Despite his triathlon victories and consistent top-ten finishes, Howard has remained, predominantly, a one-sport athlete. Because he is one of the great cyclists of the world and has the will of Attila, he has been able to compensate for what is usually a poor swim and a mediocre run. In the 1984 Ironman, for example, Howard was 750th after the swim and third to Dave Scott and Mark Allen after the biking. Until recently, he has never lost the bike phase of a triathlon. He is, heart and soul, first and foremost, a bicyclist. A world-class pedal pusher.

And will he do another triathlon? "Probably not," he says. "I like the better balance my body has as a result of cross training . . . but at forty-two, how much better am I going to get? My best-ever time in the Ironman would've put me about twentieth this year. I mean, I want to develop my full potential, but if I have no chance to win, what's the point?"

Maybe this: Howard gained more notoriety by winning the Ironman than by all his years of toil as an Olympic cyclist. As a result, he became somewhat of a hot property to sponsors of ultra-endurance events. So he took himself and his credentials to the people at Pepsi-Cola and told them that he believed he could (1) win the Race Across AMerica, (2) break the twenty-four-hour record on a bike, and (3) break the land-speed record on a bike. He sold them and became the next Pepsi Challenger. Financial backing in place, Howard took aim on goal number one. He and a few other elite cyclists established what would be known as the Race Across AMerica (RAAM): three thousand miles by bicycle, Los Angeles to New York City, stop if you dare.

Howard's second-place finish still rankles him. "My support crew was too soft on me," he is quick to say. "Instead of pushing me out of bed, they let me sleep in. I got about three hours of sleep a night." He shrugs. "It turned out to be too much."

Although he was nearly killed by a car in Pennsylvania and suffered compression damage to the ulnar and medial nerves in his hands and arms that still bothers him today, Howard completed the coast-to-coast cycle in ten days, eleven hours. "I was cooked for weeks after that," he says. "Of all the things I've ever done, the Race Across AMerica was definitely the toughest. For ten days it was just biking and eating and biking and napping and biking."

Clearly, biking thrills him. And it's more than the competition. He's simply in love with the sport, as evidenced by his paean: "There's nothing like a bike race for drama. You can watch the strategies unfold with all the variables of tactics, terrain, and riders' strengths. It's like a chess game; sometimes you don't know who'll win until the final seconds. You can be the strongest rider and still lose because of tactics.

You can't win on sheer 'horse power' alone.

"There's something about covering a lot of ground under your own power. It has to do with the blue sky, the fresh air, the gears working perfectly. When things are just right, the bike is a physical extension of yourself. Ideally, there should be a synthesis of movement between bike and rider. This gives you an incredible high. And once you've found it, nothing else will do."

But surely competition must be at the core. Like most great athletes, Howard hates to lose, and finishing second in RAAM just made him all the more determined to win a pedal-till-you-drop endurance bike race. So only a month after going coast to coast he issued an open challenge to RAAM winner Lon Haldeman and other world-class cyclists to meet him in Central Park for the Twenty-Four-Hour Bike Race.

"None of them showed up," Howard says in bully tones, his mustache bristling. "They knew what they were in for—I was in great shape."

He lived up to his own prerace hype by riding 475 miles, a new twenty-four-hour record.

The following year he was back with still another extraordinary performance. "It rained that year," he remembers, "which floated the broken glass to the surface. I had seven flat tires." And he still outdid himself, riding 512 miles—an average of more than twenty-one miles per hour and a record that stood until Howard broke it again with a 519-mile ride in Clearwater, Florida.

"No rest stops," he says, with a supercilious smile. Then, anticipating his listener's next question, he adds, "I used an external catheter."

Bonneville Salt Flats, July 1985. John Howard jammed his huge freckled hands into his leather gloves and squinted out at the shimmering salt beds. White heat wigwagged on the horizon. Utah in July: It was well over a hundred degrees, and Howard was hot and tired of waiting. For two days he'd been waiting. Now what was the delay? First they were a go, then they weren't. It was either the bike or the car or the wind or the salt. He was reminded of the old Army expression: Hurry up and wait.

He'd come to the salt flats to break the human-powered land-speed record (in the summer, because that was the only time they could count on the salt being right). But for every four-minute run there was a delay of three or more hours. It was necessary, of course, he knew that. Meticulous cleaning of salt from the bike, cooling down and checking the race car—all necessary because it was his butt on the line. But he was not a patient person, and he wished like hell they could just get on with it.

He removed his gloves and took a drink from the water bottle offered by an aide. It was hard to get enough fluids. Someone figured that he sweated away four to five pounds on every run. Part of the problem, of course, was that he was a tad overdressed for triple-digit temperatures. Colorfully garbed from head to toe in a custom-made yellow helmet, red and yellow motorcycle racing leathers, turquoise bootcovers, black cycling shoes, he looked good. Still, he reckoned, it was about the hottest he'd ever been.

At last, the green light! Howard's partner, professional driver Rick Vesco, fired up the race car, and there ensued a rumbling as if from the bowels of the earth. The car, nicknamed *Streamliner*, was a 560-horse monster machine with a top speed of more than three hundred miles per hour. Sleek and streamlined in front, the rear swooped up and out to form a boxlike chamber, behind which Howard pedaled his bike. From the side it looked like a torpedo with exaggerated Edsel fins.

Howard tugged on his gloves and helmet, then straddled his ten-thousand-dollar, custom-made Pepsi Challenger. Next to the car, the bike appeared tiny and primitive. Next to the bike, Howard, a lanky six-foot-two, looked huge. Draped over its handlebars, like an adult on a child's bike, he looked out of place.

But he was not out of place; he was right where he belonged. And in his estimation, he was the only one who belonged there, the human being most qualified to attempt to break the speed record. While it was important to Howard that he hold records at both ends of the cycling spectrum—speed and endurance—it was the speed record that truly represented the crystallization of his childhood dreams.

He'd only recently begun to realize it, but he'd been training to break the speed record for twenty years. As a kid, he had practiced drafting behind sixteen-wheelers while they careened down Highway 38 just outside Springfield. "The first time I ever tried it," he recalls, "a cop pulled me over and gave me hell. It didn't stop me, but it did keep me from doing it downtown in broad daylight."

While other Missouri kids had heroes named Stan Musial or Jim Hart, Johnny Howard used to get starry-eyed over a Frenchman named Alfred LeTourner. Who? "Alfred LeTourner was the first human to ever go more than one hundred miles per hour on a bicycle," Howard says passionately. "I read about him in a comic book insert. I was fascinated. I couldn't believe anyone could go that fast."

Imagination captured, Howard proceeded to learn everything he could about the land-speed record. Soon he could recite the list of record holders as glibly as the neighbor kids could the St. Louis Cardinals' lineup. First there was Charlie "Mile-a-Minute" Murphy, a New York City cop who chased down crooks on his bicycle. Murphy, looking to turn his cycling prowess into a vaudeville act, laid planks between the tracks of the Long Island Railroad and used the slipstream of a locomotive to cycle one measured mile in 57.8 seconds. He got a lot of ink and earned himself a nickname.

Then in 1949 LeTourner broke the century mark, doing 108.92 miles per hour behind a quarter-midget race car on the Bakersfield Freeway.

Another obsessed Frenchman, Jose Mafferet, tried for the record but crashed and nearly died. After two years in the hospital he came back with an "if-I-die" note in his pocket and broke the record: 127 miles per hour behind a Mercedes on the German Autobahn.

In 1973 Dr. Alan Abbott, a physician with an extensive background in motorcycle racing, designed his own bike, modified a 1955 Chevrolet drag racer, took both to Bonneville, and pedaled 138.671 miles per hour. Now Howard intended to add his own name to the list of record holders. Already he'd come close: an unofficial 135 miles per hour last year on uneven pavement near Mexicali (they couldn't get on the salt flats because of the heaviest rains in a hundred years). Then just yesterday Vesco had gone 137 miles per hour—but without Howard, who had fallen from the slipstream and was hit with swirling sands that blinded and choked him.

That's what it was all about: finding the perfect slipstream. Without the aid of that placid pocket of thin air that gets sucked along behind large, fast-moving objects, the record for fastest pedal pushers falls to the midsixties. Howard, who would follow a swooped-up, souped-up race car, had 152 in mind.

Howard had teamed up with Doug Malewicki, the madcap genius who had engineered a car that ran on peanut oil as well as Evil Knievel's rocket bike for the Snake River Canyon jump. Bicycle-frame builder Skip Hujsak also joined them. Together they went to see Abbott, finding him cooperative, even enthusiastic. He allowed them to photograph, measure, and test-ride his record-setting bike. The result: The Howard bike was first cousin to the Abbott. The frame had heavy, chrome-molybdenum tubes gussetted at the stress points, as well as motorcycle forks and wheel rims. The biggest difference was that Howard's bike had double-reduction gearing. Two chains and four sprockets resulted in gearing so low that one turn of the pedal translated into ninety feet of travel, gearing so low that Howard had to be towed until he reached sixty miles per hour.

An aide hooked the three-foot tow cable from Vesco's *Streamliner* to Howard's bicycle. The roar of the car was loud and deep, like a pride of hungry lions. Howard, bathed in sweat, dropped his helmet visor and flicked a switch on his handlebars that gave him radio contact with Vesco in the car.

"Ready, Rick?"

"Ready, John. You?"

Howard nodded, smiled wanly, and said, "Getting close. Got a feeling."

Nothing more had to be said. He and Vesco were by this time almost telepathic. At first they'd made a point of sharing each and every new piece of information, no matter how trivial it seemed. After all, Howard's success and safety — while they were zipping along the salt at more than two miles per minute — depended on their staying in perfect tandem at all times.

Howard sat on his bike staring into the box. The upper part of that aerodynamic structure had a Plexiglass window through which Howard could see the salty track shimmering ahead. Just below the window, orange letters read, "FASTER, YOU FOOL!"

Car and driver would have about three miles to get up speed. Then they would enter the timed mile, a surveyed section marked by electronic eyes. After the second light, they'd have about a mile to slow down and stop, which often was the toughest part.

Howard gave the high sign, and they began to move, Vesco accelerating slowly, smoothly, pulling Howard behind him. Although John could have pedaled from zero to sixty under his own power, the effort would have left him exhausted for the high-speed struggle ahead. As their speed increased, it became crucial that Howard keep the front wheel of the bicycle within an invisible ten-inch pocket. If he went too fast, he'd crash into the bumper-bar of the car; too slow, he'd fall from the slipstream, subjecting himself to the swirling turbulence of hurricane winds.

Even the slipstream itself, Howard reminded people, was not a void or vacuum, not a downhill coast. Above ninety miles per hour there was "an incredibly powerful vortex of air pushing at you."

Thirty . . . forty . . . fifty . . . So far the ride was smooth, and Howard could still read his speedometer. A wave of exhilaration washed over him. He sensed it all coming together. His body felt good, the bike felt fine, he and Vesco were in sync. What could go wrong?

The night before, while he and his entourage were camped around a fire on the salt flats, one of the motorcycle types hanging out with them had asked John if he wasn't bummed that he hadn't broken the record the first day out.

"No," he'd replied evenly, "we're here as long as it takes. It's all coming together. You need the speed to come in small doses so you can get used to it, so you can predict what's going to happen."

Someone laughed. "At 130 miles per hour, how can you predict anything?"

"One-fifty-two," Howard corrected. He'd been visualizing that number for weeks; it was now indelibly imprinted in his mind.

"Why take such risks?" someone else asked.

It was Howard's turn to laugh. "It's a risk all right but a calculated one."

It was a distinction he believed in. In the more than two years since he had begun to openly challenge the speed record, he had constantly been asked about the "danger" and whether he had a "death wish." Yet, strangely, in the previous fifteen years while he had been road racing all over the globe, danger was rarely mentioned. That in spite of the fact that road racing against others was clearly more dangerous—less "calculated"—than racing against the clock at Bonneville. In road racing, he'd seen maimings, even deaths, and had experienced a narrow escape more than once.

There was, for example, the trans-Florida race in which another rider half-wheeled him (his front to Howard's rear), forcing him into the oncoming lane of cars. Suddenly, before he could even be scared, a sixteen-wheeler roared by, missing him by inches.

In another road race, as he was careening down a serpentine

mountain road at about sixty miles per hour, he suddenly spotted out of the corner of his eye a slow-moving truck (the road was supposed to be closed!) coming up the mountain. He feathered the brake and began a semicontrolled drift that brought him nearly parallel to the truck, whereupon he struck its flank a glancing blow. He was thrown from his bike but not far, suffering only bruises and a gash on his leg. The rider on his tail, however, was not as fortunate. He hit the truck straight on, flipping over the handlebars and flying thirty yards into a pile of rocks. As a shaken and battered Howard struggled back on his bicycle (he would finish the race), he could hear the agonized screams of the other rider.

Another time, during a race in Mexico, as he led a pack of riders through a village, a dog ran out onto the road – and stopped! Before Howard could even react, a Mexican cop pulled out a pistol and shot the dog, which exploded before Howard's eyes.

Fear was no stranger to him, but his greatest fear was that he wouldn't go fast enough. For him, the desire to break the record was a stronger motivator than the fear of getting hurt. "On another level," he says, "I was afraid that the reporter from *Sports Illustrated* would leave before I could break the record."

Fifty-five . . . sixty . . . Howard released the lever that disengaged the tow-cable. While Vesco continued to accelerate . . . seventy . . . eighty . . . ninety, Howard pedaled harder and faster, trying to maintain a constant distance behind the car. He would later compare the exertion needed during this phase to riding a kilometer time trial or a four-thousand-meter pursuit on the track – although the speed on the salt flats was much more exhilarating.

One hundred . . . one-ten . . . one-twenty . . . He was caught up in the slipstream now, but staying on Vesco's tail was still a terrible strain on his arms and shoulders. This was cycling all right but also a bit of tightrope walking. If Vesco veered a few inches, Howard had to be able to adjust instantly. There was nothing in his world but the bike, the salt, and the five square feet of screen in front of his face. All motor functions that weren't needed for the task at hand were shut down. So riveted was his concentration that he didn't notice the razor-sting of salt particles that pelted him.

One-thirty . . . one-forty . . . "The record is ours," Howard thought. But suddenly, a strange sensation! As though the rear wheel were sinking into the salt and the front one about to fly into the air! Comprehension lagged behind event as he fell from the slipstream hitting a wall of wind. A swirling tumult of salt engulfed him; the bike began to fishtail. Using his cycling instincts, moxie, and considerable upper-body strength, he rode it out and brought the bike to a shivering stop.

Vesco and the crew found Howard seated amidst the great salt whiteness, a wide smile on his face. "You just set another world record," Vesco told John, eyeing the bike. "The fastest flat tire on a bicycle. I had you doing one-fifty."

Howard just kept on smiling. Most people suffering a flat tire at a speed faster than the takeoff velocity of a Lear jet would have given up bicycling for bocce ball, but not John. He was tickled by the whole thing. The way he saw it, he had just survived the worst they could throw at him. That flat tire, then, was nothing but a confidence booster.

Two tries later, Howard set a new world speed record: 152 miles per hour – the exact figure he had been visualizing for weeks. "I would have tried another run," he later said, "but by then I'd had a couple glasses of champagne. I didn't want to be unsafe."

Two years later, seated in his Encinitas home, Howard proudly speaks of accomplishments past, present, and future. "There's nothing quite so impressive to me as plain old gut-wrenching determination. I enjoy going out there and finding out just how much self-determination I have stored in me. The thing most people have never learned is how to suffer, how to push back their pain. The feeling of self-accomplishment after doing just that – it's a high you won't experience any other way. I find that surprisingly few people know what that's about. You have to do it until it hurts, then keep doing it until the hurt is part of you."

That's just the way Howard talks: direct, honest, forceful, with a sprinkling of arrogance. With his lean, firm jaw and laser blue eyes that seem to look right through you, his manner does not encourage discussion. It seems to say, "This is the way it is; if you don't like it go talk to someone else."

But there is another side of John Howard: a softer, more contemplative side that occasionally reveals itself. "I look upon the land-speed record not so much as an act of daring but as a learning experience. It helped me learn more about myself and where I want to go.

"I realized when I hadn't broken the record (at Mexicali) that a component was missing. So I sat down with a fitness guru who told me, 'You already have the hard stuff – the physical part – but what about the soft stuff?' So I started meditating on the unsuccessful attempts, trying to see it all correctly coming together. I saw myself – it was either a dream or a meditative state – doing 152 miles per hour. It seems I had programmed my subconscious mind to create my own reality."

Never before had Howard mustered that kind of mental discipline. "Before the speed project, my subconscious mind had never been used for anything but daydreaming. Going for the record helped me focus my energies, helped me gain control of my mind. I programmed it to accept nothing less than the record."

But records are made to be broken, and Howard fully expects someone, someday, to break his. In fact, he welcomes it. Those who would try have his blessing. But as he speaks he is aware of only two men – an Aussie and a Brit – who actively pursue the record. Both have called Howard for advice; he gives it freely but apparently with little effect, for neither has yet come close. "The Brit has bad equipment, and the Aussie doesn't have a good place to do it," says Howard. "I'll help them if I can, but they don't seem to have a sense of what it takes. It's a logistical and financial nightmare. To break the record cost a hundred thousand dollars (most of which came from Wendy's, Pepsi, and KHS Bikes) and two and a half years of my life.

"Of course I want someone to break the record. Where's the drama in breaking your own record? I want someone to break it, then I'll come back and put it away for good. I think two hundred miles per hour is realistic."

John still remembers the terror he felt when, as a young Olympian, he first spoke at his father's Toastmaster's Club. Now he talks in front of crowds for a living. He's started his own company, called John Howard Performance, and his job is to travel around the country and give motivation seminars and fitness workshops. He wears a suit and tie and speaks to groups of business people and athletes on subjects that include "Motivation in Sport and Life," "Focusing One's Energy," and "Developing the Winning Spirit." In short, the John Howard high-performance technique.

But Howard is much more than athlete turned salesperson. The man still performs – and performs well. As always, the ultimate competition – with himself – remains the dominant force in his life. That's evident in his favorite quote, from Norman Mailer's *The Executioner's Song*: "No psychic reward can ever be so powerful as winning a dare with yourself."

He dared himself to go one-fifty-two on a bike, took the dare, and won. Now he wants someone else to break the record, so that he can go out and do it again. But he is not sitting home waiting for the rest of the world to catch up with him. He stays busy. First there was the Daedalus Project.

In Greek mythology, Daedalus, the father of Icarus, was victimized by King Minos of Crete and forced to flee – by air! "Everybody has heard of Icarus, who flew too close to the sun and melted his wings," says Howard. "But Daedalus was the real hero; he made it – sixty-nine miles to the Greek mainland."

Scientists designed a 68-pound, pedal-powered airplane, with 104-foot wings and an 11-foot propeller. They needed someone to pedal it from Crete to Athens – the same course Daedalus flew.

John Howard, of course, wanted to be the one chosen to pilot/pedal the craft. He wanted the chance to break the world's record for nonstop human-powered flight (which was then twenty-two miles across the English Channel). He knew that the man or woman who did it would triple the world's record, possibly the greatest differential ever between best and second-best in a sporting event.

But it was not to be. Howard spent a lot of time, money, and energy training for the Daedalus Project, traveling back and forth between California and Yale University, undergoing physiological tests, but he failed to make the final cut. "They picked six guys," he says. "And all of them were around five-six or five-seven and 140 pounds. I was just too damn big for the little cockpit."

His training for Daedalus included learning to fly. He soared in sailplanes, gliders, and hang gliders. "I had some wonderful experiences in the air," he says, "but flying is just a hobby for me, not a passion."

That's unlike his new sport: pedal-powered boating – "aqua-cycling," as he has dubbed it. He has formed an alliance with Sid Shutt, a marine architect who designs such boats, and once again John finds himself in the hunt for world records.

So young is the sport that Howard sets a new record just about

Howard practices his latest passion—aqua-cycling. (Courtesy of John Howard)

every time he goes out. He recently pedaled a minimum-displacement trimaran from Dana Point in southern California to Catalina, thirty-seven miles in six and a half hours. That's some sort of an endurance record, he figures, but a veritable sprint compared to what's in store for him next. "At the end of June 1991, I'm pedaling a boat from Nassau to Miami, about two hundred miles through the Bermuda Triangle. No one has ever gone that far before."

Despite his love for, and his ability to attain, world records, Howard believes the real potential in aqua-cycling lies in the pedaler's ability to get away from it all. "This sport has a lot of what I was looking for when I first got into bicycling back in the Ozarks," he says. "It has peace and solitude, wildlife and nature. It's a natural offshoot of bicycling, which has steadily gotten more dangerous. You look at the fatality rates, and you realize that bicycling is one of the riskiest sports. Why should we have to wear helmets and risk our lives? I just don't like the odds anymore. Aqua-cycling is a much safer way to burn calories and to see new places."

Like the Bermuda Triangle?

Whether by land, sea, or air, John Howard is a man on the move. Few can keep up with him and that includes the women who have shared his life. He has been through a divorce and another painful breakup. Although he likes his life and claims he wouldn't have done it any other way, he knows he has paid dearly for the privilege of doing it his way.

"Obsessive behavior in sports is not compatible with marriage," he admits. "I was married for several years to a wonderful person, but when given the choice between my marriage and athletics, I chose athletics.

"You know, traveling is the perfect yardstick for a relationship. The first year, whenever I returned from a race, my wife would meet me at the airport gate; the second year, in the lounge area; the third, outside the terminal; the fourth, she said, 'Why don't you take a cab?' And the fifth it was, 'I don't care if you ever come home.'"

Ask John Howard and he'll say it's been a fair trade. "What I like best about my life is that it's never boring. There's a real progression. Even when I'm not improving as an athlete, I'm getting smarter, growing as a person."

He's been sitting a long time, and he's antsy to end the interview. If he doesn't leave now he won't get in fifty miles on the bike before dark. He rises, saying, "Someday I'd like to get married again, have kids, live on a farm."

For anyone else, it's a perfectly ordinary dream.

John Howard Update

Howard has put on hold his Nassau-to-Miami aqua-cycling adventure. "We are constantly upgrading and redesigning the boats, getting them ready for production. The trip from Dana Point to Catalina seemed like a more realistic goal than trying to pedal through the Bermuda Triangle in an untested craft."

Back on land, Howard competed in the 1991 Nationals, winning a gold medal in the time trial and a bronze in the road race for his age group. He is also in the process of writing an historical novel about the great black bicyclist, Major Taylor.

ELAINE MARIOLLE
RAAM Rider

Elaine Mariolle stood at the starting line of the 1984 Race Across AMerica (RAAM), straddling her bicycle and squinting east. She had no hope of seeing the finish line – 3,047 miles away in Atlantic City – but it was fun to imagine. In fact, given the monumental chore that lay before her, she was having more fun than one would have expected. As she would later confess, ignorance insulated her from fear. Ignorance of the new frontiers of pain she would be forced to explore in the next couple of weeks brought her, if not bliss, at least manageable levels of dread. "I clearly didn't know what was ahead or what to expect. I could only vaguely visualize what I'd seen on TV the year before – the glare of Las Vegas, twelve-thousand-foot Loveland Pass in Colorado, then a long blank. Well, that blank is two thousand miles long! Had I known how hard a journey actually lay ahead, I might not have accepted the challenge."

Doubtful. The five-foot-two-inch Mariolle, one quickly learns, is not big on backing down from challenges. And for a bicyclist, there is no bigger challenge than the wild, weird, gonzo endurance event called the Race Across AMerica. She recounts a personal revolution in her book *The Woman Cyclist*.

"When I purchased my bicycle in April of 1983, I had no thought of racing across the country – I didn't even know such events existed. I had been lifting weights, but I wanted to do something outdoors and thought I might take up triathlons. I mentioned my new bike to a friend at work – she was a bicyclist – and she invited me to go on a ride with her club, the Grizzly Peak Cyclists. As a result, I did my first hundred-mile ride in May, and I loved it."

She read about a race called the John Marino Open. Named for the founding father of RAAM, the JMO is a qualifying race for the Race Across AMerica. A local woman, Kitty Goursolle of Sacramento, had ridden it and qualified for RAAM. Elaine, who has never required assertiveness training, looked up Goursolle in the phone book and called her. They struck up a friendship, and Kitty invited Elaine to go riding on what turned out to be the Markleeville Death Ride, a 150-mile pedal-push over five passes in the Sierra Nevada that Goursolle was doing as a tune-up for RAAM. Although Mariolle lacked a support crew ("Goursolle had people to help her on and off with her clothes"), she finished with a smile on her face, one hour behind Goursolle. At the picnic afterwards, a video of the 1983 Race Across AMerica was shown, and Mariolle watched in fascination as the competitors flogged their bodies across the country. "They were eating and brushing their teeth by the side of the road," she said breathlessly. "It looked like the hardest thing in the world – right out there on the extremes of experience. I decided right then that I wanted to do it the next year."

When she returned to Berkeley to discuss the matter with her boyfriend, Vance Vaughan, a bike racer in his own right, she fully expected him to try to talk her out of it. After all, she had only been riding a bicycle for three months, and no woman had ever even completed RAAM. But Vaughan surprised her with his support, calmly replying, "Let's do it."

"He didn't give me one reason why not," she said admiringly. "Not one. That was true love."

She was scheduled to attend the UCLA business school in the fall. But that would have to be deferred. She called UCLA and said she was postponing her schooling for "personal growth" reasons, which turned out to be a more enduring process than she realized. As she then saw it, she'd ride across the country, get this nagging urge out of her system, then return, finally content, to business school.

The RAAM qualifier, the John Marino Open, was only one-fourth the length of RAAM. But at 792 miles, it was still nearly three times longer than any bike race Mariolle had ever attempted. The rules stipulated that a rider had to finish in less than eighty hours to be "official," so that became her goal. But deep down she wondered whether she could ride that far in a week, much less three and a third days. Despite such doubts, she finished second – thirty-five seconds behind the winner – in a time of seventy-three hours plus. She had qualified for RAAM.

California, mile 0. Before the start of the 1984 RAAM, Elaine cried in her hotel room. Then she choked down some oatmeal and slowly put on her purple and pink cycling attire. As she tried to make her way onto the pier where the race would start, a man stopped her. "Only the racers are allowed onto the pier," he said. "I am one of the racers," she replied, nervously sliding past him and finding a place in the lineup.

She couldn't blame the man; she was, after all, an unlikely competitor. In fact, she told herself, she hadn't really come to compete against the other riders but to challenge herself. "I had only been riding a bike for a little over a year," she says. "My aspirations were humble – I just wanted to see if I could make it across the country."

The Race Across AMerica had grown from the four-man Great American Bicycle Race in 1982 to twenty-three riders – nineteen men and four women. Never had so many tried to bike so far so continuously fast. The prerace atmosphere was carnival-like, with television cameras rolling and last-minute interviews and the crowd cheering best wishes to their favorite racers. "On the one hand, I wanted to get started," she says. "On the other hand, I savored every last moment before the overwhelming task began."

At nine A.M., amidst thousands of spectators, the mayor of Huntington Beach fired the gun, and the riders set out for Atlantic City, New Jersey, 3,047 miles away. They rode from the pier onto the city streets. The pace was controlled for the first forty-five miles at a comfortable speed of fifteen miles per hour. This allowed the competitors to visit with each other while the press snapped group shots and the ABC helicopter filmed the event.

Elaine, riding next to veteran RAAM racer Susan Notorangelo, asked her if it helped having crossed the country before. She said, "No, it just reminds me how much it's going to hurt."

After the forty-five miles of paced riding, the race officially began. The race director waved the flag, and everyone took off in a blur of color. For Mariolle, the blur was mostly other riders streaking away from her. Going into the race, she didn't have the experience, the training background to be a strong contender. "I just want to make it

In 1986, Mariolle completed the 3,107-mile Race Across AMerica in a record ten days, two hours, and four minutes.

across America," she thought. "I've come for the adventure, the thrill . . . and to learn."

Her plan was vague. She hoped to complete the course in eleven days. This target was born of necessity rather than any realistic appraisal of abilities. The RAAM promoters had decided that (1) only those who finished within thirty-six hours of the winner would be "official finishers" and (2) there would be no separate women's division. Elaine's camp expected the men's winner to finish in about nine and a half days, which meant she had to finish in eleven days. That translated into 275 miles per day, which translated into lots of riding, little sleep.

Mariolle and her tailing support crew rolled out of the Los Angeles–Riverside area along I-15 toward Las Vegas and beyond. As Elaine describes it, "It was hot and overcast as I started the twenty-six-mile climb out of the L.A. Basin. I was in last place as we expected, but it still upset me. No one likes to be in last place. I was convinced that I was creeping along. The crew kept trying to convince me that I was climbing and doing okay. This would happen over and over, especially on the subtle climbs where the pitch wasn't obvious. Believing I was on level ground, I got depressed because I was going so slow."

She went even slower after dark when a lashing rainstorm struck. She had no useful raingear and was quickly a study in misery. "I was disappointed that I couldn't descend as quickly as I expected because of the weather. The year before had been hot and dry, and I hoped for the same. But as sports commentator Jim Lampley says, 'You have to expect the unexpected in an event like RAAM.'"

The first attempts to cross the United States on a bicycle occurred in the 1880s. In the first half of that decade, seven cyclists tried to bicycle coast to coast, but all were turned back by a malevolent montage of bad weather, mountain barriers, bridgeless streams, and desert sands. Then in 1884, Thomas Stevens completed the journey in 103 days, during which time he frequently encountered coyotes, mountain lions, wild horses, and wolves – but almost no humans or adequate roads.

The twentieth-century rise of the automobile brought a concomitant decline in the popularity of the bicycle. But in 1982, four male riders set out to break the transcontinental cycling record in what they called the Great American Bicycle Race. Later that summer, Susan Notorangelo went the distance, only the second woman to bicycle coast to coast. She set a new woman's record for the transcontinental journey – eleven days, sixteen hours, fifteen minutes.

The following year the race was renamed the Race Across AMerica, and the field swelled to eleven men and one woman, Kitty Goursolle. Goursolle had a support-vehicle crash that forced her out of the race in Colorado.

Nevada, mile 312. Twenty-four hours after starting RAAM, Mariolle had ridden 312 miles without sleep. That was her best distance ever for twenty-four hours. She was pleased by the mileage but not by how far she was behind the leaders.

"The day was a scorcher as I pedaled across the desert north of Las Vegas, and I wondered why I had ever wished for hot and dry. The scenery was sparse. If it wasn't for my Stevie Wonder and James Taylor tapes, it would have been a long afternoon."

At the Nevada–Arizona border, the crew enacted the first in a series of state border celebrations. They banged pots and pans and put up a toilet-paper "finish line." The nuttiness was captured in full by ABC.

Elaine Mariolle's eight favorite stretches of road across America

1. The desert near Palm Springs, California ("wailing tail winds")
2. The quaint mining town of Jerome, Arizona ("perched high on a hill")
3. Sedona, Arizona ("a neat climb")
4. Loveland Pass, Colorado ("11,990 feet of grunting and screaming")
5. The rolling hills of Missouri
6. The road past Graceland, Elvis's home, in Tennessee
7. The Blue Ridge Parkway, North Carolina and Virginia
8. The final approach to Atlantic City ("Not because it's beautiful but because you're finished")

Elaine is the oldest of eleven kids, and her close-knit family is an obvious source of pride and strength for her. Although her six brothers are all jocks, Elaine's athletic background was meager until her sudden immersion in the RAAM adventure. Her father recounts the time Elaine lamented to him, "Oh, Dad, your other children are such good athletes (and then there's me)." In high school she was more academic than athletic. She attended the University of California, Berkeley, where she majored in, appropriately enough, geography. When the baby boomer fitness craze hit, Mariolle found herself adrift, without a sport to call her own. She turned to running the fire trails in the Berkeley hills and, later, to lifting weights. She developed an athletic body: slim waist, firm belly, with well-developed shoulders and thighs.

Arizona. By early afternoon Mariolle found herself in the Virgin River gorge, one of the most spectacular canyonlands in the country. "It was awe-inspiring to climb through the picturesque rock canyons ribboned with color and to watch the rusty river coursing through. It was a steady uphill for miles, but I settled into a rhythm and enjoyed the climb."

Boyfriend Vance, who was also support crew chief, described this
phase in his journal:

> I expected some great times and this is one. Elaine is
> tired. She is climbing well, but the climb is relent-
> less. From the chase car, you watch the figure on the
> bike in front of you and think this hill has to end.
> But time and time again, a turn reveals a new vista of
> uphill work. At one such point, I see Elaine slump,
> take one hand off the bar and shake it in resignation.
> I fear she will get off but she continues. About half-
> way up she hits a rhythm and really starts to move.
> It's inspiring, it makes a lump in your throat.

*Like most riders in the Race Across AMerica, Elaine Mariolle takes her refreshments on the
move. (Courtesy of David Nelson)*

Elaine Mariolle's six "other" things to bring on a RAAM adventure

1. A congenial crew of creative, independent thinkers committed to a team project.
2. Flexibility. Things just happen on the road that don't fit neatly into your plans: the motor home breaks down, the lighting system blows up, or you just get lost. The challenge lies in dealing with whatever comes your way in the most elegant, upbeat way.
3. A love of the night life. Get used to it. You'll pedal close to a thousand miles in the darkness.
4. A sense of the Big Picture. Since you don't see your competition the whole time, there's a tendency to reduce everything to your own personal drama. Remember, the rain doesn't fall just on you.
5. Focus. You have a lot of time on your hands on the roads of America, so don't let your mind go on infinite loop. Break the seemingly overwhelming task down into small segments – next town, next mailbox – without losing sight of your final destination.
6. A healthy sense of humor.

She stopped for her first sleep break at the Arizona–Utah border in the early afternoon on Monday, 406.5 miles into the race. The tiny motor home was hot, crowded, and invaded by flies, making sleep all but impossible. "We learned an important RAAM lesson on that first break: Never sleep during the day. It's better to ride when it's light out and easier to stay awake."

At first glance, RAAM would seem to be the consummate individual sporting event. After all, those bicycles are built for one, the same one who must do all the pedaling from coast to coast (about one million pedal revolutions in all). And when it comes time to battle the forces of resistance – wind, gravity – and to surmount two-mile-high passes, no substitutes are permitted.

Yet RAAM riders are not alone. They rely heavily on the kindness of others – mostly family and friends who comprise their support crew. At times, reduced by sleep deprivation to babbling incoherency, they require the aid and comfort one normally reserves for an infant. Without a support crew, RAAM, a high-risk endeavor under the best of conditions, becomes an exercise in lunacy. (Indeed, in 1985 Wayne Phillips, a thirty-seven-year-old Canadian, tried to solo RAAM. Taking sustenance and answering nature's call at local McDonald's restaurants, he made it as far as Tucumcari, New Mexico, where he was struck by a hit-and-run truck driver, paralyzing him from the waist down. RAAM has since instituted a rule prohibiting riders from going solo.)

"The crew makes or breaks a race for a rider," says Mariolle. "Whether you win or lose is determined by the crew. You're both dependent and independent at the same time. I depended on them for so many things; they depended on me to ride beyond myself. It's really a team sport—I just ride the bike."

That sentiment comes from the heart. Mariolle is a team player. A big believer in style points, she cares a great deal how she treats her teammates. "If I went across the country and was a real shrew," she says, "I swear I would rather not do it. You have to treat your crew right; I tried to entertain them as much as possible."

Mariolle's 1984 crew of seven included her little brother Matthew, fifteen years her junior and the youngest of the Mariolle brood. "I wanted him on the crew because I had left home to go to college when he was four, and I wanted to get to know him. Out on the road, we swapped roles. He told me stories, played music, fed me. He was the big brother I never had."

Utah. By Tuesday noon, she had covered 535 miles since starting the race two days before. In the last twenty-four hours she had covered 223 miles, despite two long stops. She was only one hour behind the eleven-day schedule and was occasionally passing riders, usually as they were dropping out of the race.

She had developed serious chafing from riding in the rain. It became almost unbearable to sit on the saddle. She tried creams, saddle pads, and different riding positions—nothing helped. "At six hundred miles, I was in agony. But I had barely started the race. There was no way I was going to drop out because my butt hurt. It was going to take a major catastrophe to get me to quit."

That night she had her first fatigue-induced hallucinations. Most of the time, Elaine says, hallucinations cause you to slow down. But if you get really scared, the adrenaline rush can jolt you awake, giving you another hour or so of riding time. "This happened as we approached the Green River. I was attacked by what I called the 'Lee Monster' (named after a crew member). It was a clear evening, a change from the rain I had ridden through all day. I could see stars as I rolled up and down the long grades through the Utah canyonlands. Suddenly, the large rock formations started to look like animals and monsters. I saw a large, hunched-over catlike figure that must have been fifty feet high. I was prepared to ignore it when it turned and snarled at me. I screamed and swerved toward the double yellow line. That created chaos in the chase vehicle. Liz yelled at Lee and Matthew to get me off the bike. Lee, who had been napping, jumped up and out of the bus while it was still rolling. He ate dust but wasn't hurt."

Hallucinations are part and parcel of what has come to be called "the ravages of RAAM." Competitors have reported eight-foot bunny rabbits. Two-time RAAM winner Lon Haldeman has seen dinosaurs and elephants. Explained perennial RAAM finisher Michael Secrest, "If you're not sleeping much, you're not dreaming much. Your mind wants to be – needs to be – in that dream state. And it will try to get there even when you're awake."

When you're pedaling a hundred thousand or so revolutions a day, your body burns more than eight thousand calories, which begins to deplete your stores of glycogen, the body's most efficient source of energy. In RAAM riders, these stores may disappear entirely, forcing the body to burn fat. This process requires 12 percent more oxygen, which ultimately will sap the strength of the fittest of riders. Most lose an average of five to twelve pounds, and for reed-slim endurance athletes that is a crash diet. Another health hazard is sleep deprivation. Studies have shown that going without sleep reduces performance by decreasing maximum heart rate. It also frays concentration, which increases the chances of an accident. Most RAAM riders have at one time or another fallen asleep on their bikes.

Colorado. Wednesday morning was clear and crisp. The canyonlands of Utah were behind Elaine. She was now on a high plain littered with black-eyed Susans and small red rocks. It was flat, open land, and there was a nice tailwind. She rolled along at a good clip, listening to a recording by the group Fup and anticipating the Rocky Mountains and the climb to Loveland Pass that lay ahead.

By noon she had covered 240 miles during the previous twenty-four hours, for a total of 775 miles. She was falling farther behind the eleven-day schedule. Saddle sores continued to plague her, but her feet, which had developed a few raw spots riding in the rain, were healing. "I was now going beyond my longest previous ride at the JMO. Every mile from this point on would be a new experience."

With all the excitement and work of the first few days, most of the crew hadn't slept. It was starting to catch up with them. Even the normally effervescent Elaine started to get cranky. She appreciated the crew's care and attention, but she was starting to feel self-conscious. "It was embarrassing that I was so far behind the leaders – over a day by this time. I couldn't hide the fact that it was uncomfortable sitting in the saddle. My squirming was obvious. I'm very independent, and it was difficult relying so intimately on the crew. I missed my privacy, particularly when it came to potty stops."

A serious morale crisis broke out near Rifle, Colorado, 882 miles into the race, as it began to sink in for the first time just how long a race RAAM really was. Elaine explains: "Everyone was tired; nobody had slept enough. The novelty of the first few days had worn off, and we still had over two thousand miles to go! There was dissension in the ranks. Some of the crew was ready to press on through whatever obstacles arose, but others were unprepared to cope with me when I lost the will to ride. I don't blame them. We finally pulled off the road and decided to mellow out. We didn't see how we could make the thirty-six-hour cutoff with our present pace. We decided that just making it would be a miracle. If more rest was the key, that's what we'd do.

"Lee gave me a tape his brother Calvin had made for me. The tape contained songs and motivational messages that the crew thought I could use. Lee was instructed to give it to me when the going got rough. Now was definitely the time. For the rest of the trip, I listened to that tape many times, sometimes five or six hours in a row, as a sort of meditation."

Loveland Pass, a thousand miles into the race and almost twelve thousand feet above sea level, was the highest point on the course. It had been highlighted in ABC's 1983 RAAM coverage, and Mariolle was looking forward to it. "Believe it or not," she says, "I enjoy climbing, and the elevation never bothers me. That afternoon, riding up the pass, I caught a string of touring cyclists. It felt good to catch someone. When we neared the summit, Lee and Matthew played the inspirational theme music from *Rocky*, and I felt like a hero. At the top we stopped for a few minutes, took pictures, and enjoyed the moment. Then it was off down the mountain into gathering darkness and rain, through the sprawl of Denver, and out into the plains."

Kansas, mile 1,500. Elaine had expected to make good time through Nebraska and Kansas. After all, the Midwest is flat. But she had failed to consider that it's windy. Very windy. "Oh, the wind in Kansas," she says. "It was usually a crosswind, not as bad as a headwind but bad enough."

At a quick stop at the Nebraska–Kansas border Friday evening, she watched an electrical storm roiling ahead. After some hesitation, she set off into the gloom. "It was dark, I was surrounded by clouds and lightning, and I was being blown all over the road. The veins of lightning were spectacular and scary. I saw myself as a human lightning rod. The skinny, wet sew-up tires were hardly enough to ground me. It was the kind of storm that's wonderful to watch but no fun to ride in."

Now the wind came straight at her. The crew fed her meals on the bike, bite by bite, as she was afraid to let go of the bars to eat. Crawling into a stiff headwind hour after hour was heartbreaking. It ate at her spirit – especially when she heard that the lead men, who passed through ahead of the storm, had enjoyed a tailwind. "It was," says Elaine, "a thoroughly miserable and discouraging time."

Finally, after hours of punishment, she was forced to stop just west of Bird City, Kansas. She waited out the worst of the storm in the motor home, and this time crew members Jan, Lisa, Liz, and Matt had the good sense to find a nearby motel room.

The next morning, she was back in battle, floundering through Kansas. Those middle miles were, physically and psychologically, the most difficult of the race. She was exhausted from the days of effort, but the end was still so far away that it wasn't real.

Weary of all the attention she was receiving, Elaine sent the chase crew up the road so she could ride alone for awhile. She longed to be free of prying eyes. It was then that she made what she called "the stupidest mistake in my three years of riding RAAM. I pulled off the shoulder of the road, lay down in the tall grass, and went to sleep. The chase crew backtracked but couldn't see me. They spent the next hour driving around frantically trying to find me, worried sick and fearing the worst. When they finally found me, Vance was justifiably furious. My precious purple bike got thrown on the roadside as we 'discussed' my transgression."

One ordinarily thinks of bicycling as an inexpensive sport. Mostly, you need a bicycle. The Mariolle team brought three of them to RAAM, but 99 percent of the time Elaine relied on her favorite, a custom-made Mikkelson decorated in a purple/pink/peacock-blue camouflage pattern. During the entire coast-to-coast journey, she suffered only one flat tire—when a crew member wheeled the bike off the road into a patch of thorns. Although the cost of equipment repair was negligible, it was still extraordinarily expensive to ride a bicycle across the country in RAAM fashion. "The costs mount up," Mariolle admits. "A couple thousand dollars to feed rider and crew, gasoline for two vehicles, motel rooms, airplane fares for some of the crew. We figured it cost between four and five dollars per mile." Elaine and Vance borrowed and begged what they could, then raised the remaining six thousand dollars by selling T-shirts, holding garage sales, and withdrawing what little money they had in savings.

And the payoff? Spend fifteen grand, make . . . what? If Mariolle persevered against phenomenal odds and actually finished RAAM, she would take home sixty dollars, about two cents a mile.

Missouri. As Elaine crossed out of Kansas and into Missouri, a big smile brightened her face. The crew played the songs "Surrender Dorothy" and "Escape from Kansas." "I was relieved to leave the flatlands and get into the rolling hills of Missouri. I liked the trees and the big bugs and the bullfrogs croaking in the night air."

As Mariolle worked her way through the outskirts of St. Louis, not yet across the Mississippi River, Pete Penseyres was approaching the finish line in Atlantic City. Pete was her hero, and she was glad for him, but the news depressed her. "Will I ever get there?" she wondered.

She saw a St. Louis city-limit sign early in the morning, but getting through the metropolitan area took most of the day. The city was a hot, muggy tangle of smoke-belching vehicles, but Elaine remembers one bright spot. "I was riding on a frontage road paralleling the highway. A woman pulled off the highway, got out of her car, rushed to the chain-link fence and shouted, 'Hang in there, honey!' as I rolled by. This woman, like so many other upbeat people along the way, really gave me a boost."

But she was again sitting low in her saddle by the time she got into downtown St. Louis. She was, in her own words, "thoroughly depressed. I was starting to think I'd never make it to the big river, and I was sobbing as I rode through the traffic."

St. Louis was, in fact, the emotional nadir of the journey. Once it was behind her, an unexpected transformation began to take place. She got stronger—both mentally and physically. Taking rest when she felt she needed it, she spent less time on her bike than many of the other riders; but when she was on, she was very, very on. When an ABC commentator asked her if, given her last-place status, she planned to finish the race, she answered in an upbeat tone that fell somewhere between Polyanna and the Little Engine That Could: "Oh, sure, I'll keep on going. For me, the race is just an opportunity to do this with a lot of other people. I came here to go across the country, and that's exactly what we're going to do."

In a later ABC interview, she elaborated on her New Age philosophy: "You have to be getting something out of it [RAAM] that's personal, private. I think I'm a better person for it. I think I've become a lot stronger person. It's changed my attitude and my perspective on things. I think more about every day. I try to make every day worth something. I probably won't be riding a bicycle forever, but the things I get out of bicycling are things I can use when I'm a hundred and five."

Illinois, mile 2,000. Illinois, Indiana, and Ohio were miles of undulating cornfields. In Indiana, an old man flagged Elaine down and asked her to autograph his application for his first century (hundred-mile) ride. She stopped and wrote him a short note of encouragement. It was the first time anyone had ever asked her for an autograph.

Near Terre Haute, Indiana, a local man rode beside her for awhile.

He told her how good she looked compared to the other racers who had ridden by. He asked her lots of questions about RAAM. His name was Kye Waltermire, and he would qualify and compete in the 1985 RAAM.

In Ohio, a couple of disreputable-looking guys in a beat-up truck accompanied Elaine for awhile, asking lots of questions. She worried they might mug her. But when they said good-bye, they donated a dollar for gas.

West Virginia. On a Friday afternoon, Mariolle crossed the Ohio River into West Virginia. With miles of ups and downs, West Virginia was difficult riding; but she thoroughly enjoyed the plush, green richness of the Appalachians. "It was bittersweet countryside," she says. "Such gorgeous landscape, such poverty. I saw a small child looking out through a broken window partially covered with cardboard. My heart sank.

"West Virginia passed quickly for me. Maybe because the end was near or maybe just because of the beauty of the mountains I was starting to feel spunky again. I asked in a gas station if they had seen the woman rider ahead of me, Pat Hines. 'Yesterday afternoon,' they said. Even though I had no chance to catch her, I got excited about 'competing' again. There was one goal I could still make – finishing the trip in less than fourteen days. I planned to ride the last night straight through."

Philadelphia, Pennsylvania. A mere hundred miles to go. Elaine and the crew could finally see the end, at least in their mind's eye. As Elaine recalls, "We rolled along the flat expressway nearing Atlantic City. The destination signs took on a dreamlike quality. In Atlantic City, the course reached the boardwalk, and the chase car couldn't follow. Vance got out of the car and ran alongside me, helping me elbow my way through the Labor Day beach crowd. I didn't know where I was going, so I rode into some open-air casino looking for a pier like the one at the start of the race. We finally asked a janitor if this was where the bike race ended. He said, 'What race?'

"In a way, that summed it up for us. The officials had left, there was no trace of a finish line, no confetti, no cameras."

As she crossed the finish line – final time: thirteen days, twenty-three hours, thirty-six minutes – a weary, relieved smile lit her face. "We did it!" she mouthed, issuing her favorite pronoun. She had finished a race that almost anyone else with her conditioning, with her experience, would never have started.

Despite the lack of public acclaim for doing something only a handful of women had ever done, despite what could have been an insulting monetary award, Mariolle knew, right down to her sinew and synapses, that she would be back to have another crack at RAAM the following year. She had been stronger at the finish than at the start, which boded well for the future. Business school would just have to wait.

She returned to RAAM in 1985 with the same goal as the year before – to finish in eleven days. This time, however, having learned a lot about training, she had a realistic chance of achieving it. In the year preceding the race, her practice mileage almost doubled to about 500 per week, and in May she tuned up for RAAM with a record-setting Seattle-to-San Diego ride – 1,300 miles in less than five days. That represented a 280-mile-per-day average, just what was needed to go coast to coast in eleven days.

The Mariolle crew for 1985 was increased to eleven; the vehicles, to three – chase car, errand car, and motor home. Everyone was assigned a job – masseuse, cook, mechanic – with scheduled shifts and planned rest time. Improved logistics and fitness paid off, as Elaine finished in a time of ten days, twenty-three hours, and forty minutes. She was pleased with her time, which represented an extraordinary three-day improvement, but not pleased with another third-place finish. Despite damage to the ulnar nerves in her wrists ("I couldn't turn keys or unscrew jars for months") and doctors' recommendations that she never do a race of such magnitude again, it wasn't long before she had resolved to do next year's race.

During 1985 and 1986 Mariolle concentrated more on speed, less on endurance. Over the years RAAM had become more than just an exercise in sleep deprivation. Now plenty of riders could stay on their bikes twenty-plus hours a day, but how many could average fourteen or fifteen miles per hour all that time? As a two-time RAAM finisher, Mariolle figured she'd take her chances on endurance. "My attitude

Both Mariolle and her bike are in road-ready condition. (Courtesy of UNIPRO)

was, I know I can do the distance; now let's see if I can do it fast. Six weeks before the 1986 RAAM, I topped out at a thousand miles in a single week. After that it was speed, speed, speed. That gave me time to recover from the aches and pains of the endurance work, but I still had it in my system."

She rode century and double-century races as fast as she could. Every Tuesday and Thursday, she took a train to the town of Fremont and rode back to Berkeley via Mount Hamilton, a 150-mile joy ride. "By the 1986 RAAM I was in the best shape I could be in. All the planets were properly aligned. As Vance says, 'I was dialed in.'"

Mom and Pop Mariolle—as well as third-timer Matthew—signed on for Elaine's support crew that year. "I wanted them to see what I did every year for my summer vacation," Elaine said, with a dimpled laugh. "They were real helpful." She paused, apparently deciding if it were appropriate to provide more detail. "The thing about my parents is that they always treated the eleven of us as individuals. They let us live our lives, which means everything to me. It was great having them along on RAAM at a time in my life when I didn't have to worry anymore what the folks thought."

By 1986 scientific methods were being applied to RAAM, and Mariolle, as much as anyone, benefited from that explosion of knowledge. Taking advantage of speed training, sleep pattern analysis, liquid carbohydrate drinks, the latest bicycle technology, and good weather, she won the women's division of RAAM in a new record of ten days, two hours, four minutes. Sleeping but two hours a night – three after building a five-hour lead – she averaged fifteen miles per hour for the crossing, finishing seven hours ahead of second-place finisher Sue Notorangelo.

In the wake of her extraordinary victory and storybook comeback she said, "I did the 1984 RAAM on a wing and a prayer. After I finished third again in 1985, I looked at the race and decided 'I want to win.' Then I asked myself, 'What do I have to do?'"

In a remarkably short time, she had sprinted from the huge pack of recreational pedal pushers and joined an elite group of world-class endurance cyclists at the very forefront of the sport. How did she do it? What synergistic mix of mental and physical skills gave her the impetus she needed?

"Well, first of all, I have a strong constitution," she explains, seated in her Berkeley apartment, next to a desk heaped with books, papers, and magazines, emblematic of a fledgling writing career. "My body handles stress. It doesn't break down, doesn't get all torqued out if the bicycle is a millimeter out of sync. Even at the end of RAAM, I wasn't bobbing and weaving; I wasn't hallucinating."

When pressed, she speaks perfunctorily of the importance of "good quadricep muscles" and "good aerobic capacity," but her heart isn't in it. Her speech, uncharacteristically, lacks passion. Her tone remains downbeat when pressed to talk about slow-twitch muscle fibers, which endurance athletes are supposed to have in such proliferation. She's never been tested for such things, she says, and doesn't have the foggiest idea how she would rate. Nor, her tone implies, does she much care. Clearly, physical skills do not pique her interest as much as mental ones. "I have the right frame of mind for a race across America," she says, her usual animation returning. My strategy is to nickel-and-dime my way across, breaking down the overall goal into small, manageable segments.

"All this really stems from my philosophy that we're capable of doing a lot more than we think. We first have to set goals, then follow through and work hard. In my case, I have some talent, but mostly it's perseverance. I tend to want to show that little voice in the back of my head saying, 'I wonder if I can do that.'"

The trouble with an event as long and potentially heartbreaking as RAAM is that a little voice like that gets a lot of air time. For some, it never shuts up. And the wonder inherent in the question "Can I do it?" can easily turn to doubt. For the undisciplined, it becomes refrain, dirge, death knell.

A defense against such defeatist emotions, and one that Mariolle regularly employs, is to "enjoy the heck out of your work. I am neither insane nor a masochist. I just really think RAAM is fun. Sunrises, sunsets, watching the days roll by, looking at the map and knowing I've crossed the country – it's a sort of frontier mentality.

Elaine Mariolle, now thirty-four, has, in Freudian terms, a well-developed id. Her instinctive energies are forever on simmer, her passions never far below the surface. Called bouncy, vibrant, dynamic, spirited, a firecracker, her enthusiasm is downright infectious. She is having a love affair with life that could give the most hardened of cynics pause.

After three times across the country on a bicycle with almost no financial compensation, most people would have called it a career and taken their slide show on the circuit. But Elaine has kept a whirlwind pace. Besides writing bicycling articles for newspapers and magazines, she can list the following among her post-RAAM achievements:

She rode from Moscow to Leningrad as part of a group of twenty-five Americans and twenty-five Soviets, a cultural exchange program. "I went out of curiosity rather than with some big political message. My background is geography, and I loved going to places that had been closed to foreigners since World War II. I do think, though, the bicycle is a great tool for bringing people together."

She led a tour of amateur bicyclists across the United States, often on the same roads she had traveled on RAAM. "It took us five days to reach the place where I first slept," she laughs. The sixty-six people in her group ranged in age from eighteen to seventy-four; most had never done a century ride before, and most didn't believe they could make it. That's where Mariolle, a natural cheerleader, came in. "It was great going from ocean to ocean and watching their confidence grow, celebrating that at the end. We took longer than I took on all three of my RAAMs put together. But everybody made it."

She rode the Iditabike, the 210-mile, winter, off-road Alaska bike race. Battling the most snow ever in Iditabike's five-year history, the riders lost the race to Mother Nature. Says Mariolle, "We faced six feet of snow that never set up. I rode one mile, then pushed my bike the next fifty-one (in twenty-seven hours). We all had to be airlifted out."

It sounds like a disaster, but Mariolle doesn't think so. "It was the neatest experience of my life," she bubbles. "It was so beautiful—I saw the northern lights, which captured my heart. Several of us banded together, trudging through the snow; we were all scared, but no one spoke of it. In all these things I do there is a sense of linking up with humanity. The physical risk was definitely a notch above anything I've ever done before. It all seemed tame by comparison.

"RAAM, the Iditabike, they changed the way I see myself, changed the way I live my life. And when I find myself stuck, I try to remember them. They kind of give me that can of spinach, like Popeye. I'm more willing to take risks now, calculated risks. I'm willing to really try, and if I fail I know that I really tried, that I extended myself. I know what I am, one way or the other. And that's all I really want to know. I want the truth and the courage to just keep going."

Whew! Why demand so much of yourself? "Because I want to know I've been alive. I want to know I've felt something. Win, place, or show, there's no way you can find out what you're made of unless you put yourself out there. I'll know when to stop. When my days of actual competition are over, I'll know they're over, and it'll be okay. This is, after all, just one chapter in a whole book of adventures."

ERIC HEIDEN

Rebel with a Cause

Eric Heiden jerked the handlebars of his mountain bike hard left, stood up on the pedals, and assailed the steepest trail in the Windy Hill Recreation Area. Heiden, five-time Olympic gold medalist, former U.S. Pro Bicycle champion, was in yet another race. This one, however, was not about medals or ribbons – he never cared much for that anyway. It was instead about the satisfaction of winning.

His pursuers were rangers who wanted to ticket him for riding on trails recently closed to mountain bikes. The way Eric saw it, he'd been legally riding those trails for years with no problems – so why change the rules? He wasn't going to take it – not without his usual jab at authority.

The guys in uniforms had a big advantage: cars, radios, weapons, and personnel. Heiden, dressed only in shorts and running shoes, had his bike, his wits, and an intimidating physique. It was a mismatch: If it were a basketball game, Heiden would spot the cops points.

Eric Heiden had a ninety-mile bicycle "fun" ride the morning we were scheduled to meet, so he asked if we could postpone our visit until midafternoon. It was a warm Indian summer day when I arrived at his Woodside, California, home, an A-frame mountain retreat nestled in the cool shade of the redwoods.

Heiden drifted out of his house, directed me to park next to the pool, and called off his dog, Ursa, a 110-pound Akita that had been barking threateningly at me, effectively holding me prisoner in my car. Reassured by his master's touch, Ursa was instantly transformed into a friendly giant.

Heiden was wearing shorts, and I immediately found my eyes drawn to his famous legs. Impressive ankles and calves, shapely and tanned, but g-a-a-a-d those thighs! World-class quads. Why, the man's rectus femoris and vastus externus could make Michelangelo reconsider David. Muscles so well defined, so bursting with vitality, they appeared to breathe. I'd last seen them wrapped tightly in a Spandex cycling suit; but here, in the naked flesh, the definition was theatrical. They bulged Schwarzenegger-like, disproportionate with the rest of his six-foot-one-inch, 195-pound body. Muscles run amuck.

We didn't shake hands; Eric, in fact, barely nodded in greeting. Somehow, though, with him it wasn't rude or unfriendly but a manifestation of his low-key, casual nature.

"That's quite a drive. You're a damn recluse," I said, gazing on the grounds.

He smiled.

"Nice spot – if you like natural beauty."

He nodded.

In at least one of the many interviews Eric had given after his five gold medals in the 1980 Olympics, he had expressed the simple desire to own a redwood tree. Well, he had certainly achieved that goal – there were dozens on his three acres. To the east, the trees thinned, permitting a view of the smog-shrouded southern Bay Area below. He motioned for me to sit, and we dropped to the porch.

"I bought this place four years ago," he said, "but I've been coming up to this hill for about ten." He gazed east at the sinister brown haze below. "Ten years ago, the air wasn't bad here. Now, this is a typical day." His still youthful face showed mild disgust. He was thirty-two, but except for a subtle dusting of gray hairs on the temples of his brown mop, he looked five years younger than that. The forelock of his hair looped over his forehead like an afterthought; his thin face was punctuated by a strong nose and jawline and, frequently, a boyish grin. His eyes were an unusual mix of green, yellow, and brown. The overall effect was distinctly, powerfully, handsome.

I started at the beginning: I asked him about his genes. As we talked, Heiden warmed to the task.

"I don't think you can be a good athlete and not have good genes.

But it's certainly more than that. I also had great parental – and grand-parental – support. Both of my parents were real active in sports."

I had read that Dr. Jack Heiden, an orthopedic surgeon, had run cross-country and been cocaptain of the Wisconsin fencing team for two years in the fifties. Now, in the nineties, he was a cyclist. He had once broken three ribs in the Masters Time Trial Cycling Championship; another time he won the national Road Race for Masters. Eric's mother, Nancy Heiden, is a formidable recreational tennis player. "And my grandfather," he added, "was a hockey player, a swimmer, and a gymnast. That group had Beth and myself on skates when we were two." He smiled sheepishly. "I wasn't very good then."

His father confirms that: "Eric fell down a lot, whined a lot. 'I'm too little to skate,' he said. So I told him, 'Okay, then we'll come back next week.'"

Though Mom and Dad raised two world-class athletes, both kids concur: Their parents were supportive but not pushy. "We got to try a lot of things when we were growing up," Eric said, "skating, hockey, running, tennis, soccer, swimming, diving, and skiing. My dad organized the youth soccer in town; my grandfather organized the youth hockey program."

The family converted a large room of their house into a gymnasium, and there Eric and Beth (sixteen months younger than Eric) had their pullup contests, their wrestling matches, their incessant games of skill. It was there that they kept their slide boards for speed skating training, their rollers for stationary biking. "For awhile we had a basketball hoop up, too," Beth said, "but the dining room was just a Dutch window away and the ball kept landing on the table. That got old with my mother."

The Heidens' grandparents lived on a lake, and like most Wisconsin lakes it froze in the winter. Eric's tawny eyes brightened in fond recollection. "The ice was crystal clear on Lake Mendota. It was so clear that we had to skate with a hockey stick ahead of us to make sure we didn't skate right into open water. You could see to a depth of at least twenty feet."

The Heidens gravitated toward boisterous pack racing, where they quickly excelled. "When I was seven and Beth was six, my uncle entered us in the Madison city races. We each did two races, a fifty- and seventy-five-yard sprint. Mostly I remember standing at the starting line shaking in my skates. But I won both my races, and I think

Eric Heiden's three favorite things to talk about while cycling

1. Girls
2. Girls
3. Girls

Beth won hers, too. After that, we were both recruited by the Madison speed skating club.

"Now my mom had to drive us not only to Monday hockey but to Wednesday speed skating. And from the time I was thirteen, speed skating meant traveling to Milwaukee, a three-hour roundtrip, five days a week. Beth and I would go to school until noon, then off to Milwaukee, where we'd skate from about 2:00 to 6:00, then the drive back."

"Boy, long day for Mom. What did she do while you were skating?"

He shrugged. "Read, knit sweaters, played tennis." (Mrs. Heiden reacted as though it were a question devoid of reason: "There are always things to do," she said. "Write down that I mastered ground strokes.") The question had made Eric think. "As I look back on how good I was able to become, I couldn't have done it without my parents. They were so supportive. And I just don't think that's the norm anymore."

The Heidens progressed from pack racing to metric skating, the Olympic-style event in which only two skaters, confined to a particular lane, are on the ice. Like the little kid who can unhesitatingly recall his first baseball game, Heiden carries the memory of the first world-class skating event he ever saw. "I went to Milwaukee as a teenager to see the World Sprint Championships," he said with recollected awe. "Holy smoleeee, there were some big boys there. Strong, well-developed, with skin-tight suits that really accentuated the butt and thigh muscles."

When he was sixteen, he made the Junior World team, which

included the chance to go to Europe, all expenses paid, no parents or school for three months. He chuckled. "I said, 'Where do I sign up?'"

I asked him about Europe as a teenager. Was it a learning experience?

"Well, I learned how to get hammered. France . . . cognac . . . very nasty."

"And the racing?"

He wrinkled his forehead, as if to say, "That's harder to remember." Finally: "I did well but not spectacularly. I won some junior races. Sometimes we competed against the big boys. I can still remember my first race against the seniors in Inzell, West Germany. We were skating around the rink in warmups, and I came up behind this huge Russian skater. I thought, 'God, I've got to compete against that guy!' When I got around to the other side and looked back—it was a girl!" He laughed gleefully. "I thought, 'Thank God I don't have to race against her!'"

At seventeen, he competed in the Junior World Championships in Heerenveen, Holland. "Europe was a good reward for working so hard during the year," he said. "But for me, the best experiences that year were not on the ice."

He fell in the world championships, finishing a disappointing tenth. Nevertheless, he was optimistic about the future. "I felt like I was over the hump. I now believed if I worked hard, I could make the Olympics."

He had the talent, the winning attitude, now all he needed was a coach. "The coach is everything in speed skating," he said, a mix of humility and hyperbole. "You rely on the coach 100 percent—never doubt her."

I was curious how much credit he assigned parents, coach, and genetics for his success.

He considered this. "For me, coach 50 percent, parents 30 percent, genetics 20 percent. When I was fourteen, speed skating gold medalist (1972 Olympics: women's fifteen hundred meters) Diane Holum came to Madison on a phys. ed. scholarship. The Madison Speed Skating Club recruited her as coach. She was great. Over the next six or seven years, fifteen Madison skaters made the world team—all because of her."

Diane Holum brought to the Heidens a systematic discipline that would spill over into other areas of their lives. Added to their physical skills and their aggressive spirit, the effect was synergistic. Both Heidens began doing two-a-day workouts, intense and varied. The workout schedule was written out on charts, so the athletes knew a month in advance what they would be doing. Every week there were sessions of lifting weights, running sprints, running hills, running distance, running stadium steps, circuit training, dry skating (jumping from one leg to the other in the skating position), track skating, slide boarding (another skating simulation drill done in the stocking feet), and lots and lots of bicycling.

Long before the Heidens' Olympic success, Holum recognized that they were special. She spoke to *Sports Illustrated* writer Kenny Moore about the intangibles that separated them from the other young skaters: "Both Heidens have exhibited an ever-increasing capacity for work. . . . They were thirteen and fourteen, in with a lot of other kids who started training hard at the same time. Most of them leveled off after one year. The Heidens did, too. A lot quit then. Eric and Beth didn't. They just kept on. They have always had perfect racing temperament. There is little visible emotion; it's all submerged in concentration, but the key was back when they hung on. You have to hang on. It's the hardest thing to teach, that you will make that jump, that sudden improvement. It's like faith. Inside themselves, they believed."

Back in the redwoods, Eric was still thinking of Diane. "She was the one who got Beth and me interested in bicycling. It became our most important off-ice workout. One exercise was to bike from Madison to Northbrook, Illinois—two hundred miles away.

"I started racing bikes when I was fourteen. Speed skating was still number one, but bicycling was sure a lot of fun. But I always had to worry about falling off my bike and ruining my skating career.

"My dad worried about it even more than I did. He thought bicycling was just too dangerous. Finally we were at a junior race in Milwaukee, and I talked him into buying me a decent bike. He gave me a check for $250. While I was gone, he witnessed this terrible accident on the track. He searched high and low for me to get that check back." Heiden smiled. "It was too late. By the time he found me I already had my used Falcon.

"The high point of my early phase of bicycle racing came when I was fourteen. It was the Wisconsin State Championships, and I was trying to qualify for the nationals, intermediate division. I needed to get third. It was a dead heat, a photo finish, between myself and this other guy. I didn't make it. I finished fourth." He looks up with the calm of a yogi. "But that's okay."

With the 1976 Olympics approaching, Heiden intensified his focus on skating. Just before the Olympics, he finished second in the Junior World Championships to a South Korean skater.

"Then on to the Olympics."

"Innsbruck, Austria. I had a blast," he said. With the impish grin, the rising inflection, he suggested a little kid recalling his trip to Disney World. "Inside the Olympic Village, it was our own little town. Good food, free pinball and tunes – you picked up the earphones when you came in." His face took on a somber look. "Of course, I also remember the security: metal detectors, dogs, machine guns, big fences. It was four years after the Munich Olympics (when terrorists killed eleven Israeli athletes), and they weren't screwing around."

The smile returned. It was the devilish smile of the unindicted prankster. "Of course, that didn't stop us from having fun," he said. "Some friends and I ripped off five huge Olympic flags. The cops spotted us sawing down a flag pole, but I pulled up the whole thing – pole and all – and sprinted away from them." He laughed. "It might have been my best race of that Olympics." He looked down at the ground; this was one story he wasn't proud of. "I was just happy to be there. My goal had just been to make the Olympic team – I forgot there was more to be done. I finished nineteenth in the five thousand meters. In the fifteen hundred, I actually had the best time with two laps to go. But then a big windstorm came blowing in. Winds were up to forty miles per hour gusting. I came around a turn expecting a big tailwind and almost got knocked over backwards. At the end, I had nothing left. I finished seventh. I remember because they gave some neat diplomas to the first six places, and I just missed it."

When he went back to high school in Madison, a girl he knew said, "Wow, the Olympics. How you going to top that?" "You wait," he replied, "I'm going to be world champion."

One of his dad's favorite lines was, "If you want to be a champion, you have to train like a champion." Eric was, at long last, receptive to that advice. He put his training regimen in Diane's hands. Her philosophy was to slowly increase the workouts. So each year he was with her, the training got more intense. It went from five days a week, to six, to seven. Two workouts on six days, one workout on the seventh.

It paid off. In 1977 Heiden, age eighteen, went to Heerenveen, Holland, for the men's World Speed Skating Championship. In pursuit of the all-round title, he won the five hundred meters, placed third in the fifteen hundred and ninth in the five-thousand. That sort of fade on the longer races is characteristic of American skaters. With only the ten thousand meters remaining, few gave Heiden any chance of winning the race or the all-round title.

His best time ever in the ten thousand was 15:27; he needed a 15:02 to be all-round world champion. As if any further incentive were required, he was paired with Olympic champion Piet Kleine. Heiden matched Kleine stroke for stroke for the first five miles. Every lap they alternated inside and outside lanes, a graceful weave with a practical effect: Keep the distance equal. Jack Heiden compared it to "watching geese in flight." At the end, Eric tapped a new source, put on a powerful sprint, and won in 14:59.

His time was an incredible twenty-eight seconds better than his personal record. "That's why it felt like a fluke. The guys I beat had been beating me by twenty or more seconds in the five thousand." He was, in fact, the first American since 1891 to capture that speed skating title.

Eric's championship encouraged him to work even harder to prove that it wasn't a fluke. "Now I was beginning to believe that I really could expect something in return for all that training. It made all the hard work worthwhile."

For the next three years, Heiden was the dominant speed skater in the world. From 1977 to the 1980 Olympics at Lake Placid, he lost only two individual races. One of the losses, in the 1978 World Championship in Gothenberg, Sweden, gnaws at him more than any defeat in any sport in his life, and it says loads about his character. "Back then, the rule was that if you won the first three races, you were automatically World Champion. Just show up and finish the fourth race, that's all. So I won the first three and finished eighth in the last race. Afterwards, I couldn't believe I had blown a race that way. I was world champion but real disappointed in myself. I never failed to go all out again. It taught me that you have to please yourself." He launched into a quick chorus from the Rolling Stones: "Can't get no satisfaction . . ."

Speaking of satisfaction, most people can't get past the training, the arduous workouts, necessary to be world champion. I asked him what his secret was.

"The secret is liking it. I like setting goals and accomplishing them. If someone asks, 'What makes you happy?' I say, 'Accomplishing something.' I like the sense of accomplishment I get from doing workouts."

Good thing. Because with Diane Holum for a coach, Heiden had plenty of workouts. "During the year, I'd miss maybe four days – two to being sick, two to just being lazy."

Lazy? It wouldn't compute.

"One reason I like workouts is the feeling at the end of the day, when you've trained as hard as you can, and you sit down with that big plate of food. You feel sooo good about it." He chuckled in happy reflection. "One time, after a major workout, two other guys and I bought a whole cake, split it into three equal parts, and ate it all."

I agreed that it was a heck of an accomplishment, then urged him on to the 1980 Olympics.

"Lake Placid," he nodded, lips pursed. "This time I was all business, really focused. I know I walked through town, but I don't even remember it. I was so intent on skating. Oh, but I do remember the live shows – Harry Chapin, Tina Turner – and shooting off a flare gun in the Olympic Village. Oh, and I stuck a live lobster in Beth's bed. They were uptight about security, too, but I had to give them a little jab."

Not all of Heiden's pranks have been without malice. There was, for example, the case of the pushy Norwegian journalist who would habitually knock on his hotel door late at night, rudely demanding a story. "He got his payback," Heiden said in a businesslike tone. "I doused him with a bucket of water from above. Got him good. He was pissed.

"The hardest part of the Olympics was racing every other day. I never really had a day off. I was either getting up for the race, doing the race, or coming down from the race. And always worried about the next one. I didn't sleep much, though I did get better at that."

In between naps, Heiden put up some big numbers: five races, five gold medals, five Olympic records, one world record.

"After it was all over and I was leaving the rink I thought to myself, "This is the best shape I'll ever be in my life." He laughed that infectious laugh. "I demonstrated that immediately. I'd gotten a bottle of champagne for each race, and when it was all over Tom Plant (a fellow racer) and I drank every drop in about two hours." He chuckled. "We were toasted."

But then he sobered up for the first day of the rest of his life, and the endorsements started rolling in. He had an agent, an attorney named Arthur Kaminsky, who fielded offers. At Eric's request, he turned down most of them, including 7-Up and several camera companies. Was it a moral issue?

"Well, I don't drink 7-Up," he said. "And back then I didn't know anything about cameras. I don't feel right pretending to know something when I don't. I have to believe in it – that's my standard. Now I'd feel better doing it because I've gotten into photography.

"I did some work for Schwinn and Descente (cycling clothes) and Crest toothpaste. But I turned down corn flakes – they were going to pay half a million – and I even eat corn flakes. But I didn't want to be on a cereal box." He paused, not so much to gather his thoughts as to find the right words. "I don't want to be that . . . popular.

"It wasn't a hard decision. I've never had a problem with money. I've always gotten what I needed. When you start doing endorsements, the companies think they own you. Instead of hanging out on Windy Hill, you have to show up for meetings. I'd rather hang out on Windy Hill.

"I want privacy. I don't want to hang out with vice presidents. When people know who you are, you have to watch every move. If I want to pick up a piece of chicken with my fingers, I don't want to be wondering who's watching."

This guy was for real – as down-to-earth as he appeared. In 1980 the Associated Press and United Press International, in separate polls of European sportswriters, chose him as the world's Outstanding Male Athlete of 1980. But in the United States, where the gold medal in hockey stirred nationalistic fervor, the votes went to the members of the hockey team. Most athletes with his achievements would have been annoyed, but Heiden breathed a huge sigh of relief.

As he told the *New York Times*, "All that publicity for the hockey team is great. It saves me a lot of hassles. I don't have to worry about people knowing who I am. If people don't know I'm in town, they don't recognize me. If they know I'm there, it's autographs and the same questions over and over and 'Would you please pose with me for a picture?' It gets kind of boring – except that sometimes I get to meet some nice girls."

To *Sports Illustrated* he elaborated on the downside of popularity: "All the attention can be a drag. I really prefer being obscure. I liked competing in a sport that was obscure – at least in the States it was. But now people are beginning to recognize me around Madison, and it's kind of hard. I like to be myself and do what I like without being watched – or even being noticed. I'm planning to quit racing. . . . Maybe if things had stayed the way they were and I could still be obscure in an obscure sport, I might want to keep skating. I really liked it best when I was a nobody."

Heiden was no longer a nobody. As he was the first person in history to win five gold medals in the Winter Olympics, the spotlight found him. Like it or not, his days of complete obscurity were as dead as disco, and in places like Oslo and Amsterdam he was more famous than rock stars or soccer players. In most European cities, he could no longer sit quietly quaffing beers in a favorite pub. "I'd have to sign coasters all night." As a measure of his fame, when the Soviet wrestling team came to Wisconsin, they identified Madison not as the capital but as the birthplace of Eric Heiden.

Throughout all the tumult, the hero worship, the crush of people trying to make money off his accomplishments, he has remained, well, Eric. He let the first photographer who reached him snap his picture with five gold medals garishly dangling from his neck, but he regretted it and was never that tolerant again. Today he is an absentee curator of his own museum, claiming that he doesn't even know where to look for his gold medals. "I'm not impressed with gold medals," he said evenly. "I'm impressed by people who work hard. If you win but don't work hard, so what? I guess I inherited that attitude from my dad."

Nor is he terribly impressed with victory banquets, of which he has endured plenty, most recently when he was inducted into the Wisconsin Hall of Fame. "I always have to sit at the front table with the mayor and other bigwigs, and the conversation can get pretty lame. What do you say? Please pass the butter? Meanwhile, at the back of the room, my friends are having a great time, laughing, throwing rolls."

Actually, as Heiden would discover, some tolerable side effects did accompany the Olympic hoopla. When applying to medical schools, for example, it didn't hurt to have five gold medals on the old resume. Then, too, there were the women.

"I got to go to Hugh Hefner's mansion," he said brightly, like a kid who just found his first *Playboy* magazine. "An agent in L.A. set it up. I went to breakfast there . . . saw a playmate through a doorway. It was fun." There followed a stint on the Johnny Carson Show. "I told them I'd do it only if I could talk to Johnny – no substitutes. It was fun, too."

After the 1980 Olympics, Eric celebrated for a while – a short while. He partied and backpacked and kayaked and bicycled, gener-

Eric Heiden can always handle himself in a crowd. (Courtesy of David Nelson)

ally doing the things he'd put off while he was busy becoming the best speed skater in the world. But he is not by nature hedonistic and could not drift for long. He is one who needs specific challenges. Goal in place, course plotted, his accomplishments can be prodigious. And that is when he is the happiest.

In the long term, he had an extensive life blueprint: finish college, go to med school, become an excellent orthopedist like his dad. But because that would take about a decade to accomplish, he needed to fill the holes with short-term challenges.

Then one day he thought, as almost no one else could think, "Wouldn't it be a gas to go for the Summer Olympics, too."

He knew the sport had to be bicycling, but which event? Although he was most experienced in road racing, he decided his best chance to make the Olympic cycling team was in a track event. "I'm really too big for a bicycle," he admitted, "especially climbing hills. On the track there are no hills, plus I figured I had track sense from skating."

He finally settled on the one-kilometer (thousand-meter) time trial because, he said, "In that race I'm out there alone and can't hurt anyone but myself."

So off he went to San Diego for the Olympic trials. He made up for a total lack of experience with overpowering strength, great instincts, pure athletic prowess, and that competitive intangible that scientists are still trying to identify. The combination enabled him to finish second, a remarkable, infinitesimal fourteen hundredths of a second behind the leader. In the time trials, Heiden discovered, only the winner goes to the Olympics, so he became an alternate. But few call in sick to the Olympics, and he knew his chances of staying home were excellent.

As it turned out, all the American athletes stayed home. The United States boycotted the Moscow Olympics in protest of the Soviet Union's invasion of Afghanistan. Heiden, however, is used to achieving his goals, even if they have to be altered slightly to fit reality. Focused like a laser on going to the Summer Olympics, he succeeded four years later as a capable TV broadcaster, a color man in bicycling. He also did TV work at two more Winter Olympics – 1984 and 1988 in speed skating.

His life seemed to be full. But despite the TV work, the endorsements, and the school work, he decided to get serious about bicycling. "I wanted to be a respectable cyclist," he explained. "That was my goal. I had a couple of friends who were racing in Europe, and it sounded like a good life; I thought I'd give it a try for a while. The racing was mostly circuits – criteriums – and I had a blast traveling. I even won a race or two. Then in 1981 I turned pro. Soon after, I started racing with the 7-Eleven team and got to go back to Europe."

He set another goal for himself. "I decided I wanted to ride in the Tour de France. That was the ultimate. I think every cyclist dreams of that. I had no thoughts of winning it; I just wanted to finish."

Tour de France, stage eighteen. Eric Heiden, with a flat tire, waited impatiently for the team mechanic to arrive. If he were Greg LeMond, he thought without bitterness, the mechanic would have been here by now. But in the pecking order of big-time team bicycling racing, he was not top chicken. As one of the domestiques on the 7-Eleven team, his ultimate responsibility was to help Alexi Grewal win the race. In the strange, rarefied world of European road racing, he was both an individual racer and a team player. Sweating profusely in the golden glare of the French summer sun, he took off his helmet and waited.

The flat tire was a shame – he'd felt great. Mountains were usually his biggest problem, but today he'd had a good, strong climb to the top of Mount Glabier. But now the pack in which he was traveling was miles ahead. He felt thwarted, adrenaline backing up in his system, like gasoline in a clogged carburetor.

Ten minutes later, flying down the mountain at about fifty miles per hour, Heiden was desperately trying to regain his group. The gale-force winds created by his moving mass blew through his hair, ears, and nose, drying out his mouth. He leaned into turn after turn, alert to animals darting across his path. Do a header here and they'd be digging pebbly asphalt out of your skin for a year. Knowing that, he slowed down not a whit.

He was going much too fast for the turn—thirty-five miles per hour, he would later estimate. He saw the guard rail all right but couldn't avoid it. Clipping it with his derailleur, he was launched from his bike, over the guard rail and down a cliff. He rolled over and over, like a folded-up newspaper, coming to rest at the bottom of a ravine. Somewhere on the marquee of his rattled brain, the thought appeared: "God, I wish I'd put that helmet back on."

He lay there for a moment, inventorying body parts. Dazed and shaken, he was not, as far as he could tell, seriously hurt.

Ten minutes later, he was back on his bike. In the chase mode, surges of adrenaline temporarily masked other symptoms. In thirty minutes he caught his original pack. One of the European riders looked over at Heiden, whose eyes were beginning to roll around their sockets like loose marbles. "Eric," he called. "What's wrong?"

"Wrong?"

His next clear memory was of waking up in an ambulance. His first thought: He had failed to finish the Tour de France. "I wanted to finish so bad," he said. "Medical school was starting, so I knew it would probably be my only chance. It was the last racing day in the mountains, and I dumped it big time."

It was a disappointment, as was the entire 1986 season that followed. "I never felt right," he admitted. "After that concussion I had headaches, and then later that season I took another header in the Coors Classic in Reno. This time I was wearing a helmet, which was a good thing because the impact cracked that sucker. I clipped my pedal on a sharp left turn. The back tire flew up in the air, and as I tried to turn into it, the front tire hit a pot hole. I got launched. Hit the pavement and slammed into a curb. I was frowning on life."

Frowning or not, Heiden got back on his bicycle and finished the race. "You put so much into stage races, you gotta finish them," he said.

Besides mammoth physical skills, Heiden brought to bicycling the requisite belief in training and a willingness to do it long and hard. "I've been criticized for not training enough, but most days for two years I biked nine to five. I try to go all-out, no matter what I'm doing, and I gave bicycling 100 percent for two years."

U.S. Pro Cycling Championship, Philadelphia, 1985. Though few people gave Heiden a chance of winning the 156-mile criterium, he found himself in the lead pack late in the race. For fifty miles, he had been looking over his shoulder, expecting to be overtaken by his top team-mates, Davis Phinney and Ron Kiefel, both bronze medalists in the 1984 Olympics. His initial assignment was to try to control the pace of the front-pedalers to assist his 7-Eleven mates.

But as they began the last 14.4-mile circuit, six hours after they had started, Heiden realized that he had a real shot at winning the race. Phinney and Kiefel were not making their move, and the closer the lead pack got to the finish line, the more the race favored him. He was, after all, a fast-twitch kind of guy.

Coming off the last turn, he was sitting third in the five-man lead group. Having passed this spot ten times, he had already picked out his marker: He would make his move at the Swedish flag – one hundred yards from the finish.

It was as though the ending were choreographed. A seamless moment. As he reached the flag, the riders ahead of him moved to the right, leaving just enough of a gap for him to slide through on the left. The rest, a full-bore sprint to the finish, was no contest. As Eric's front tire crossed the finish line, a bike length ahead of Danish rider Jesper Worre, he thrust his arms into the air, acknowledging the cheers of the crowd, reveling in the achievement of another goal: Respectability was his. He was national champion.

He trained hard, he had ability, and he had luck. But he also had something else going for him that allowed him to win what was then the richest one-day cycling event in the world. He had a psychological edge. There was an undeniable tendency among the other riders to take Eric lightly. "He's talented but doesn't train enough," was the consensus. "He's involved in too many things."

It was true that Eric had a lot going on in his life. He had worked for ABC during the last two Olympics and done other TV work; two months earlier he had taken his medical school entrance exam; and just two weeks before the race, he had attended graduation exercises at Stanford. The following week, he was scheduled to cover the Tour de France for CBS. But then, for Heiden, none of that mattered. During a race, you shut everything else out; you stayed focused; you simply did your best.

"People have trouble believing this," he said, "but in speed skating, in cycling, I wasn't out there competing against the other guys. I just wanted to go as fast as I could."

We were now sitting in the sunburned grass on Windy Hill. Facing west, we watched the sun set in a blaze of reds and purples. Heiden's elbows rested on his knees, his arms dangling. Ursa ran the hillside like a puppy. "That's why I was so disappointed in that race in Sweden (in which he won the world championship but finished eighth in the final race.) I didn't go as fast as I could. I didn't do my best."

Listening to him, with the firm set to his jaw, the steely edge to his voice, it was easy to believe that he wouldn't let it happen again. I could see the headline: "Eric Heiden, Eighty, Hasn't Failed in Fifty Years."

Heiden powers his bicycle past a crowd of spectators. (Courtesy of David Nelson)

I was curious how much carryover there was from skating to bicycling. Did dominance in the former assure success in the latter?

He thought about it. "Well, physically, I went into bicycling already in pretty good shape from skating. I already knew how to train hard. The important muscles in skating – quads, butt, calf, back – are important in bicycling, too, and the amount you use them is about the same. Mentally, I had the ability to focus. I tend to commit to what I've decided to do, at the expense of just about everything else. I'm not saying that's good – you sacrifice some things, like partying – but it will make you a successful athlete.

"Another thing that enabled me to reach my full potential was what they call visualization. The night before, I'd go through a race in my mind, from beginning to end, down to the second. I would mentally diagram the perfect race. They've discovered that muscles have the same electrical potential when you're thinking about a race as when you're actually racing.

"Another key is being able to relax the right muscles. Being able to conserve energy by saving the parts of the body you don't need. When you're good, you use only the muscles you need for the specific exercise and relax the ones you don't need. I was able to do that in skating, but it's harder for me in bicycling."

In his final year of Stanford Medical School, his life seems as rooted as it's been since he was a wee skater. He's had a fairly serious romance for the past two years with Karen Drews, a second-year medical student. They are close, but he brushes off any talk of marriage. The problem is a mix of goals and geography. "I may be moving back to Wisconsin to study orthopedics," he said. "So who can say?"

Returning from Windy Hill in Heiden's pickup truck, with Ursa yelping joyfully in the back, Eric, not surprisingly, drove aggressively. As we were barreling down the hill, like Calvin and Hobbes on a runaway sled, I couldn't help wondering how big the explosion would be if Eric met Eric on this skinny, serpentine mountain road.

"Once a sprinter, always a sprinter, eh?"

He chuckled. "I used to have the hottest car, and I always drove it too fast. One time, I went all the way to L.A. going about 120 miles per hour. Outran a couple of cops. That's why I got this truck – so I wouldn't go too fast."

My fingers tightened around the door handle. I tried to relax by changing the subject. "Still planning a career in orthopedics?

"Or maybe emergency medicine."

"As in drug overdoses? gunshot wounds? car accidents?"

He nodded, mercifully keeping his eyes on the road, his classic profile in twilight silhouette. "I love it. The action, the intensity. It's like a race. Walk through the doors, and it's time to turn it on; walk out those doors, and it's 'Ahhh' – time to relax."

We squealed around another couple of turns, but listening to Eric, I began to relax. My knuckles regained their color, and I stopped biting my lip.

We were just chatting now. "You went back to the Tour de France as a medic, didn't you?"

"Yeah, that was fun. Three years – 1988 to 1990 – I worked for the 7-Eleven team as an assistant to the team doctor. I organized medicines, helped the cooks and mechanics. Once the race began, I'd oversee the mixing of the carbo drinks, drive the second car, and serve the pack guys."

Heiden was downright garrulous on this point, as though someone had zapped him with a current. "At the Tour, you gotta be prepared for anything. At some points, we're three days away from a pharmacy. There's daily weigh-ins, charts so that we know how much everyone drinks, colds and flu, crashes, abrasions and stitches, wear-and-tear injuries like tendinitis, and dehydration – that's the biggest worry. I'm like a general practitioner on the road, and I've gotten to see France. It's been a blast."

Heiden works hard, trains hard, studies hard, and yet all the man can talk about is how much fun he's having. That, I suppose, is what happens when you do what you love and love what you do.

For so long it was athletics that brought that twinkle to his eye, that bounce to his step, but now it is orthopedic medicine. Given Eric Heiden's perseverance in the development of his gifts, his unremitting reverence for his craft, and his persistent love of excellence, I'd put my bones in his hands.

Windy Hill Recreation Area. Heiden crested Windy Hill and began a switchback descent on his fat-tire bike. As he slid around a corner, he saw something that made him skid to a stop. In the parking lot below, a grim-faced ranger waited for him.

Heiden decided to skip that meeting; instead, he turned around, headed back up the hill, found an old, overgrown fire road that he was sure the rangers didn't know about, and descended that route. Emerging onto the paved highway, he shifted into high gear and cruised past the parking lot. The ranger was still there. Heiden smiled and waved to him. The ranger stared back balefully, his face a portrait of resentment. It conveyed the message "Nobody but nobody deserves to have that much fun."

KENNETH CRUTCHLOW

Adventure Cyclist

It was dark—can't-see-your-hand-in-front-of-your-face dark. Kenneth Crutchlow, twenty-eight, was reevaluating his position, which at that moment lay somewhere in central Oregon, alone, on a bicycle, pedaling slowly up a mountain that seemed like Everest. His position might have seemed tenuous to some; actually, when he thought about it, it seemed a bit tenuous to him. So he tried not to think about it.

It was around four in the morning, and he wondered if he were the only person still awake in this time zone. His partner and teammate, Pax Beale, and their two-person support team were no doubt asleep twenty miles ahead in their Old Cortes motor home. No car had passed in more than an hour; there were no other cyclists. And besides the erratic chink-chink-chink of his chain and his own mutterings, the only sounds were those of other species. "Animal sounds," he thought, but that was about as far as his knowledge took him. On the other hand, his imagination ran wild and free.

Experience and philosophy prodded him forward, like a hand to the back. "Just keep moving," he would tell himself, ad nauseam. "You'll never get anywhere if you get off and push. Keep those legs moving, moving." He had become a two-wheeled version of the Little Engine That Could.

He comforted himself with the knowledge that eventually his four-hour stint would pass and he would get off his bike, slap hands with Pax, crawl into the motor home, and sleep. Ah, sleep! The word was a lullaby. It wrapped itself around him like a down comforter. Hard as he tried, he could not remember the last time he wasn't sleepy. He closed his eyes, then quickly caught himself. "Not my turn . . . wait your turn." The agreement with Pax was four-hour shifts—no exceptions. And an agreement was an agreement. End of story.

With maybe two hours to go, he knew he had to get tough. But he also knew—a confidence born of experience—that he would get tough. Shifting artlessly to his lowest gear, he settled into a sputtering sort of rhythm, sufficient to keep the bicycle inching up the mountain road.

The lamp mounted just below the handlebars cast a slim shaft of light on the road ahead. It offered a slight beacon to the night, a buffer against loneliness, but no clues as to what lay on either side of the road. Forest, he figured, just as it had been for the past five hundred miles.

"Bloody hell, my back aches, my butt aches, I'm sleepy, tired. But I shouldn't complain. After all, I volunteered for this mission. I wanted to do this. Yes, but . . . why? Damn, I've forgotten, and there's nobody around to remind me . . . except me. Okay, get a grip, lad. You can't make it to Alaska, can't beat the ship, with negativity. And you have to make it—Pax is relying on you, you're relying on yourself. So unless you want to pedal back from Alaska, let's get something positive going. Whoa, what was that sound—an elephant? So anyway, if we're going to finish this—and we are going to finish this—must improve the ol' attitude. After all, it could be worse. I'm healthy. I'm free. I wanted to do this. I want to do this. Maybe a little song. Yeah, everybody join in, all together now:

> *Pack up your troubles in your ol' kit bag,*
> *and smile, smile, smile . . .*
> *While you've a lucifer to light your fag.*
> *Smile boys, that's the style.*

Why had London-born Kenneth Crutchlow undertaken such an ordeal— a two-thousand-mile bicycle relay race against a ship? It had begun innocently enough—a chat with fellow Englishman Troy Garrison, the public relations officer for a shipping company, P&O Lines. Like all PR people, Troy was forever hunting for new publicity angles. Knowing something about Crutchlow's penchant for betting on adventure, particularly his own adventures, Garrison was ready when Crutchlow admired one of his sleek white cruise ships, the *Arcadia*.

"Why don't you race the ship from San Francisco to Ketchikan, Alaska?"

Ken Crutchlow's four lessons of the road

1. Always know where the next water is because it's too heavy to carry.
2. There's nothing wrong with luxury accommodations – especially if someone else pays for it.
3. You can't stop until you get to the end.
4. It's better to have traveled and suffered than never to have traveled at all.

"Race? It's too bloody far for me to swim, Troy."

"No, run it. Or maybe bicycle. Do a relay with another cyclist. Beat the ship, and I'll get you fifteen hundred dollars and first-class passage back to San Francisco. If you lose, you pedal back."

To a man who once hitchhiked around the world to win a bet of a pint of beer, that sounded generous enough. He accepted. And he recruited his pal Pax Beale to be his relay partner.

Says Beale, now sixty-one and a world-class bodybuilder, "At first Crutchlow wanted to run against the ship. I told him, 'No way.' Then he came back to me and said, 'It's a bicycle race!' Even with bicycles, experts said that we didn't have a chance. The capacity of the ship was absolutely known. The *Arcadia* would do four hundred miles a day. What could we expect to do? Well, if we expected to win, we'd each have to cycle two hundred miles per day. That's quite a load, even for big-time endurance bicyclists, which we certainly were not."

A strategy meeting was called, and Crutchlow and Beale made the following deal: One, they would spend any amount of money necessary to win the race, even if it exceeded the fifteen-hundred-dollar prize. (It would eventually cost them – Beale, actually, since Crutchlow didn't have any money – four thousand dollars.) Two, under no circumstances would they concede – even if it got to the point that it was a mathematical impossibility to beat the boat to Alaska. They agreed they would pump the bicycles all the way to Alaska even if the ship had left the port and they had to pump them back again.

So while the ship had steady, constant speed on its side, the bicyclists had spirit, guts, ingenuity, and teamwork on theirs; what they lacked was preparation. Beale had been on a bicycle twice since elementary school, and Crutchlow was only slightly more experienced. The Englishman would later admit, "The Ketchikan adventure wasn't thought out too well. We didn't know exactly where Ketchikan was or that the AlCan Highway is, in some places, a narrow gravel road. Of course, the ignorance was partly intentional. I've found that if you know too much prior to the venture, good sense will tell you not to do it. You'll talk yourself out of it." Beale concurs: "If I'd thought much about this bicycle race, I wouldn't have done it."

"Up . . . up . . . up . . . down . . . down." On the freeway in northern Oregon, Crutchlow was drafting less than a foot behind the motor home, relaying speed changes to the driver. "Up [faster] . . . down [slower] . . . down . . . down." They had begun the journey drafting more than two feet behind the vehicle but soon discovered that inside twelve inches the vacuum tightened, and the drafting effect improved dramatically. On the freeway, they regularly hit speeds of thirty, forty, fifty miles per hour. (Pax Beale briefly hit sixty-two after being goaded on by some reporters.) But their hunger for speed, their gutty inclination to go all out to win the race was tempered by a sincere belief that if either rider actually hit the rear bumper of the Old Cortes, he would die.

"Down . . . down . . . down."

The day of their San Francisco departure dawned sunny-side up. There was a dockside champagne party for them, with dozens of friends and reporters milling about beneath festooned streamers. Their opponent, the huge, white cruise ship *Arcadia*, loomed nearby, casting a behemoth shadow over the festivities. Docked next to Beale and Crutchlow's bicycles, the ship fulfilled its role in the exaggerated David-and-Goliath tableau.

While Beale wore a red-white-and-blue cycling outfit, complete with stars and stripes, Crutchlow mingled and flirted in his usual pinstripe suit, doffing his bowler hat, mugging for the cameras, lobbing one-liners to the scribbling scribes, and generally playing the ham.

Outward appearances suggested the prototypical English adventurer, with stiff-upper-lip confidence; inside Crutchlow, however, a debate raged. At one point, amidst the tumult, he glanced at the bikes parked on the dock and the realization hit him right between the eyes: They had to ride those bikes all the way to Alaska! For a split second, his face sagged, his mustache drooped, and he took on the look of a man whose life expectancy is measured in days.

Festivities over, Crutchlow and Beale sat astride their bikes, joking with the crowd, awaiting the release of the final bow line, which was the agreed-upon signal to start the race. Finally, the huge rope splashed into the water and Crutchlow and Beale began a slow pedal cadence, all the while waving to the crowd like two Miss America candidates.

They rode together as a team past Fort Mason and onto the Golden Gate Bridge. It was a dreamy May day of exquisite proportions and vibrant colors: moderate temperature, light breeze, shimmering blue bay, white sailboats, the distinctive orange of the span itself. Crutchlow always felt a special rush around the bridge—he had run across it, rowed and swum under it. But this time his exhilaration was tempered by a very sobering thought: "Jesus Christ! We've got to pedal all the way to Alaska? This is going to be bloody tough!"

Looking west from the Golden Gate Bridge roadbed, 248 feet above bay level, Crutchlow and Beale could see the white hull and yellow smokestack of the *Arcadia*. She had already passed under the bridge and was nearing the Pacific Ocean. Beale thought, "God, look how far she's gotten already! Wait until she really gets fired up." Crutchlow thought, "Once the *Arcadia* really gets going, she'll do four hundred miles a day. She has an engine that will keep her going and going. But what do we have? No engine. Can I keep going?"

After the heady ambiance of the Golden Gate Bridge, the reality of Interstate 101 north brought them crashing to earth. After the partitioned cycling on the bridge, they suddenly merged with frenetic freeway traffic. Motorized vehicles ripped by them. The road began a steep climb. And after the bright sunshine that anointed them on the bridge, they now rode in cold shadows.

They exited at first opportunity and began weaving through Marin County. After a frustrating hour of trying to find frontage roads that parallel 101, they pulled over and held a team meeting. Crutchlow

With his girlfriend and Crutchlow looking on, Pax Beale is questioned by a policeman. (Courtesy of Kenneth Crutchlow)

said, "If we don't use the freeways, we might as well call it quits. We'll never get there."

Beale agreed. "The crowning, the potholes, the cross-traffic of these side roads makes traveling them ridiculous."

"It's illegal to bicycle on the freeways," said Linda Elaine Peterson, driver, nurse, gofer, coordinator, and Pax Beale's girlfriend. "You can't do it."

"Today we can," announced Crutchlow imperiously, and the motion was quickly passed. By the time they reached the Canadian border, they would be stopped by the authorities eighteen times, escaping each time by promising to end their life of crime at the next exit, which they did for a mile or two. "Ironically, we thought the freeways were a lot safer," says Crutchlow. "Despite the speed of the cars, the freeways were straight with no intersections or potholes, and people could see you. It's a shame the cops never saw it that way."

Near Eureka, a California Highway Patrol officer stopped them. He approached Beale, who was on the bike at the time, with a haughty swagger. "I'm writing you up," he said arrogantly.

"What for?" said Pax.

"Hanging on to a moving vehicle. It's illegal to hang on to a moving vehicle."

"Hanging on? I wasn't hanging on. I was drafting behind the motor home."

"Drafting? Don't shit me! I wouldn't drive my car six inches behind another vehicle, and you're telling me that you're doing it on a bicycle?"

"That's right."

"I don't believe you."

"Well, it's true. And if I can prove it to you, will you tear up that ticket?"

"You're on."

"Rev it up, gang!" Beale shouted. "Here we go!"

While the cop followed, Beale drafted behind the Old Cortes, raising his speed ("Up . . . up . . . up") to twenty . . . twenty-five . . . thirty. Then the red light went on, and the cop again pulled them over. This time, as he approached Beale, the arrogance was gone; in its place, bemused irritation. "Okay, I'm not going to write you up," he said. "And I've called ahead to all my boys from here to Oregon. They'll wave you right through." He turned to go, then turned back with a parting shot: "Oh, by the way, you're going to kill yourself."

"He didn't even say goodbye," said Beale, and he and Crutchlow enjoyed a good laugh over that.

The driving force in Crutchlow's life and the urge that defines so many of his adventures is "an intense desire to go from somewhere to somewhere else." In school, geography was the only subject in which he thrived.

He got his first travel fix when he was thirteen: a school trip to Belgium. "A great part of the fun for me was getting there. We took the ferry across the Channel." He takes a deep breath. "I can still remember the strong smell of the Gitane cigarettes."

When he turned twenty-one, his family threw a large birthday party for him, at which time he blithely announced that he was going to travel around the world. "It came as a complete shock to everybody, because for the past six years I had been an apprentice printer, and normally the next step was to start earning big money in the print. But I was not enamored with slaving away for the rest of my days. I had only completed the apprenticeship because I had been taught that if you start something you better finish. I finished the apprenticeship but discarded the possibility of spending a lifetime working as a printer. I wanted to see the world."

Crutchlow would see it—many times over. For the next seven years he lived an itinerant life, more-or-less continuously on the road, save the brief and occasional rejuvenating return to London. While his mates were digging in, he was roaming free. While they were establishing work and family goals, he was setting somewhat less traditional ones. "I decided I wanted to spend every New Year's Eve in a different country. I managed it about eight years running." In all, he chalked up about one million miles, sixty countries, eight arrests ("there was always an explanation"), and more adventures than he could count.

The press reported regular sightings of Crutchlow—"Crutchlow Fired Upon in Singapore," "Marooned and Suspected of Murder on 'Round the World Trip"—mostly because he made for such jolly good reading. The lad was a regular magnet for trouble, a scandal waiting to happen. In defense, Crutchlow admits to having endured more than his share of brushes with the law but insists that "I've almost always been innocent."

He was held for assault in Sydney, detained for five days as a spy in India, and in New Zealand he hopped the wrong fence while waiting for customs and was arrested as one of the Great Train Robbers. The topper, though, occurred while climbing Mount Fujiyama in Japan. A small rock slide carried Crutchlow a short way down the mountain, dropping him atop a dead body. He took the fellow's boots (his were ripped by the fall) and wallet to identify him to the authorities. As he tells the story, "A patrol met me as I was halfway down the

mountain and accused me of killing the bloke for his wallet. Compli-
cating the matter considerably, I couldn't speak Japanese, and they
couldn't speak English. They were frustrated, and so was I. One of
them sort of pushed me – not hard – but I whacked him in the face,
which is out of character for me. It was a big mistake because they
immediately arrested me."

On one of his many visits to India, he met an American named
Dennis Kirby. "Dennis became my mate. The question came up between us, 'How far can you get with no money?' With money you
could obviously do anything, so that was no challenge."

On one of his R and Rs in London, he watched an American kid on
TV bragging about his ability to travel on the cheap. Crutchlow, who
had already thumbed twice around the world, didn't much care for the
fellow's attitude. "His very tone was a challenge to me to race him
around the world. I called him and accepted the challenge. We agreed
to meet at a London pub on Drury Lane, but the Yank didn't show.
That really agitated me."

Sometime later, Crutchlow was in the States, and he complained
of the incident to his friend Kirby. "We had an agreement, but the
bloke didn't show," he groused. "You damn Yanks are all the same."

"You can't come over here talking like that," Kirby replied with
mock anger. "Dammit, then, I'll race you around the world."

"What stakes?"

"A pint of beer."

"Done!" said Crutchlow.

The rules were simple: (1) Each contestant will leave London with
ten pounds (twenty-four dollars) in his pocket; (2) no flying, no stealing, no borrowing; (3) each traveler must go through Sydney and San
Francisco.

And so it went, both men locked in intense combat over a matter
of principle and national pride. Locked, that is, for five days, until
Kirby got a gagging dose of reality that threw his principles helter
skelter. Stuck on the side of the road in a pelting rainstorm in Yugo-
slavia, the successful electrical engineer kept asking the question,
"Should I be doing this?" until *no* bullied *yes* into submission, whereupon he immediately quit the race and returned to his high-paying job
in America. Crutchlow, ignorant of Kirby's early retirement, carried on
with trademark doggedness, overcoming one seemingly insuperable
obstacle after another. He was shot at while trying to take a boat from

Singapore to Indonesia, had a ship captain take an axe to the door of the stateroom he occupied (it happened to be the captain's own stateroom in which Crutchlow was stowing away), worked his way across the Pacific Ocean as a deckhand, then hitched across the United States in seventy-one hours (an unofficial world record). To support himself, he sold blood, ate infrequently, and relied constantly, heavily, on the kindness of strangers. He slept whenever and wherever the situation permitted. His autobiography could appropriately be entitled *Around the World by the Seat of My Pants.*

Speaking of pants, it should be noted that Crutchlow disdained the traditional hitchhiking costume – T-shirt and jeans. Instead, "Sir Kenneth" always thumbs nattily attired in a bowler hat and pin-striped suit, carrying a rolled umbrella. "The idea came to me years ago in Afghanistan," he says. "I was hitching outside of Kabul, along with about twenty other travelers, when it hit me that I needed something to set me apart from the masses. I wanted some way to distinguish myself as British, but I didn't have what it takes to wave the British flag. I thought, 'What do people associate with the English?' Of course: bowler, pinstripe, and umbrella. So I went back to London, got a bowler, pinstripe, and umbrella and changed from a backpack to a suitcase and" – he laughs – "it changed me life. Everybody thinks my Rolls just broke down." He laughs again. "Absolutely, I tell 'em."

From New York, it was once again necessary to stow away, this time aboard a ship bound for Europe. "It was near Christmas, so I took my luggage – six shirts, a pair of pants, and some socks – to Saks Fifth Avenue and had them gift wrap them. They thought I was crazy. But dressed in my suit and carrying these Christmas presents, I walked right on board with no one questioning me."

As he watched the Statue of Liberty recede into the hazy soup that engulfed New York, it occurred to him that he was "doing the Ellis Island thing in reverse." He was stowing away to get to the *old* country. But unlike the tired, poor, and huddled masses, Crutchlow had his sights set on a stateroom. In pursuit of that, he befriended two English women, told them his story, and asked if he could sleep on their floor. They thought the whole thing too romantic for words and immediately assented.

The next challenge was to get off the ship. "When the ship docked at Cherbourg, France, I tried to walk down the gangway, but an immigration official asked me for my pass. I occasionally make a stab at some quick thinking, and this was one of those times. I remembered that Ginger Rogers was on board, so I told the officer that I wasn't a passenger but a journalist who had just bribed one of his men to let me on the ship so that I could interview Miss Rogers. He was upset and asked me to leave the ship immediately, which is, of course, exactly what I had in mind."

Crutchlow hitched to Paris, then on to Dunkirk, where he stowed away on the cross-channel ferry. Another hitch to London and on to the Thames Rowing Club, the finish of the race, where he arrived at 11:00 A.M. on December 22, exactly ninety-seven days after leaving. With visions of Phineas Fogg dancing in his head, Crutchlow had set aim on eighty days. But unlike the deep-pocketed protagonist of Jules Verne's novel, Crutchlow made the journey on a pittance. When he danced into the Thames Rowing Club, he still had seven pounds ten shillings in his pocket. "I had traveled thirty thousand miles on two pounds ten shillings," he likes to say.

When Crutchlow inquired about Dennis Kirby, he was handed a cable from him that read, "Amazingly well done, you're a world-class hitchhiker."

"He later sent me a dollar for my winning pint of beer," says Crutchlow with a satisfaction scarcely diminished by the passage of twenty years.

"I have no regrets," he adds. "I did what I set out to do. I proved a point – that the body can stand a hell of a strain and that one does not always have to have a plane ticket and money to travel."

"Up . . . up . . . up." Crutchlow, staring at the rear bumper of the Old Cortes, leaned into a downhill right-left-right turn. The scenery of southern Washington was probably impressive, but he couldn't afford to sightsee. He had to stay focused on that bumper.

He was feeling a little light-headed from exhaustion but relatively chipper. Even with the added risk, downhill sure beat hell out of uphill. And nature was, for the moment, favoring him. It was neither cold nor dark. The sun was expected up soon, and the violet haze on the horizon augured for a beautiful spring morning. After more than three hours of night riding, he could at last see a dim outline of the road. Best of all, he would be off the bike in thirty minutes, asleep in forty.

> *What's the use of worrying,*
> *it never was worthwhile.*
> *Sooo pack up your troubles*
> *in your old kit bag . . .*

In the seventies Crutchlow added athleticism to adventure. His resume should properly include the following accomplishments from that decade:
- Raced across Death Valley in the summer four times.
- Ran from Los Angeles to San Francisco.
- Bicycled from Death Valley to Las Vegas.
- Rowed a small skiff from San Francisco to Sacramento.
- Swam from Alcatraz to Aquatic Park, San Francisco.
- Did his own personal triathlon, bicycling from London to Edinburgh, running from Edinburgh to Dundee, swimming the Firth of Fourth.
- Bicycled from Los Angeles to Mexico City.
- Ran from San Francisco to Reno.
- Bicycled from San Francisco to Ketchikan, Alaska.

Film and photos of Crutchlow in the seventies reveal a spidery young man with long arms and legs, modestly muscled. Ichabod Crane on a bicycle. How could a man of such, well, ordinary physical prowess push his body to such extremes? "I never trained much for those things," he says, by way of explanation. "But I would schedule them close enough together so that I'd still be in decent shape from the previous one."

Crutchlow snorts derisively at critics who claim that his antics rightfully belong in a supermarket tabloid rather than on a proper sports page. He has something to say in response to the claim that they are nothing but publicity stunts to cash in on what Andy Warhol promised us: fifteen minutes of fame. "Any adventurer, I think, would be disappointed to do something that absolutely nobody notices. Of course you want to read about it in the paper—that's just human nature. It's flattering to have a Steve Boga call you up to do an interview, but fame? Naah, not really.

"I'll give you the perfect example. John Fairfax rowed six months, from the Canary Islands across the Atlantic, and landed at Hollywood, Florida, on the exact day the bloody astronauts stepped on the moon. What was going to be a page-one story was relegated to page sixteen (though Fairfax did get a congratulatory note from the astronauts). Fame, ha! Now I won't say it's not a dream that we all have for a while, but very early in the piece we recognize that it's dubious at best, that you can't count on it. You might start with the thought 'I'm going to be the world's greatest adventurer, and they're going to make a movie out of my life.' But you don't have to go very far down the path before you realize you've been beaten out by the really big story: 'Eagles beat Giants.'

One gets the feeling that if Crutchlow, who is amply blessed with the gift of gab, can't sell himself well enough to make a living in adventure, the odds are long on anyone else effectively doing it. Bruce Maxwell, against whom he twice raced across Death Valley, believes that Crutchlow, if he'd put his mind to it, could have replaced Muhammad Ali as the world's greatest self-promoter. "At our press conferences," says the soft-spoken Maxwell, "we were exact opposites. He had the media wrapped around his little finger. Charming—always kissing the ladies' hands—gregarious, dressed in his pinstripe and bowler. And that English accent doesn't hurt either. What's more," continues Maxwell, "although I think Ken is a very moral person, he isn't afraid to play with reality a bit if his version is more newsworthy. For example, before our first race across Death Valley he and I made a private $100 bet on the outcome. At that time it was a lot of money to both of us. Well, he told the press that the bet was $500, which had me worrying that he would hold me to it. But no, it was just his way of drumming up interest."

Crutchlow carries on about fame and fortune: "As for money," he snorts derisively again, "there's no money in adventure. Never has been, never will be. Even if you write a book, it won't sell well enough to make much difference. And these stunts cost a ton of money. The one I'm working on now—Peter Byrd rowing from Siberia to San Francisco—I have to raise a quarter of a million dollars. The guys I know—like John Fairfax, Peter Byrd—none of them make money. They may get expenses." He laughs. "They may even get a bicycle."

"This is about as real, about as authentic as it gets," thought Crutchlow, deep in a cycling crouch. "And probably about as dangerous." He was wheeling down the side of a mountain somewhere in Canada inches behind the rear bumper of the Old Cortes motor home, his heart in his mouth, his body draped over the bike like a giant crab. "Up . . . down . . . up . . . down."

His mind clicked off the stats like an odometer:

Top speed: about fifty miles per hour.

Distance from the four-thousand-pound Old Cortes motor home: about eight inches.

Time to react if anything bad happens: approximately one nanosecond.

Risk factor: off the meter.

What happens to my body if I splatter: a million pieces.

Closest previous experience: in my dreams.

Crutchlow is nothing if not adaptable. If one of the adventure schemes that define his life isn't a go, look for him to conjure up another, like a magician pulling scarfs from his sleeves. In 1970, for example, he returned to America to try to drum up a corporate sponsor for his latest idea. He wanted someone to subsidize his participation, as a rookie driver, in the World Cup Auto Rally—London to Mexico City. "As an Englishman, I had this streets-paved-with-gold image of America, complete with the notion that I would just call up Ford and tell them I wanted to enter this auto race and would they please give me a Bronco for that purpose."

When the inevitable refusal came, Crutchlow accepted failure with his usual good grace. "However, I also had to accept the fact that I was flat-ass broke and without prospects." He thinks about it. "God," he adds, mustache bristling, jowls shimmering like Jello, "poverty gives you an incredible freedom. When you don't have very much to lose . . ."

That's pretty much how he looked at it one day in Los Angeles when Dennis Kirby goaded him with the words: "I'll bet you can't bicycle from L.A. to Mexico City and get there before those auto rally cars do (about three weeks later)."

"The World Cup Soccer finals are in Mexico City," Crutchlow said, thinking aloud. "And y'know, the English are picked to win it."

"So take the bet."

"Kirby, you have at last maneuvered it so that I do all the work and you don't even have to leave home."

"For a pint of beer?" said Kirby, hand extended.

"Done," said Crutchlow.

Two days later, after another in a long line of champagne sendoffs, Crutchlow pedaled away from the Great Scot Pub on Los Feliz Boulevard, Los Angeles, waving ta ta to his friends, the press, and a motley assortment of bemused onlookers. As usual, he got the best-dressed award in his full pin-striped suit, punctuated by the bowler and umbrella. Such sartorial splendor would not last.

"I got my first surprise when I got to the Salton Sea," he says. "I'd hardly pedaled out of Los Angeles, it seemed, when it turned into a bloody desert. It was sooo hot, I had to take my jacket off."

The shock reverberated when he crossed the border into Mexico and the desert conditions intensified. The heat shimmered on the horizon in a variety of hues, all of them shades of brown. "I had anticipated going from village to village, natives waving to me, stopping where I wanted, but that wasn't to be for a while."

When he saw the Green Angels – "government trucks that patrol the roadway to bring aid to desperate, stupid people who venture out into the noonday sun unprepared" – he realized that a potentially serious problem existed. "If it hadn't been for the Green Angels," he admits, "I would have run out of water."

Farther south, the Mexican geography began to conform to Crutchlow's expectations. The climate mellowed; there were villages and towns and, yes, the local people waved to him. About half the nights he threw down his sleeping bag somewhere ("Crutchlow," Beale says, "can sleep anywhere. The man's like a piece of luggage"). The rest of the time, he knocked on strangers' doors and asked for a bed. Both worked. "I never had a problem," he says. "I did worry a bit about banditos until I realized that I had nothing anyone would want to steal."

As he neared Mexico City, elevation 7,500 feet, the needle on the fun meter dipped. Besides the climbing ("on and on and on, up and down but mostly up") there was the retching pollution ("so bad I'd literally disappear into a cloud of black smoke from all the trucks"). But he just coughed and kept pedaling.

A hundred miles from Mexico City, Crutchlow stopped and called the office of a London newspaper, the *Daily Mirror*. They showed interest in this latest Crutchlow escapade, even promising to send out a reporter to meet him en route. "He was supposed to accompany me to the soccer stadium in Mexico City," says Crutchlow. "The whole thing was a fiasco. The reporter didn't find me. And when I arrived in Mexico City, I had no clue where they might be playing the World Cup. I asked directions but couldn't seem to get the same answer twice. By the time I found the stadium it was dark – not a soul around. They eventually got a photographer to me."

Photos were nice, but that *Daily Mirror* reporter, named Hitchins, was the bloke Crutchlow really wanted to see. With England the favorite to win the World Cup (they would win it), the London newspapers were hungry for human-interest stories. Given the Super-Bowl-level hype of the event, there was a demand for the story of a mad Englishman in a pinstripe bicycling from L.A. to Mexico City to see his team play in the World Cup. Crutchlow was once again newsworthy. And available. "Hitchins had promised me that while we were doing the story, his newspaper would put me up in a hotel room. After twenty-one days on the road, I very much wanted to find that reporter. I finally did and got that hotel room – with the shower, ahhh, and break-

Bowler and umbrella held aloft, Kenneth Crutchlow celebrates the completion of his Los Angeles to Mexico City ride. (Courtesy of Kenneth Crutchlow)

fast the next morning. And y'know, I never did make it to the World Cup." He laughs. "England won the bloody thing, and I never even made it back to the stadium. I guess the whole trip was really a journey in self-discovery." He laughs again. "I discovered I'm not really much of a soccer fan."

"So far, Canada looks a lot like the States," he thought. "Dark, uphill, lots of trees. Y'know, maybe this trip wasn't such a good idea? Maybe it wasn't. What happens if something, y'know, happens. Whoa, what was that? How agitated an animal makes a sound like that? Pax and the crew are somewhere ahead, all tidy and warm, but what if something comes out of the forest, hits the bike, and knocks me off? Who'll know? It's absolutely pitch black. Who'll know and when will they know it? Why am I doing this? Bloody hell, I'm tired, and my back aches and my legs, too. But the worst by far are the blisters on me bum. 'Like raw meat,' Pax called it. Nah, maybe I shouldn't do this anymore. Why am I here? I should at least be able to remember that, but I'm so tired. Oh, stop the defeatist talk and pedal. Yeah, pedal. Ha, pedal your bloody arse off.

*Pack up your troubles in your ol' kit bag
and smile, smile, smile . . .*

Kenneth Crutchlow was born March 18, 1944, in London, England. He was the oldest of four children – two boys and two girls – born to Lil and Alf Crutchlow. Though none of his siblings have ever tuned in to the call of adventure, Kenneth's father and grandmother were forced by the exigencies of World War II to live life close to the edge. "Emma Crutchlow was in charge of serving school lunches during the war," Kenneth explains. "She became the head school lunch lady, getting meals to the people bombed out by the Germans in London's East End. She wasn't afraid of much. Her attitude was 'The bloody Germans were a bloody nuisance always bombing the place.' It was so dangerous and she did such a good job, they gave her the British Empire Medal. A bloody big deal, it was. She had to go to Buckingham Palace to collect it, but when I asked her how she got to Buckingham Palace, she said, 'I went on the bloody bus, what do you think?' She was terribly put out that I would think anything was different than usual."

Crutchlow's father also squared off with danger during the war. "He was a police administrator. His job was to replace the road signs around Berlin torn down by the Germans in the last two days of the war to confuse the Allies. He was working in areas mined by the Germans. It was very dangerous, and he relied a lot on his instincts. Whenever it didn't feel right, he would stop and fix a cup of tea – like any civilized Englishman. At least once, that habit saved his life. He stopped and prepared his tea, while some others, who lacked his instincts, went on ahead and were killed by a land mine. His axiom was 'When in doubt, brew up.'"

As a kid, Crutchlow did not at first distinguish himself as an athlete. "I tried," he says, "but I wasn't any good. I didn't make the football [soccer] team. I swam but never won. I had virtually no athletic history until I was fifteen."

It was then that he finished school and became a printer's apprentice. His uncle George, who was captain of the workingman's rowing club, urged him to try crew. "I found I liked the competition," he says, "but also the traveling that went with it. My interests became twofold: one, trying to win, which I did not always do; two, getting away every Friday night to be somewhere else Saturday morning."

As a fledgling oarsman, Crutchlow came under the tutelage of rowing coach Sid Price, who would have a huge impact on the young man's life, though arguably not in the manner he intended. Although it was more than thirty years ago, neither Price's words nor message has dimmed with time. "'Crutchlow, you just think you're going to die!' he would shout at me. While we rowed until we ached, Coach Price rode his bicycle on the path next to the river, staying alongside us, shouting, 'No one ever dies of exhaustion! We've never had anyone die down here! But we've had lots quit! Anybody can quit!' It is a way of thinking that, with an exception or two, I have stuck to."

When Crutchlow and Beale arrived at the Alaska town of Prince Rupert, they were startled to learn that, although Ketchikan was only fifty miles away, they couldn't get there from here—at least not by bike. Ketchikan, it seemed, was surrounded by water. That left only a ferry or seaplane—two choices that quickly narrowed to one. Because the ferry wasn't running that day, they would have to take a seaplane if they wanted to win the race.

At Pax's suggestion, they composed an ad for the local radio station, an attempt to attract a pilot and plane to fly them to Ketchikan: "Dear Good People of Prince Rupert, we are in a race against time and need your help . . ."

How is it that Crutchlow's adventures always seem to contain hefty elements of misadventure? "It's the nature of this field," he says. "That's what adventure is. It has to do with"—he ticks them off on his fingers—"risking your life and the unknown. Adventurers don't sit around with the atlas whining, 'Well, this route might not work if there's an earthquake, and this one has better weather.' What you do is get underway, and when you come to an obstacle, you figure it out then."

One obstacle Crutchlow has repeatedly, intentionally confronted is heat. Desert heat. Inside-your-stove heat. Like the kind he faced running across Death Valley four times under a blistering summer sun; like the kind in which he immersed himself bicycling from Death Valley to Las Vegas in—when else?—summer.

"That was another bet," he explains, "with the manager of the Sahara in Vegas. Free room and meals if I pedaled from Death Valley to the Sahara. When I finished, I rode my bike through the casino, while the PA announced, 'Kenneth Crutchlow just rode his bike from Death Valley to the Sahara.' A couple of blokes gave me poker chips.

"The ride wasn't that far—only about 250 miles—but that's as hot as it gets. And it had never been done before. That's how I got most of the seven world records I held—doing things nobody else had thought of yet. I've always liked being the first one to do something. It feels good knowing I'm going to get the record."

The seaplane dropped Crutchlow and Beale in Ketchikan. All told, they had taken five days, five hours, seven minutes, beating the *Arcadia* by eight hours. When the ship arrived, Crutchlow and Beale hotpedaled back down to the dock to collect their winnings: a first-class stateroom. Much to their dismay, the captain greeted them like stowaways. "He wasn't happy to see us at all," Crutchlow says. "And even less so when I celebrated by riding my bike around the deck of the ship. He was an unpleasant bloke and not a bit impressed or amused by our efforts." Says Beale, "Crutchlow tried to appeal to the captain's sense of honor, Englishman to Englishman, all that rot, but he got nowhere."

Ill will or no, the boys received first-class passage out of Ketchikan, bound for San Francisco. But, as usual for Crutchlow, first-class passage did not equate with trouble-free travel: He and Beale were rudely dumped from the boat in Vancouver because of an arcane law that demanded cruise passengers return to their port of embarkation. The ship would not take them back to Ketchikan, and the Canadian authorities would not allow them to go on to San Francisco. Before they would leave, however, they did a little demanding of their own: airplane tickets to San Francisco.

Crutchlow and Beale now speak to each other through their attorneys. Their grudge concerns overlapping business interests, but it in no way diminishes the respect Crutchlow has for Beale's guts, or Beale for Crutchlow's. "Ken is a terrible guy to be in business with," Beale says. "But he is the greatest guy in the world to do an adventure with. He has limited physical skills, but he will never quit—never. And the man doesn't feel pain—not in the ordinary sense. I don't mean he's heroic; *I mean the man does not feel pain.* If you had seen the saddle sores on his ass . . ."

Crutchlow is sitting in my house in northern California's wine country telling me story after story, many of which are accompanied by laughter. We've finished dinner and are doing mortal damage to our third bottle of wine (though my wife, Karen, and Kenneth's girlfriend, also Karen, have contributed nominally to the demise of the first two).

Crutchlow is clearly feeling no pain, but he is in full control of his ample faculties and shows no sign of being drunk. Nevertheless, it requires a staggering leap of faith to accept the 1990 Crutchlow participating in any of the activities he's been describing. At forty-seven, he has lost some youthful luster. And at 220 pounds, he is at least 40 pounds over his prime playing weight. His hair and mustache are graying, and his hairline is in general retreat. His bushy eyebrows arch over close-set eyes, and he has a large head, nose, and ears. Dressed in a pullover sweater and a striped tie, he suggests a librarian or perhaps a tenured college professor. When he speaks, particularly of his adventurous past, he reminds me of a Monte Python player: "So this bloke in Singapore said he had a rubber dinghy, said he could take me to Indonesia under cover of darkness. Ideas with me have always come and gone rather quickly, and that's one that should have gone right after it came. So when the machine-gun fire started, the captain yells, 'Hide!' Hide? Bloody hell, we're in a rubber dinghy — where you going to hide?"

In response to my question — "How do you manage to get out of all that trouble?" — Crutchlow replies, "Ingenuity is the main ingredient. If you're inventive enough, you can always find a way out of any situation."

Crutchlow has had a lot of situations with which to practice. That's because he has spent the better part of two decades regularly putting himself "out there," where, as the saying goes, Shit Happens.

Further into the wine bottle, I ask him, "Just how does a fellow with such prosaic physical attributes consistently go the distance?" After all, Crutchlow himself has described his body at its peak as only "halfway decent," adding however, "I've always had the essentials of strong legs and good heart capacity. And I've been healthy. Take a healthy body and be prepared to push it — that's the engine that drives it. I guess it's really just having the ability to suffer."

Let the record show that Crutchlow is speaking of more than just physical suffering; endurance athletes must confront the mental privations, too. How, for example, does one combat the mind-addling repetition of running/walking across Death Valley for fifty hours? or a succession of solitary days pedaling a bike from here to there? Far from the Zen ideal of quieting the mind and minimizing desire, Crutchlow takes a refreshingly hedonistic approach. "I think of the future a lot," he admits. "It's usually so uncomfortable out there that I think of clean white sheets. I think of showers, drying off with a white terry cloth towel, breakfast in bed, getting laid."

Night has turned to morning. The wine is finished and so am I. The capillaries in my eyes are popping so loud it sounds like New Year's Eve. But I have two final questions, and I reach deep inside for that last vestige of strength. This is the journalistic equivalent of getting up for the big one. "Would Coach Price be proud of you today?"

"Ahh, good one, mate. You finished strong." He thinks about it before answering. "Y'know, I believe so, though not necessarily any more than some others who have done different things with their lives. I think his message was 'Get out and try something. Then, when you do try something, give it your best.' Well, I've at least gotten out and tried something. And I've always given it me best. Whether I've accomplished anything – that's for others to decide."

"A good answer," I say, chuckling. "Humble yet effervescent. And your next adventure?" "Well, I'm very involved with this Peter Byrd row from Vladivostok to San Francisco. I'm hard at work trying to dredge up the sponsors, and it's looking like I might be off to Vladivostok.

"But I recently told Karen that if all that unravels, I'm going to take off this forty extra pounds of weight I'm carrying. And y'know how I'm going to do it? I'm going to buy a bathroom scale and head south – running, walking, skipping, pogo sticking, whatever. And one of two things is bound to happen: Either I'll lose forty pounds or I'll get to bloody Tierra del Fuego." He thinks about it, then pounds the table with excitement, laughing. "Y'know, I could live with either one."

MARTHA KENNEDY
Iditabiker

It's a lot of fun, the
shortest way to inner
peace, a whole new
experience.
—writer/bicyclist
Rob Van der Plas
answering the question,
What is a mountain bike?

Knik Lake, mile 0, twenty degrees. Straddling their bikes beneath an incongruous yellow banner that read "MOUNTAIN BIKES OF ALASKA IDITABIKE START," a motley collection of colorfully garbed riders joked and laughed and wished each other luck. They were a nervous mix of people – twenty-one men, five women – none of whom had the slightest idea what lay ahead. Adventure had brought them there, and adventure bonded them, for their mainstream avocations differed widely, ranging from mountain biking to triathlons to cross-country skiing. The convivial atmosphere of the starting line would contrast sharply with the silent, semisolitary nature of the race itself.

Favorites were difficult to figure in this first-ever Iditabike, but in the women's division, twenty-nine-year-old Martha Kennedy probably had the edge. She was, after all, the winner of the women's expert class at the NORBA (National Off-Road Bicycling Association) Nationals. A woman with superb stamina, the longer the race, the better she fared.

In preparation for a 210-mile bicycle race over ice and snow, Kennedy wore Lifa long underwear, cycling shorts, Patagonia top, wool and polypropylene sock liners, wool hunting socks, Plumline three-season pants and jacket, fleece-lined snojoggers and burleigh shoe covers, and Lifa cap, headband, and balaclava.

An avalanche of whoops and hollers accompanied the yell of *Go!* as suddenly everyone became riveted to a like task: propelling a bicycle loaded with fifty or more pounds from a standing start to maximum speed, while balancing, steering, and keeping in mind the old adage: *The shortest distance between two points is a straight line.* Riders' legs churned like pistons, driving their bikes across a ghostly white expanse of hard-packed, undulating snow, maybe three hundred yards across frozen Knik Lake, before the course funnelled into a snowmobile trail, making passing tough but not impossible. From the air, the start of the race appeared somewhat orderly – black dots on a white background – and you could imagine the bikers in composed, rhythmic control. From the ground, however, one could almost feel the teeth-rattling ride these hardy souls endured while navigating the synclines and anticlines of rutted snow. It was like riding over a drain grating the length of three football fields.

The course narrowed and the pack stretched out, with Dave Zink in front and Kennedy about a third of the way back. For now, the race was fun. The snow was firm, the weather was fine, and the riders were rolling easily through pine forests. After all the training, the buildup, it felt exhilarating just to be outside working the pedals.

California, forty-one degrees. "God, it's cold," Martha Kennedy said, her teeth chattering like castanets. It was indeed cold – by California standards. It had been the Golden State's chilliest February in recorded history; yet it paled in comparison to places like Canada (where Kennedy was born), Minnesota (where she trained), and Alaska (where she had twice entered the Iditabike, a grueling 210-mile off-road bicycle race – in the *winter!*).

At five-foot-four and 120 pounds, she was courteous and soft-spoken with an intelligent face framed by large wire-rimmed glasses. She did not, at first glance, appear to have the stuffing of those mountain bike fiends you occasionally see on TV, the kind who ford creeks, skid around corners, and jump fallen trees in a single bound of their fat-tire bikes, screaming like banshees, as if to proclaim, "Nobody has ever had this much fun before!" I tried to imagine her in the heat of competition – muscles twitching painfully, eyes glazed with determination, rivulets of sweat pouring from her scalp. But I finally decided I needed to know her better in order to complete the image.

Growing up, she said, she was an active kid usually cross-country skiing, skating, or hiking. A self-described tomboy, she loved being in the woods and didn't love the team sports they made you play in gym class. "I played a little field hockey, but it seemed so out of control with all those people running around." Her first time on a bicycle was similar to the experience shared by millions of kids: she got on, she fell off, she cried, she got back on.

The difference is, Martha Kennedy got back on her bike plenty. For her, cycling quickly blossomed into something more than just "kids on bikes." Having no taste for circular track races, she was drawn to longer rides and to companions who shared her love for them. In 1973 and 1974, while she was still in high school, she began formalized competition by entering the Belle Isle Marathon near Detroit. The challenge was to ride a five-mile loop continuously for twenty-four hours, most mileage wins. In her sophomore race, she won the women's division, setting a record of 267 miles.

"About eight hundred people started the race," Kennedy remembers, "and about two hundred went the whole twenty-four hours. It was May and pretty warm, and the track was nearly level. Technically it was not a difficult race."

The Belle Isle Marathon sounds strenuous, even a bit daring, but not terribly risky. Kennedy, however, goes on: "That particular time in the Detroit area, the racial situation was very bad. When it got dark, gang members started jumping out from the bushes and yanking riders off their bikes. They probably saw it as, 'Here's a bunch of white kids from the suburbs, let's disrupt this thing.' No one was seriously hurt, but it was unnerving, to say the least. I decided to stop and sleep for four hours, until it was light."

Martha was a good high-school student, taking college-credit classes and finishing with a 3.6 GPA. In spite of her academic accomplishments, she wasn't wild about high school, confessing that she often felt like a social misfit. "I was real shy then," she says. "Sports gave me a chance to fit in a little. When I wasn't playing, I was learning how to be alone."

In addition to her other activities, she swam and rowed crew and in the latter found a team sport in which she could excel. In her senior year she was stroke for both four- and eight-woman boats. "Crew was great," she effuses. "I got to do a little traveling, and we did real well. We had a new team, but we worked together and won. Crew is so much more of a team sport than mountain biking. But I was stroke,

Martha Kennedy's seven training tips

1. Take care of your body. This includes eating right, getting massaged, and resting.

2. Take care of your mind. Sometimes I think this is more important than the physical, because even when the physical is there, your head can totally screw up your performance. Work on concentration, visualization, relaxation techniques.

3. Define your goals. This can work closely with number 2. Make goals challenging but not unreasonable. Both monthly and yearly goals are good. They can be anything from completing a certain ride in a certain time to completing the Iditabike to just finishing a race season feeling strong.

4. Keep a training journal. It should include the kind of workout; the time, distance, and intensity; how you felt before, during, after. You can also go into diet, weather, weight, etc. With a journal, you can look back and figure out what you did right and wrong in a season, what led to an injury or a poor performance. Review your notes in the fall to plan next year's schedule.

5. Keep the intensity up. Especially for working folks, go for less time on the bike but greater intensity.

6. Invest in a heart rate monitor if you're serious about training. You can use it to figure your maximum heart rate and also the rate at which you race and blow up. Then use those figures to decide at what rate to train.

7. Take breaks. Don't let racing and/or training be the only thing in life. Everyone needs a break once in a while, mentally and physically.

---

so I did find my individual position in the boat—the others had to follow me."

Kennedy's parents were less-than-enthusiastic supporters of their daughter's athletic pursuits but not because she was a girl. They believed the "jock" life inappropriate for any of the eight Kennedy kids. Having in mind for Martha a more conventional life of college and career, they grudgingly tolerated her devotion to sports because they figured it kept her off the streets. "To this day," Martha says with lowered eyes, "my parents have never seen me race. Yeah, it bothers me some. It's changing, though, mostly because I don't seem like such an oddball anymore, because I have, in some sense, 'made it.'"

The trail to the top really began at the University of Minnesota, where Kennedy was going to school when she became a full-fledged competitive mountain biker. She quickly rose to the pinnacle of the women's field, Midwest division. In late 1986 she saw an ad in a biking magazine for the first-ever Iditabike. It's safe to say that her first words were the same ones every human being utters upon seeing a come-on for a winter bicycle assault of the frozen tundra of Alaska: "That is completely nuts!" Kennedy, a self-described "winter burnout," dismissed the race from her mind and made plans to move from Minnesota to California.

The Iditabike covers 210 grueling miles of the Iditarod Trail. The boxed area has been enlarged on the facing page to show the route in detail.

A week later, however, Kennedy's friend Dave Zink, a canoe mara-
thoner from St. Paul, announced, "I'm going to do the Iditabike."

That race, the idea of that race, had been haunting her all week.
"Okay," Kennedy said, almost involuntarily, "I'll do it, too."

The Iditabike was spawned by the Iditarod, the 1,100-mile sled-
dog race. Billed as "the ultimate challenge of cross-country mountain-
bike racing," the Iditabike begins 60 miles northwest of Anchorage at
Knik Lake, follows the Iditarod trail 106 miles to Skwentna, then returns along the frozen Yentna River to Knik Lake. Total mileage: 210.

Only six weeks before the race, Kennedy and Zink began training
for an event five times longer and exponentially harder than anything
they had ever before attempted. They worked out feverishly, lifting
weights on weekends and a couple of nights a week, running, bicycling outdoors in the frigid Minnesota winter and indoors on rollers.
They worked their minds as well as their bodies, sharing ideas on race
philosophy and discussing such things as how cold affects the extremi-

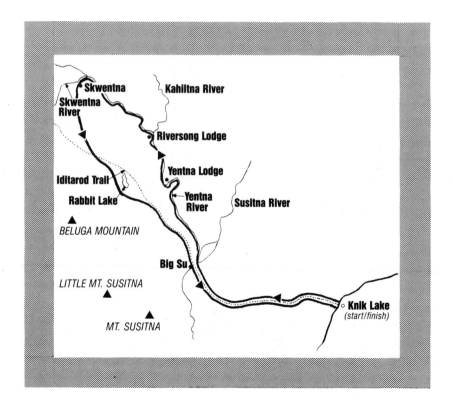

ties and what to do about it. "Mostly what I did was ask a lot of questions and listen."

There was one problem she didn't know what to do about – money. "It was a problem because I didn't have any," she says. "I couldn't even come up with the $500 air fare. Then a friend said to me, 'You know, if you got just $5 from each one of your friends, you'd make it.' I was reluctant to ask friends for money, but finally sent out flyers to about eighty people. I raised $850, enough to go to Alaska. It was like sharing the experience with a whole bunch of other people."

Knik Lake. For Martha Kennedy, waking up on race day produced a liberating sense of freedom. "Mostly I felt relief that the race was finally going to start and there was nothing more I could do. I couldn't go to the store for another pair of socks." It was 4:00 A.M. and still dark. Although Kennedy had butterflies, she knew she had to eat – it would be, after all, her last real meal for a while. Accordingly, she had a hearty breakfast of oatmeal, cereals, and fruit, which, mixed with those butterflies, immediately sent her scurrying to the toilet.

Before the race organizers would allow anyone to ride off into the Alaskan wilderness, they let them know what they were getting into. A University of Alaska professor who had done extensive research on the effects and treatment of frostbite lectured them: "Frostbite is basically a result of poor circulation in the extremities. A lack of moisture. When you constrict the blood to the center of the body, you have very little moisture in the extremities, and it's similar to being freeze-dried. Worst thing you can do is to freeze your extremities, thaw them out on the trail, then refreeze them."

A question was raised about moose attacks. Alaskan moose, it seems, can be rather stubborn, even confrontational, when it comes to trail right-of-way. Two years earlier, Iditarod champion Susan Butcher's team was attacked by a moose that killed two of her dogs and injured a dozen others. The latest and best advice for dealing with a defiant moose: "Yell at the animal and hope it goes away."

An hour or so before the race, officials began going through the riders' gear. Kennedy didn't mind this invasion of privacy because she understood the motive – the race organizers wanted to conduct an event in which everyone came back alive.

The Iditabikers, who would face subarctic cold, sleep deprivation and cruel, capricious conditions, were expected to be self-sufficient,

Martha Kennedy's three reasons to mountain bike

1. To get out of traffic and into nature; to make your exercise less stressful than your daily life.
2. To have pure, unadulterated fun; to feel that childlike freedom and exuberance!
3. To explore. Get a map; pack lots of water, food, tools, and spare tubes; and go out and explore new areas.

except for a twenty-pound supply cache that was air-dropped at Skwentna, the approximate halfway point. They were expected to start with at least twenty pounds of gear and finish with fifteen pounds (not counting water). Required gear included the following:
• signal flare and whistle
• sleeping bag (four-pound minimum)
• one-day supply of food at all times
• capacity to carry sufficient water
• tent, bivvy sack, or two space blankets
• matches, stove, and a minimum of one pint of fuel

Kennedy also carried a change of clothing, extra socks, duct tape and wire. There was a last minute flurry of, What did I forget? Sure enough, she had forgotten something – her mittens. She'd left them in Anchorage, and after a brief panic she borrowed a pair from a racer's girlfriend.

For food, she would rely mostly on a liquid diet. Along with some dried fruit (power bars would come next year), she carried Ultra-Energy, "a food replacement designed to power the accelerated metabolism during training and competition." Since Iditabikers would burn about five hundred calories per hour, there would definitely be "accelerated metabolism," necessitating serious "replacement." She would drink every half hour or so.

Two notable items the race officials did not insist upon, both of which Kennedy chose not to carry, were helmet and compass. An all-nighter in the winter wilds of Alaska without a compass? Kennedy shrugged in her no-big-deal way. "I talked to some people and decided a compass wouldn't really help me," she explained. "I'd only need it if I got lost, and I didn't figure I'd get lost. The trail was supposed to be pretty well marked with orange reflectors every two hundred yards or so. (As it turned out, those reflectors were for the Iditaroders, who didn't return on the same trail, so they only aided the *outgoing* bikers.) As for the helmet, about 60 percent of our heat loss is through our heads, and helmets are designed more to keep sharp objects out rather than keep heat in. I knew there would be more falls than I could count, but in the snow they wouldn't be hard falls – or so I hoped."

En route, mile 5, twenty-five degrees. Kennedy had been worried about her back, but thus far she felt fine. For a week prior to the race, she had been ibuprofen-loading, taking six to eight Advil a day for a chronic lower-back problem, and she was pleased that the pain was absent. "I guess I've been lucky," she thought. "Never had any major injuries, never broken a bone. Just bruises, bruises, and more bruises. And, of course, injuries from overtraining, like tendinitis in the knees, lower-back aches, and neck and upper-shoulder problems from gripping the bike too hard. Yeah, I've been lucky."

Lucky, talented, or both – in any case, Kennedy recognizes the enormous potential for corporeal damage inherent in her sport. "Most problems occur when you get in over your head," she explains. "In mountain biking, there are lots of broken legs, ankles, and collar bones. One guy who fell on rough terrain lifted the skin off half his face."

Like most risk athletes, Kennedy is self-effacing when it comes to rating her own courage. "I'm a real chickenshit," she says without a trace of irony. "I've only recently gotten faster on the downhills. I've always tried to ride with people who are faster than I am, and with time, my bruises have gotten bigger, my fears smaller."

Kennedy expresses surprise that more mountain bikers aren't seriously damaged. "It seems to me the potential for disaster with mountain biking is greater than for, say, rock climbing, mostly because of all the other people on the track."

In the Iditabike, though, with its peculiar hazards, having other riders around can significantly reduce risk. In the 1988 race, Nels Johnson hooked up with Jim Lewis of Racine, Wisconsin, a decision that may very well have saved Lewis's life. During the last quarter of the race, he became hypothermic. Confused and disoriented, he fell

Martha Kennedy's six favorite mountain bike rides

1. Porcupine Rim (Moab, Utah)
2. White Rim Trail (Moab, Utah)
3. Eldorado/Sullivan Canyon (Carson City, Nevada)
4. Palisades Loop, Old Stagecoach Trail (Calistoga, California)
5. Hermosa Creek (Durango, Colorado)
6. Secret rides that I don't want anyone to know about because then they'll get too popular and might be shut down.

---

from his bike and refused to help himself. Johnson was faced with a decision that, in any other sport, would be no decision at all: (1) go on and finish the race, or (2) stop and aid his fallen rival/companion. Said Johnson, "It's night; it's Alaska. You don't just abandon someone out there. If I had, Lewis could have died."

For those ardent athletes and die-hard competitors who have trouble understanding Johnson's decision to return with Lewis to Big Su and finish the race the next morning, consider the Nels Johnson philosophy, a prototype for the Iditabike breed: "The struggle [in the Iditabike] is unbelievable. And when you're finally there and it's over with, it's total relief, total self-satisfaction. In this race, it's not just the person who finishes first who wins; in this one, everybody who finishes is a winner."

Off-road bicycling reached Alaska long before the 1987 Iditabike. The Klondike Gold Rush of 1897–98 coincided with the bicycling craze in the United States, when millions were riding "wheels." Many gold seekers around the turn of the century brought their bicycles with them to Alaska. They were relatively inexpensive and easy to repair. The early models were strong and simple, with no gears and few complicated parts. An Alaskan bicycle ride could be a rugged journey, but frozen rivers and dog-team trials made pretty fair bicycle paths. Even a novice cyclist in Alaska could travel faster than most dog teams.

Nevertheless, the bicycle was never warmly embraced by the average denizen of Alaska. For one thing, severe cases of frostbite and snow blindness plagued early riders; for another, bicycles tended to break down in the worst weather, usually far from town and even farther from a ready supply of spare parts. And a below-zero fall on the ice could seriously damage a bike – as well as the precious bodily parts of the person riding it.

The Iditarod trail, which passes through the town of the same name en route from Anchorage to Nome, first gained notoriety in 1925. In that year twenty mushers and their dogs used the trail to carry 300,000 units of diphtheria serum to an epidemic-threatened Nome. The Iditarod trail fell into disrepair with the arrival of the bush plane. But in the 1950s a fellow named Joe Redington became interested in it and made efforts to ensure its survival. In 1973 he guaranteed its fame by organizing the first Iditarod Sled Dog Race of the modern era, an eleven-hundred-mile mush into the foreboding maw of Alaska.

For Alaskans, the Iditarod has become the hottest ticket in the state, drawing ever larger entry fields and spawning a host of other winter races along what has become a National Historic Trail. First there was Iditashoe, then Iditaski, a two-hundred-mile Nordic ski event. Then in 1986, the seventy-three-year-old Redington bought a mountain bike, loved it, and told the Mountain Bikers of Alaska that they should organize a race on the trail, too. The MBA accepted the challenge, making a statement that would be echoed by virtually everyone involved in the race: "We don't have any idea what's going to happen, but we're willing to give this thing a try."

En route, temperature unknown. After a little less than an hour, Kennedy came to the dreaded Nine-Mile Hill (nine miles from the start). It was steep (that was expected) and thrashed (that was news). It seems the Iditarod sled dogs that had passed through the day before had, in the words of rider Mike Kloser, "just tore the hell out of the trail." Another unpleasant side effect of following on the heels of about a thousand juiced-up dogs was the pervasive odor of feces and the yellow cross-stitch of snow that assaulted the senses.

Because it was impossible to ride up the hill, Kennedy got off and pushed her bike. The downside was just as difficult – hard-packed and slick – and it forced her to remain a pedestrian. She dug her heel into the icy hill, eased the bike down, dug her heel in, eased the bike down.

Big Su checkpoint, mile 41, thirty-five degrees. She reached the first checkpoint in about four hours, the seventh person to check in. Staying near the front of the pack had helped her enormously because the snow was firmer than that confronted by the rearguard. At Big Su, which was nothing more than a couple of bedraggled tents manned by a checkpoint person, she filled her water bottles, mixed her Ultra-Energy drink, and listened to news from the front. "It's kinda nice hearing voices after four hours of being alone," she thought.

After a forty-five-minute rest stop, she mounted her bike and pedaled out into the wilderness. Ten miles outside of Big Su, the snow really deteriorated. The combination of warm weather and approximately four thousand dog legs that had churned through there the day before had conspired to render the trail unridable for anyone beneath the stature of Robobiker. "It's like pedaling in six inches of sand," she mumbled.

The Iditabike had become the Iditawalk.

She soon ran into Laddie Shaw, who was returning on foot. Shaw was a search-and-rescue specialist for the Alaska State Troopers and a top-ten finisher in the Ironman Triathlon. He was also a big-talking guy and a media favorite who, before the race, had predicted an Alaskan sweep, with himself the winner: "The cowards won't show and the weak will die," he boasted, sending scribes to scribbling. Now, one-quarter of the way into the race, he was turning back, complaining, "I expected a bike race, and this isn't a bike race." The implications of such a defeat were not lost on him. "I guess I'm going to be eating my ego for a while," he admitted to Kennedy. "I admire you for going on; I'm just not prepared." Then, as though realizing how much he had exposed, he added with characteristic cheek, "No one will finish this race."

(If it were notoriety Shaw sought, he garnered far more by quitting the race than he ever would have gained by winning it. A Laddie Shaw Award was subsequently established, to be awarded each year to the rider who was "humbled the most.")

Day drifted to night. The sun disappeared behind a mountain, but the winter sky in Alaska was not as dazzling as one might expect—something about there being fewer gaseous imperfections in the atmosphere to reflect light. On the other hand, beauty surrounded Kennedy, and that helped get her through what she now called the Iditatrudge. Mostly, though, her attention was on the auditory: the sound of her feet squishing in the snow, the howling wind, an occasional rustling in the bushes. Despite the darkness, the loneliness, she was able to find a plodding rhythm, and the steady sound of her footsteps imposed a reluctant discipline on her fatigue.

Every so often, she would become convinced all over again that she could ride. In the faint glow of a quarter-moon the snow didn't seem so bad, but each time she mounted up she was able to go only a few feet before she sank to her hubs in crystalline snow the consistency of sherbert. The effort exhausted her so that she soon had to get off and push. *I came to ride, not to push. Just a little farther, just make it to the next checkpoint, just make it respectable. God, it sure is beautiful out here. Gotta try to remember that, concentrate on that. Be here now.*

Rabbit Lake, mile 72, five degrees. At first, Kennedy refused to believe the race official when he told her she had truly reached Rabbit Lake, the second checkpoint.

Martha: How much farther to Rabbit Lake?

He: This is it—come on in and get warm.

Martha: But I didn't think I'd get here until one in the morning. Where are all the bikers?

He: They left for Skwentna.

Martha: They're walking the whole way? They're nuts!

He: Come in and rest. In an hour or so, you'll be ready to get back out there again.

Kennedy thought that highly doubtful.

Mile 80, zero degrees. *This is ridiculous! This is beautiful! There! A little bit of the northern lights, or am I seeing things? This isn't a bike race. Why didn't they check out the trail? Ah, biker's footprints—at least I'm not the only crazy one out here.*

The rise of Martha Kennedy to the apex of the women's mountain biking pyramid has made her a fairly hot prospect to sponsors. She was a member of the first sponsored women's team in mountain bike history: Team Salsa (cycles). Her other sponsors have included Sun Tour, Giro Helmets, Specialized (tires and helmets), Klein (bikes), Campagnolo (components), Expressline (gloves), Champion Nutrition, Suspension Eyewear, and the Ralston School of Massage.

She has also become a bigger draw to the media, which has recently been devoting more and more coverage to the women's races. With her boyish haircut and librarian glasses, she is not the stuff of high glamour — but then, neither is mountain biking. The other side is that she is smart, articulate, deceptively tough — and above all, a winner. And she has learned to handle reporters' questions.

What were you doing before you started racing?

"I was in art school doing lithography. I've been riding bikes since I was in the seventh grade, but back then I didn't race much. I did a lot of touring where we would try to get to the finish as fast as we could, but they weren't really races."

Do you consider yourself a competitive person?

"I'm definitely competitive. I like to finish a race and know that I've pushed as hard as I could. And finishing first makes it feel that much better."

Why aren't there more women in mountain biking?

"Maybe because it's not a 'glamour sport' and people still expect women to look a certain way; because aggression isn't stressed as a 'womanly' attribute, yet is needed to compete. One theory is that bike maintenance intimidates women. Mountain biking has the reputation

In the game of follow-the-leader, Martha Kennedy prefers to be the leader. (Courtesy of Larry Lebiecki)

of being a real macho sport. The lack of women has made me work harder, because I've had to race against the guys."

Has being a woman presented obstacles in mountain biking?

"Well, it's getting better, but the attitude of some guys is that women are like 'kids on bikes,' not to be taken seriously. Winning – and beating a lot of the men – has brought me some respect within the sport. Outside the sport, I'm sure most people think I'm crazy."

What about prize money for women?

"There's still a real bias in that area. I came from the Midwest, and back there I had a reputation for always complaining about the differences in prize money for men and women. Race organizers say there are fewer women competing, so there should be less prize money for them. I say, we train just as hard, work just as hard, and should get the same money for winning.

What's so great about mountain biking?

"The people you meet. Being out in the woods. Because I was racing every weekend, I spent most of the summer camping. I like to be away from the traffic, and I really like the kind of people off-road racing attracts. The women's field is really friendly.

"I want to compete on mountain bikes for another couple of years, then work as a team manager/masseuse for a mountain bike team and just do long-distance specialty races – 'go where no woman has gone before.' Then maybe I'll do RAAM [the Race Across AMerica]. I'd like to specialize in the weird events."

Mile 88, minus ten degrees. *Where is everybody? Haven't seen a soul in ten hours. Trudge, trudge, trudge, I-did-a-trudge. I can't believe I've pushed my bike forty miles, mostly in the dark. Probably isn't any such place as Skwentna anyhow. They lied to us – probably have to push this bike the whole entire eleven hundred miles to Nome. Whoa, there's a moose! There's a moose! What am I going to do? No, no, it's just a tree. Relax, relax.*

Kennedy estimates that her success in mountain biking is three parts strength and one part technical skill – "and lots and lots of mental stuff. The strength needed in mountain biking is more full-bodied than in road racing," she adds. "You use the upper body a lot to keep the bike upright. Still, it's mostly the legs and more specifically the quads. You have to have great leg strength to climb those long, steep hills and to be able to ride on rough terrain – over rocks and tree roots – without falling. I lift weights, and I also run — though I hate it unless it's on trails with my dogs."

In the Iditabike, other skills are required, too, such as the ability to withstand cold and the ability to pass hours and hours in wilderness solitude without going stark-raving mad from loneliness and fear.

Mile 100, minus twenty-two degrees. *I'll just make it to the next checkpoint, then it'll be all better. Sure, that's it, there'll be a plane at Skwentna (if there is a Skwentna) that'll take us out. Just think, my friends are all home in bed, warm and comfortable. Yeah, my friends. The same ones who helped me get here. Gotta keep moving, moving. The snow looks okay here, maybe I'll try and ride. Oops! It's nice lying here looking at the stars. Maybe I'll stay awhile. No, no, can't do that. Gotta keep moving, keep moving or die. Don't want to die.*

Mile 105, minus fifteen degrees. *Got to get to Skwentna before the moon sets and it gets really dark. Why can't I be thinking profound, interesting thoughts out here? Where are all the meaningful revelations I'm supposed to have this close to the edge? I'm tired, but that's no revelation. My legs hurt. I wonder how far I've come. Gee, maybe the snow's hard enough now to ride . . .*

Approaching Skwentna, a dozen buildings near a plowed airstrip that could pass for a town only in Alaska, Kennedy was once again able to ride her bike. The temperature around Skwentna, which sits in a topological bowl, had plummeted, firming the trail considerably. After nineteen hours of pushing her bike almost sixty miles, Kennedy was finally able to do what she does best — ride. As she neared the tiny schoolhouse where she would take her six-hour layover, she passed the home of Joe Delia, who had been postmaster of that outpost for forty-nine years. He and his wife had moved there "to be north of it all."

Delia happened to be looking out his window at the exact moment Kennedy rode by on her bike, muttering to herself. Delia returned to the bedroom, woke his wife, and said, "It's time to move north again, dear."

A trail-weary Martha Kennedy pulled in at the schoolhouse just as the leaders, Mike Kloser and Dave Zink, were rising from their naps.

While she shed layers, they dug into their "turnaround breakfast": moose stew, French toast, pork sausages, cinnamon rolls, lemon-meringue pie, Ultra-Energy drink, and coffee. As she watched them leave, she marveled at their get-up-and-go, hoping that she would eventually be able to duplicate it. In the meantime, she desperately needed a nap; boots off, not wanting to walk barefoot through the snow, she accepted a piggyback ride to an outbuilding, where she was helped to bed.

Outsiders see very little humor in a guts-out winter endurance event like the Iditabike, usually calling it something like "The Toughest Mountain Bike Race in the World." But insiders typically engage in a type of gallows humor by referring to it as the "Why Did I Bike?" or the "I Did A Hike." *Mountain Bike* magazine called it "the toughest thing they'll ever attempt . . . unless they go to war." And bumper stickers have recently appeared in Alaska that read "The Brave and Strong Will Show . . . and Still Might Die."

That expression—and the concomitant doubt—flitted briefly through Kennedy's mind soon after she awoke from her turnaround nap. But she received a boost to her spirits when race officials informed her that the closest woman was seven hours behind her and that the route home would be along the frozen Yentna River, a fast track in good shape. That meant no more pushing.

Leaving Skwentna, Kennedy realized for the first time that she would finish. As she descended the frozen Yentna, she was excited to once again be involved in a bike race. For a time, all was right with the world.

Yentna checkpoint, mile 142, twenty degrees. Kennedy pulled off her gloves and stomped into the Yentna Lodge where two people sat at a bar watching the video *Star Wars*. The incongruity of that scene made her feel as though she had just gotten a walk-on part in an extraterrestrial stage play.

After a forty-five-minute rest, she was back on the trail—or rather, trails. The greatest threat to safety and sanity on this fifth of six legs was getting lost on one of the many snowmobile tributaries that masqueraded as the main route. For a full two hours, as she lost and regained the trail, Kennedy could see the orange glow of the Big Su tent, flickering alluringly in the distance, like a polar oasis. "It was very frustrating," said Kennedy afterward. "I felt like I was never going to get there. Finally, a checkpoint person came out and guided me in."

Big Su checkpoint revisited, mile 167, twelve degrees. Anxious to put the race behind her, Kennedy planned to go right back out on the trail. But the checkpoint was abuzz with the news that two of the racers were believed lost, so she hung around for a while to hear the outcome (they were found). There was another punch-drunk racer there who had dropped out at the first checkpoint and was babbling on about which event—the Iditaski or the Iditabike—produced the finest hallucinations. He loudly concluded that the Iditaski—with its tarantulas and grazing dairy cattle—had created the most extraordinary mental images.

Kennedy decided that her hallucinations were disappointingly tame. "I figure if your eyes are going to play tricks on you, it should at least be interesting. I just saw moose, lots and lots of moose."

The final sprint—Big Su to Lake Knik—was forty miles long, and Kennedy hoped to do it in less than four hours. She later wrote, "This was the fun leg of the journey—mostly hardpack and rideable, lots of hills with lake stretches in between. Mostly pine, some birch. Snow, snow everywhere." She took a few "fliers" on the steep icy patches, an inevitable result of what she called her "gonzo enthusiastic riding," but it was nothing serious until one time, plummeting to earth, her right eye landed inches from a sharp stick that pierced the blanket of snow. After that, she calmed down a bit.

So strong did she feel that she chose not to stop and drink her last bottle of Ultra-Energy. She was seventy minutes from the finish, with a sizeable lead over the nearest woman, but it was just too much of a hassle to stop and find the bottle. She decided to push on.

Fifteen minutes from Knik Lake, she wavered and toppled. On a dark, narrow stretch of trail, she took a fall, not unlike many others she had taken. But this time, she had hit the Wall. She got up shaking and disoriented. "I was totally bonked," she later said. "I was cold, even though I hadn't been cold the whole race. I knew I was nearing my limit, so I gulped down a bottle—four hundred calories—of Ultra-Energy, had some dried fruit, and put on my extra jacket. After fifteen minutes I started to feel OK again. It was just inexperience. The moral of the story is, never stop intake of fuel even when you think you're almost to the finish."

Knik Lake, mile 210, twenty-five degrees. *Two tiny blue lights ahead. Eyes? Wolf? No, now it's one eye . . . or a light . . . and a voice saying, "It's over." I finished? I won!*

She finished the 1987 Iditabike as first woman, sixth overall (thirteen of the twenty-six riders quit early, ten by the first checkpoint), in a time of forty-two hours, fifty-nine minutes. In 1988 she returned to the Iditabike and successfully defended her crown, bettering her time by seven hours but winning by a mere six minutes over Sara Ballantyne, who strayed off the course and lost several hours. Overall, the two women had finished eighth and ninth out of a field of fifty-two mostly male riders.

To get a fix on the degree to which some mountain bikers love (some would call it love/hate) their sport, consider the aforementioned Nels Johnson and his friend Mark Frise, also from Wisconsin. In the 1987 Iditabike, Johnson was evacuated with a case of frostbite and Frise finished seventh. Both returned in 1988, hoping to improve on their previous performance. Both said they had thought about the race every single day for the past year. Said Nels, "It's billed as the world's toughest mountain bike race, and if you consider yourself a true avid mountain biker, this is something that's irresistible. It's the toughest race, and am I, as a mountain biker, tough enough to do it?"

Buoyed by her second win in the Iditabike, Kennedy recently entered and won a novelty race that is, geographically and meteorologically, in stark contrast to the Iditabike. The Coors American Original 150 Desert to the Sea Mountain Bike Race is a 135-mile (they cut off 15 miles to avoid some deer hunters but didn't change the name) bike ride that has a little bit of everything in it. It runs from Palm Springs to the Pacific Ocean on a course that is 40 percent pavement, 60 percent dirt and rocks, and takes the rider through five cities, three counties, and two national forests.

Said an exhausted, dirt-caked but still glib Martha Kennedy after the race, "Believe it or not, I do these races for fun." She laughed. "I think I'm going to have to reconsider that."

After winning the first two Iditabikes, Kennedy was the clear favorite to do it again. Furthermore, as the 1988 winner, she had earned airfare to the 1989 race, so there would be no need to pass the hat among her friends. But it wasn't enough incentive. When the Iditabikers went off in 1989, she and her bike were back in California.

"If you could just go do the race, it would be fine," she explains. "But the preparation is ridiculous. Last August while I was doing training rides in the blazing heat, I found myself thinking, "The Iditabike is earlier this year. It'll be colder. What am I going to wear on my feet?'

"Then a friend said, 'You know, Martha, you don't *have* to do it. Not if you don't want to.' And it was like I had never considered that. 'Oh, freedom? I don't have to? Well, OK then.'

"But the thing is, when the time came I kicked myself for not going. Mentally I was up there the whole weekend. I missed it! I missed those hours alone in the middle of the night. That event is sort of—how do you say it?—self-affirming. You're on your own and you're doing fine. There's no more preparation; you're just doing it. Now!

"I also missed the parties—especially after the race, when everyone tells their stories. All those great stories."

From the frozen wilds of Alaska to the parched and dusty arroyos of Texas, Kennedy will ride just about any terrain Nature throws at her. But still the question nags, Why? She answers unhesitatingly. "I just love the sport, love the feeling of being out there in the wilderness, on my own. It's that high I always seem to get when everything's flowing just right. Every time I do something like the Iditabike, I learn more about myself. Boundaries get expanded." She thinks a moment, tries a different angle. "It's like you've been training for months, and you're finally seeing the results of all that work. It's the big payoff. You are firmly *in* and *of* this moment."

And what about all those later moments? The future? Will Martha come to her senses, get serious about something besides mountain biking? More to the point, will she finally settle down, get a conventional job, and conform to her parents' view of what life is all about?

Only if pressed will she look that far in the distance. Finally she smiles wisely. "I see myself as an eighty-year-old woman, tooling around on my mountain bike, my pit bulls trailing after me."

The smile remains. She is contented, self-assured. It is an image she can live with.

Martha Kennedy Update

"The last couple of years on the race circuit have changed me from a fresh, naive competitor to a jaded old-timer.

"Well, it's not that bad. But it's no longer just train, have fun, race your hardest, and win a lot. It's much more competitive. And we've moved on to scientific training (Let's see, today I have to do forty-five minutes at anaerobic threshold in the A.M. and ten 90-percent heart-rate intervals in the P.M.) and specific nutrition (low fat, high carbs, not too much protein but not too little. Am I hydrated? Did I take my vitamins and supplements? Is my body fat low enough?).

"Condos with kitchens have replaced tents and camp stoves. I fly to most races, not just because the budget is higher but because the races are so spread out around the country.

"It's hard out there. But what a challenge! Top five is now considered doing well, whereas two years ago if I didn't place top three I was severely depressed and wondered if it was worth it to race anymore. Amazing.

"So I'm still in it for another year or two and hoping to move into a coach/team manager/soigneur position on a team after that. I still love the sport and the people in and around it. Although we all look and act on the outside like 'professionals,' that wildness still lurks just below the surface.

"And I still love to ride. Fall, my favorite time of the year here in Nevada (I moved to Carson City—a great place for a mountain biker), is when I rejuvenate myself. It's when my bike and I become buddies again, going off into the wilds, exploring new trails and rediscovering old ones. I may get burned out on competition, on four- to six-mile-circuit courses, on never being home, but I always love moving around on my bike."

DAVE SCOTT

Mere survival is an affliction. What is of interest is life and the direction of that life.

——Guy Fregault

Ironman

Moments before the start of the 1984 Hawaiian Ironman Triathlon, Dave Scott waded into the Pacific Ocean, drawing stares and murmurs of recognition. Standing knee-deep in the warm, blue water off Kailua Pier, he adjusted his swimming goggles and shook out his well-developed shoulder muscles. It was 6:55 A.M., and although the sun had not yet crept over Mount Hualalai, the day was already warm. In an hour, when Scott was due to emerge from the 2.4-mile ocean swim, it would be hot and humid.

He kneaded a tight hamstring muscle and thought, "The weather favors me. I'd rather do a triathlon in the Sahara than the Arctic any day." After a while, old doubts began to assail him: Was he strong enough today to win? Would he feel bad early and embarrass himself? Why did he put himself through all this? Seeking ablution, he dived into the water and washed away his fears.

Submerged to the neck, he looked around at the other competitors—more than a thousand well-toned bodies, men in yellow bathing caps, women in red—moving into the sea like so many lemmings. What drove them? Most, he figured, got by with what he called the "Rocky philosophy"—just try to go the distance. How different it was for him; he raced to win, especially in the Ironman, where he had done just that in three of the last four years.

It all began one night in 1978 when some Navy boys were whooping it up in an Oahu bar. Which of Hawaii's punishing endurance events, they wondered, was the toughest. The 2.4-mile Waikiki rough-water swim? The 112-mile around-Oahu bicycle race? Or the 26.2-mile Honolulu marathon? One of the men, Commander John Collins, suggested they separate the men from the boys by combining them all into a continuous three-sport event. "It won't answer the question of which is the toughest event," he said. "But it will sure tell us who's the toughest human."

Thus the Hawaiian Ironman was born. Fifteen men competed in the premiere contest. The battle for first was between two graduates of Navy "tough guy" squads, who nearly killed themselves trying to beat each other. The twelve finishers received a tiny trophy made of nuts and bolts with a hole in the top—that is, in the head.

In 1979, fourteen men and one woman competed in the second Ironman. Despite the eleven- to sixteen-hour "gruelathon" that the competitors faced, most brought a rather light-hearted attitude to the starting line. One man competed in a superman outfit; another, in cow horns. A third had taught himself how to ride a bicycle just the day before. But Tom Warren, who had once won a beer bet by doing four hundred situps in a sauna, was dead serious. He finished first in a time of eleven hours and fifteen minutes.

Sports Illustrated covered that 1979 Ironman, and in 1980—the year "Wide World of Sports" began televising the event—108 competitors showed up. By 1982 the field had grown to 850. The following year, the Ironman started turning away thousands of applicants.

One of those who had read the *Sports Illustrated* article was twenty-six-year-old Dave Scott of Davis, California. He was particularly moved by the description of one of the competitors, a man so depleted at the end of the race that he was stumbling into parked cars and accusing his support crew of trying to poison him. Certain that he could do it better, Scott immediately went out and bought a bicycle and began training for the 1980 Ironman.

"Ever since I heard about the Ironman, I thought I could do it," he says. "I've always been a workout freak. In high school, whatever the coach said was gospel. I looked at Warren's times—3:50 in the marathon, which translates to nine-minute miles—and thought, 'I can do that.' I can be an exercise machine if I want to—and for the 1980 Ironman I wanted to."

He developed a three-sport exercise regimen so rigorous that it became legendary within the inner world of triathletes. Every week

Dave Scott's two funniest (in retrospect) happenings on a bicycle

1. The time Scott Tinley urinated on him
2. The time a fan released a battery-powered mouse that darted in front of him

he bicycled four hundred miles, swam thirty thousand yards, and ran sixty to seventy miles. In his spare time (raised eyebrows), he lifted weights. All in all, he devoted seven to eight hours a day, six days a week, to training. "I had this idea that if I trained more than anyone else, I was bound to succeed. If I found out that Scott Tinley or Mark Allen was working out fifty hours a week, I'd work out fifty-one. The real challenge of endurance sports lies in mustering the discipline necessary to train enough to win."

He was, as he says, bound to succeed. In the 1980 Ironman he led from start to finish, beating his closest competitor by more than an hour and shattering Warren's Ironman record by nearly two. "I knew the record was soft," he says modestly. "No one had ever seriously trained for a triathlon before. I realize now I'd been working out my whole life for that event. The Ironman allowed me to show my true colors, to find my niche.

1984 Ironman: mile 0. As the clock ticked toward zero, some of the competitors began a countdown, while others prayed or cheered. "Five . . . four . . . three . . . two . . . one." The cannon boomed, launching more than a thousand swimmers as though shot from it. Beating the water to a white froth, they suggested fingerlings fighting for survival at a fish hatchery. In the vanguard, where the population density was lower, Scott and the other seeded athletes swam in water that was still blue and relatively calm. Hawaiian waters are noted for their waves, but this day it was all roll and no chop. Scott figured he'd be out of the water in less than fifty-two minutes.

He slipped into third place in the lead pack of four. He was content there, bulling his way through the water with a powerful, steady eighty-four strokes per minute. He made by far the biggest splash, slapping the water each time as if the ocean were his enemy. It was Dave Scott's way of "beating the course."

He was fourth out of the water, but his transition (a freshwater rinse, slip on socks and cycling cleats, eat a banana, pocket some figs) took less than two minutes, and he was the second one out on his bicycle.

At the early stages of the ride, his "sea" legs were sluggish and unresponsive. Also the muscles of his upper body—the deltoids, the lats, the triceps—were pumped up, and he knew it would be several miles before they could relax. As he pedaled out onto the paved lava flats, one minute behind Mark Allen, he glanced at the second wave of athletes scurrying awkwardly toward their bikes, bananas in their mouths. Head down, he burrowed into a headwind.

Dave Scott lives in Davis with his wife, Anna, and their two children. The clues to his avocation are scattered throughout his house. The front porch is littered with running shoes and bicycle gear. The coffee table features magazines of his sports—*Runners World, Triathlon, Bicycling*. The medicine cabinet is crammed with untold vitamins and minerals, as is the refrigerator with exotic health foods. The bookcase contains—besides the physiology tomes and the suspense novels—a dozen highly organized scrapbooks and videotapes cataloging Scott's athletic career. "My mom did it," he says. "She's my biggest fan. Both my mom and dad come to most of my races." One senses that, in Dave Scott's relations with his parents, the direction of influence has reversed itself. His mother has recently taken up running; his father, who has been the president of the U.S. Triathlon Federation, is an accomplished cyclist, one of the best in the country in his age group.

Scott's parents, recognizing athletic prowess in their only son, encouraged—but never coerced—him. He started swimming when he was seven and continued in age-group competition until he was seventeen. "I've spent a lot of time in the pool," says Scott. "But I never really felt that swimming was my forte. I've always had a horrendous stroke." At the University of California at Davis, he discovered another way to be competitive in the pool—water polo. He excelled to a point that in his junior and senior years he was named to the all-American team.

Meanwhile, as a physical education major, he was learning a lot about physiology and kinesiology, useful knowledge for a triathlete. "I think my education gave me an enormous advantage over others," he says. "It gave me insight into the science of training. Knowing what muscles to emphasize, what foods to eat and supplements to take—it's enabled me to train more efficiently."

When you put in as many hours on the road as a triathlete does, minor orthopedic distractions can become full-blown injuries. "Triathlons magnify problem areas," says Scott. "You have to know how to train to avoid injuries. Ideally, runs should be first, swims last, because running pounds on your legs, and if you do it after cycling you risk injury. But swimming—aahhh, it feels so good. Even when I feel fat and lazy, I can always swim."

Dave Scott lazy? Fat? At six feet and 163 (he balloons up to 165 in the winter as training time drops off), he appears to be all muscle, vein, and sinew. He has the body of the classic male triathlete—with the thighs of a cyclist, the calves of a runner and the shoulders of a swimmer and lifter. The incongruous bulge around his middle—at first taken for a pot—is actually an extra ridge of muscle. "I hate doing situps," Scott explains, "so I invented my own abdominal exercises. I do them in the pool."

Mile 20. Alone on the lava flats, five minutes behind Mark Allen, Scott pedaled smoothly, almost jauntily. He had a natural rhythm in cycling that he seemed to lack in swimming and running. Reaching into his pocket, he pulled out a fig and popped it into his mouth. Two squirts from the water bottle brought life back to his desiccated tongue. Suddenly the road dropped off, necessitating a gear change. Then another. He put his teeth to the bar and roared down the hill, imagining himself a torpedo slicing through the heavy air.

At the bottom of the hill, a right turn reared up. Scott leaned that way (threatening the "tire-adhesion breaking point") then coasted through the turn without braking, his pedal an inch off the pavement. Righting himself, he shifted gears then relaxed his grip on the handlebars and thought, "That was dangerous. Damn near planted a pedal. Yeah, dangerous . . . and exciting."

People meeting Scott for the first time after viewing him on TV are invariably struck by his all-American good looks. At rest, his short

Dave Scott (right) and Mike Pigg compete even when training on rollers. (Courtesy of Centurion Bikes)

blond hair is so tidy that he could be a model for "The Dry Look." He has a prominent nose, chiseled facial features, and the healthy, bronze glow of a man who spends a lot of time outside. His expressive mouth, easy with a smile, reveals extraordinarily large white teeth. When he hears—as he often does—that he's "much more handsome in person than on TV," he smiles and says, "When I'm doing the Ironman—tongue hanging out, eyelids drooping, sweat dripping from every orifice—I just don't look my best."

Nor does he always feel his best. Competing in and training for triathlon events—especially the cycling event—is inherently risky. Once, while returning from a frigid cycling workout, Scott skidded on a pile of crushed olives and hit the pavement hard, gashing his left elbow and badly bruising his right hip. That kept him out for a month. Later, with the hip still healing, he was time-trialing, cycling smoothly at twenty-five miles per hour, head down, eyes on the white line, when he hit a dead possum. He did a half-gainer over the handlebars, landing again on the pavement and reinjuring his hip and elbow.

Another time, near the finish of a 200-kilometer bicycle race, Scott foolishly opted to bypass the last aid station – and became both dehydrated and hypoglycemic. Starting down a hill at twenty miles per hour, his eyes blurred and he drifted off the winding road, crashing into a rock. He required sixty stitches in his head and a year to heal but still refuses to wear a helmet unless the rules demand it. He explains, "I never train with one. It causes discomfort, which is the last thing I need out there."

Some would say that discomfort is part of the Ironman's weave. The race takes the average competitor more than thirteen hours to complete, and the heat and humidity of Hawaii mix malevolently to sap him or her of precious bodily fluids. Every year at least 10 percent of the starters aren't finishers, and many more require medical care the moment they stumble, crawl, or fall across the finish line.

Though Scott is often accused to being a mental freak (as in "anyone who pushes himself so hard must be wrong in the head"), he is just as much a physical freak. Along with only a few elite triathletes, bikers, rowers, and cross-country skiers, he has a state-of-the-art respiratory system and a musculature dominated by slow-twitch fiber. And why does he excel in Hawaii? "My sweat glands work pretty well," he says with typical Scott humility.

Mile 58. Scott, halfway through the bike race, was experiencing leg cramps. The wind had picked up and was gusting to fifty miles per hour. No longer did he appear jaunty. His face had hardened into grim determination. What he was doing was just plain hard work. Ducking his head, driving his legs, he wondered just how far ahead Allen was. Nobody was around to tell him. Nobody was ever around. One thing about being a world-class triathlete, you had to get used to competing alone. Back in the pack, it was a more convivial affair; near the front, there was only the metallic whirring of a bicycle sprocket, the roar of the wind, and the beating of one heart. Scott dug deep within his well-developed imagination, focusing his mental pictures until he clearly saw himself gaining on Mark Allen.

Scott feels that he gets the greatest respect for his cycling. "It's hard to gain much time in swimming," he says. "Wetsuits are so widespread, and their buoyancy gives an advantage to weaker swimmers, who can draft and stay close. In the Ironman bicycling, I tend to dictate the pace. If I hold back, others hold back. That respect is like a red flag, telling them, 'You better not blast out now or Dave Scott will catch you at mile 90.'"

A great bicyclist needs a great bicycle, and Dave recently signed a contract with Serrato, a small bicycle builder who, like Scott, gets loads of respect. "He builds top-end bikes, all handmade," Dave says. "A lot of cyclists have used them for years. I'm not going to make a million dollars with Serrato, but I will get a lot of credibility. We figure to sell 250 Dave Scott models the first year; my last year with Centurion, we sold 33,000. But he's the best choice to build a specialized triathlete bike. The first prototype is due out in a month; it will have a twenty-six-inch wheel base, a much bigger chainring, be more responsive, better on hills."

Equipment is important and makes you look sharp, but in a race as long as the Ironman, the winning ingredients are within the individual. When Scott explains his success in terms of nature and nurture, he gives greater weight to the latter. "I think my diet makes a big difference. It's about 75 percent carbohydrate, 10 percent fat, and the rest protein. No sugar, oil, white flour, or red meat." Scott's daily workouts help him burn more than six thousand calories a day, yet he refuses to eat most high-caloric foods. He compensates with gluttonous quantities of fruits and vegetables. "I like fish, but I won't cook it myself. I eat chicken a couple of times a year. Mostly it's fruit and vegetable salads, tofu, rice crackers, yogurt, and cottage cheese."

The Dave Scott legend includes sensual tales of his downing seventeen bananas for an appetizer, eating five salads for dinner, and washing his cottage cheese. Washing his cottage cheese? "Yes, I wash my cottage cheese," he says with a shy laugh. "Rinsing reduces the fat by about 10 percent and eliminates some of the salts. I mean I don't hose it off in the front yard or anything; I put it in a strainer.

"I eat well, but I'm not a fanatic. I'll drink wine and beer when the time is right. I even go to parties once in a while, though I'm not the type to writhe around on the floor. People ask me what I think about while I'm training. I tell them I think of my body rhythms . . . and lunch."

Before a "short" triathlon—anything less than three hours—Scott runs on empty. "I consume only water," he says. "For an Ironman, I'll eat heavily up to two days before. On the morning of the race, I'll have three bananas, toast, water. Then during the race, it's about twenty figs and a couple of bananas on the bike, a banana and some orange slices on the run, and lots of water! At least a couple of gallons, more if I can get it."

Viewers of the 1983 Ironman saw an annoyed Dave Scott – 22 miles into the run, 136 miles into the race – throw down the cup of Gatorade he'd been handed and call for water. "The electrolyte drinks are a lot of bull," he says. "They have too much sugar and too high a concentration of minerals. They can't be assimilated into the body quickly enough. They'll actually draw water from the muscles to the stomach, making you more dehydrated."

Mile 78. Scott, calves bulging, stood up in his stirrups and pedaled powerfully up the hill, trying to slice into Mark Allen's ten-minute lead. He felt strong, much better than in 1983. Now he'd lost eight minutes to Allen on the bike; but it was okay – he wasn't worried. The bike was Allen's best event, the run was Scott's. And best of all, only he knew it.

He and the bike were working as one now, a fluid, efficient machine, needing lubrication. He sucked on his water bottle and searched for an aid station.

Just then he spotted Allen, who was heading back from the turnaround at Hawi. Scott knew that this moment of passing had great psychological importance. It was one of the few times in the race that competitors were able to see one another, to get a fatigue reading. Allen had the lead, but he had to be hurting, too. If he saw pain or weakness in Scott's face, it could give him the boost he needed to win and vice versa. As they passed, both men wore masks of stolid indifference.

Winning the Ironman in 1980, 1982, and 1983 brought Dave Scott fame but no fortune, prestige but no prize money. Until recently, the Hawaiian Ironman had never offered a purse, apparently on the theory that just having the opportunity to "go the distance" is reward enough. Although most triathlons now offer some prize money, purses are still quite small, and as yet no triathlete has been able to make a top-flight living from his winnings.

Scott has found other ways. The quantitative leap in the popularity of triathlons brought out neophytes in droves, and soon budding triathletes were pestering him to design training programs for them.

They phoned from all over the country, asking for his secrets; at first he gave them away, then he began charging – two hundred dollars to design a one-year regimen, five hundred dollars to run an all-day clinic. He also came out with a Dave Scott line of sportswear, which has done very well.

After his first Ironman win, Scott attracted four sponsors, each of whom paid him "a little" money. Nike, Bell (helmets), Peak Performance (vitamins), and Anheuser-Busch each paid him about fifteen hundred dollars. "Triathletes aren't yet identifiable to the masses," says Scott. "But our day will come. Right now, there are about twenty triathletes making a living off the sport. Make that a partial living. Sharing houses, driving old cars."

Triathletes would seem to have plenty of products to endorse. During a race they are forever changing outfits, and in the area of gadgets they use everything from swimming goggles to bicycle helmets. That is, most do. Dave Scott doesn't. While it's not uncommon to see the other top triathletes wearing wet suits on the swim, Scott wears only trunks. On the bicycle, the latest craze is the sleek, aerodynamic tear-drop helmet, but Scott rides bare-headed whenever he can. Although it may hurt his advertising, he believes it helps him race.

Until recently, when legal troubles intervened, a handful of top triathletes were being subsidized by the sport's sugar daddy: JDavid, an investment securities company based in San Diego. JDavid had under contract five of the top six male triathletes and two of the top five women. The members of Team JDavid were treated with the veneration of potential Olympians. They trained and traveled together; they received equipment, free clothes, and all-expense-paid trips to Nice and Hawaii for competitions, as well as a stipend of about twelve hundred dollars a month. They typically arrived in Hawaii ten days before the Ironman, with an entourage that included a cook and a team bike mechanic.

The comforts and advantages afforded Team JDavid make Dave Scott's accomplishments all the more remarkable, for he was the lone top male triathlete absent from the team. Yet in 1982, training alone, he won all ten of his races, including his second Ironman.

On a cold, wet, windy morning, a lone runner jogs down a narrow country road. A tulle fog hangs low over the rice fields, creating a monochromatic moonscape. The only splashes of color are the runner's green vest and blue gloves, antidotes for the damp cold that seeps into his bones. Head down, he plows ahead on his eighth mile of the day, his sixty-second of the week.

He's tired – dull from fatigue – and glad it's Saturday. Sixty miles to go on the bike, a two-mile swim, then he'll take Sunday off. Spend some time with Anna, maybe watch a football game. Be an ordinary person for a day.

His run turns to a plod. He is still two miles from his apartment, but now he's just putting one foot in front of the other, trying to go the distance. His thoughts are uncharacteristically negative: "Why is it always windy in Davis? Maybe I'm training too much."

Suddenly, ahead in the distance, he spots another runner, a gray ghost shrouded in mist. He squints to make sure, then confirming that he and the figure are moving in the same direction, he begins to sprint, to close the gap. The race is on, and he is born anew.

Scott says it would be a mistake to label him a recluse. "Contrary to what is written about me, I do miss the human contact of training with others. It's lonely out there on the windswept roads of rural Davis. But there are competitive advantages to the solitude and the bad weather. The members of Team JDavid knew about each other's strengths and weaknesses, but they didn't know about mine. Working out alone, I've been able to maintain a certain mystique. For example, there was a time when running was my weakest event. But I worked on it and got better and even had some races in which I caught Tinley, Allen, or Molina on the run. Sure, those guys trained under perfect conditions in San Diego, but when they got to the Kona Coast for the Ironman, it must have seemed like the moon. I was already used to the moon."

Despite JDavid's attempts to instill camaraderie into the sport, world-class triathletes remain highly individualistic. Like most triathletes, Scott was drawn to a sport that forces the athlete to work things out for himself. "In a triathlon, it's all up to the competitor," he points out. "The longer the race, the greater the challenge. I think I have the mental perseverance to out-endure anybody in the Ironman. For most, the topography at Kona is mentally stifling, and they lose their concentration after about five hours. They give up."

His appreciation of individual effort is one reason he has no interest in bicycle road racing. "It's too frightening with all those people," he says. "And I don't like the team tactics in criteriums. It doesn't necessar-

A friendly Dave Scott signs autographs at a trade show. (Courtesy of California Bicyclist*)*

ily bring out the best individual cyclist. In a triathlon, there's nobody to help — you just go for it." Scott's sensitive side is always nearby, alert to possible offense. "That's nothing against cyclists. I'm sure many of them are more explosive than I am. But I don't think they develop the mental tenacity of triathletes — except, of course, for the guys in the Tour de France."

Mile 92. Approaching one of the twenty-eight aid stations, Scott signaled to the volunteers, and when he pedaled by, they were dutifully lined up, reaching toward him with cups of water and wet sponges. Slowing only slightly, he deftly snatched the prizes from their hands. While he cooled himself with the water from a sponge, he drank two cups of water. He knew about dehydration.

Dave Scott — handsome, humble, articulate — is the perfect triathlon ambassador. In numerous interviews and articles, his infectious enthusiasm for the sport spills forth. He once said, "I encourage all of you Ironmen – and other triathletes – to strive for your goals, whether they be to win or just to try. The trying is everything."

During Scott's reign as Ironman the sport has evolved from an activity perceived as suitable only for the type of people who howl at the moon or laugh at the wrong parts of movies to one in which millions of people in at least thirty countries now participate. In 1982 in the United States alone, sixty thousand people participated in 250 triathlons. A year later, the numbers were four times that. And in 1986, 1.2 million Americans took part in 2,100 triathlons, making it the fastest growing participatory sport in America. "It's exploding," Scott says. "Someday it will be as big as tennis."

Scott envisions the day when world-class triathletes will command the six-figure appearance money that, say, Joan Benoit got for running the Chicago Marathon. "It'll happen," he says. "The sport is still in its infancy. Running has taken years to advance to the point of high recognition. One of the problems with triathlons has been that there are no standardized lengths or world records for people to identify with. The transitions are all different, the water temperatures are all different."

The athletes, too, are different. Research indicates that triathletes have slower metabolic rates, stronger hearts, denser bones, and more money than the average person. According to *Triathlon* magazine, the average triathlete makes forty-five thousand dollars a year, has graduated from college, and carries an American Express card. Over a third of the entrants in the Ironman are attorneys, airline pilots, doctors, dentists, engineers, business owners, educators, and stockbrokers. As one race organizer explained, "It's a natural extension of the aggression those people take to their careers."

But when you're Dave Scott, professional triathlete, the sport is a career. And getting up at 6:30 on a frozen foggy morning to bicycle eighty solitary miles is part of it. Like all workers, Scott sometimes feels like calling in sick. "I'm human," he insists. "Some days I just feel like sitting in my beanbag chair and letting the day go by."

In spite of those feelings, Scott lets few days go by. He is used to digging deep within for that wellspring of strength. Moreover, he believes that if you're in shape, an Ironman is not just 140 miles of pain and mental anguish. If you're in shape, his theory goes, there are morphinelike highs to be reaped. You gain a sense of power, a feeling that you can go on forever.

But what if you're not in shape? The other side of the sport is some kick-ass lows. "The 1983 Ironman," Scott says, nodding his head. "My hardest race. No one believes it, but I was in lousy shape. In the previous six months I had missed more days than I had trained. And the winds that day were the worst. I won the race, but when I got to the finish I had absolutely nothing left. Everything was a blur. I tried to wave to some friends and nearly tipped over. I beat Tinley by thirty-three seconds (in the closest Ironman ever), but if the race had been a hundred yards further it would have been his. They carried me to the medical tent and pumped me full of glucose. I was in bad shape."

Mile 112. With a little more than two miles to go on the bike, Scott lowered his head into a fifty-mile-per-hour gust of wind. Focusing on the white line, he cautioned himself, "Be patient. Allen is great on the bike. Don't burn out with a final sprint. There's still a marathon to go. Pace!"

He knew to win he'd have to be the consummate tactician. Ease up too much on the bike and you need five-minute miles on the run. Ride too hard and you die on the run. Don't drink enough and you don't even get to the run.

"I always have a race plan when I begin," he has said, "but with so many variables, that race plan usually gets tossed early. Your goggles get knocked off. Someone crosses in front of you. A flat tire. It's very important for a triathlete to be able to adapt. Other competitors let those unanticipated events wear them down. I can see it taxing them, and I guess I delight in being a part of that wearing-down process. I'll think to myself, 'I feel as bad as they do, but I know I can go a little further . . . then a little further.' It's not pain if you're in shape – it's only high-level discomfort."

While most triathletes worry only about completing the race, Scott regards that as a given. He finished ninety-eight of the first one hundred triathlons he started. Explaining his remarkable inner drive, he says, "I get a self-satisfaction in pushing myself to the near-limits of my capabilities. When I do that, I find I can be among the best in the world. I have an ego like everyone else.

"I think Allen is my most formidable opponent, the most mentally tough, but even he doesn't scare me. I do. Myself. I can talk myself out of training, working hard. My primary motivator is to live up to my own standards. I create the fear that lives within me."

When Scott began doing triathlons, his best sport was swimming, his worst cycling. In response to that, he worked hard on the bike, and after a while cycling was his strongest event. But this made his running look shabby, so he went to work on it. "I think it's interesting that I'm basically mediocre in three events, yet when you put them together I can be the best in the world. I tend to work close to my limits at all times.

"Well, maybe not mediocre, but hardly world-class. My best time in the marathon is 2:33. If I worked at it, I could probably get down to 2:25 – but that isn't even 'United States-class.'"

Mile 114.4. Scott rolled into the bike-run transition area in five hours and ten minutes. Before he had come to a stop, he had already kicked off his cycling shoes, and his sweat-soaked jersey was up around his neck. He was eleven minutes behind Mark Allen, solidly in control of second place. His look of grim intensity suggested he was dissatisfied but not discouraged. As he hustled inside to towel down and speed-tie the laces of his running shoes, TV commentators outside reminded the public that running was Dave Scott's worst event. Scott knew better.

Starting the run, his legs were rubbery, defiant. He was well aware that the most difficult transition was from bike to run. For five hours his leg muscles had been repeating a specific motion; for 112 road miles the bike had supported his weight – but now his legs had to do that. Leaving the hotel parking lot, the road immediately began to climb. Dave Scott followed, searching for an easy running rhythm. He knew it would be several miles before he found it.

Mile 120. The heat shimmered off the pavement, creating mirages in the distance; the only sound in the hot heavy air was the steady squish-squish-squish of Scott's shoes as they hit the pavement. Nearly six miles into the run, he was striding smoothly – as smoothly as he was able. For under the best of conditions, his technique in the run, like the swim, is heavy, brutish. The way he pounds the pavement and swings his head from side to side is not textbook stuff. He is, in fact, a classic example of strength and endurance taking precedence over form.

Although Scott is thirty-seven, married, with two young sons, he doesn't talk retirement. "First of all," he says, "motivation is the biggest thing, and I still have that. And my age won't be a factor for a long time. The peak for triathletes is going to be older than for most other sports. It takes years to become proficient, plus there's no real physiological reason to collapse."

Easy to say, hard to prove. After winning the Ironman in 1986 and 1987, Scott returned to Hawaii for the event in 1988. He never got to the starting line. A bothersome knee flared up, and he decided at the last minute to withdraw. Despite continued discomfort in that knee, he had a pretty good season in 1989. He finished second in the Gold Cup Race in Australia and returned to Hawaii feeling pretty good.

"In the 1989 Ironman, Mark Allen and I got out of the water at the same time, got off the bike at the same time, then ran shoulder-to-shoulder for the first twenty-four miles of the marathon. On an uphill stretch Mark attacked, and I couldn't stay with him. I broke my course record (previously 8:28) by eighteen minutes; he broke it by nineteen."

In 1990 Scott had the worst year of his athletic career. The knee problem returned with a vengeance, and he was only able to race twice all season. The results were, as he puts it, "fair to awful," though so accomplished an athlete is the man that, even hobbling, he finished fifth at Nice and eighth at Vancouver.

It's 1991 and Scott is back, brimming with ambition. After visiting countless doctors and therapists, he has finally found his orthopedic guru in San Antonio. The good doctor diagnosed the problem as a "tightness in the patellar region due to a muscular imbalance" and is working with Dave on a combination of strength and stretching exercises. "That's the biggest thing I'm doing differently now," says Scott. "After years of telling others to stretch, I'm finally doing it myself. I'm also getting massage twice a week – that really seems to help."

He figures swimming is the easiest to get back after a layoff – "I'll be swimming faster than ever" – and running is the hardest. As for cycling, he has increased his mileage weekly and is now up to about 240 miles a week. It's a far cry from his once-upon-a-time 400, but he now spends more time than ever standing up on the pedals and working a big gear. He plans to do about twelve races in 1991. "I'd like to be strong at all distances," he says, "not just the long, endurance races, where only 'empty-headed Dave Scott' can do well. I'd like to win every triathlon I enter this year." But most of all, he wants to be at the line in October when the cannon booms the start of the Ironman.

Mile 130. The ABC people, cruising around in their flatbed trucks, told Scott that Allen's lead had shrunk to six minutes, that he was complaining of leg cramps, that at times he was slowing to a walk. The news gave Scott a remarkable jolt. He could feel it entering his body, like some wonder drug, like some magical combination of cortisone and adrenaline, working its way through his heart, lungs, legs, and mind. Like a cheetah stalking his prey, he picked up the pace and set out after Allen.

SALLY VANTRESS

Round the World on a Wing and a Wheel

Auckland, New Zealand. Straddling her mountain bike, Sally Vantress secured her right foot in the toe clip and raised her leg for the first downward stroke. Pushing on the pedal reminded her of lifting weights back home. "This can't be," she thought. "The resistance is amazing. How am I going to ride up small hills let alone mountain passes?"

Her new red bike and bright red touring packs wobbled left and right as she cycled away from the airport. "Why didn't I practice riding my bike loaded with all this gear?" she groused. "Maybe if I had practiced, I'd have realized how difficult it was and stayed home."

She thought of other things she had plunged into without considering the alternatives, things she would not have done if she had analyzed everything – flying an airplane, for example. "Clearly, I am a doer, not a thinker. Sometimes this works to my advantage, sometimes not."

Her boyfriend, Mark, rode ahead, excited to be out of the airplane and on the road. She lagged behind, learning to ride all over again. She was wobbling so, she started to think the white line was painted on crooked. Adding to her confusion, everyone was driving on the "wrong" side of the road. She stopped and changed her rearview mirror to the right side. Still, each time she glanced in it and tried to make an adjustment, it was the wrong one. "I am an accident waiting to happen," she thought.

118

After stopping for vegetable pies and fresh blueberries, Sally left quiet country riding and turned on Route 2, where Mark was waiting for her. He had stopped to show her the effect passing trucks can have on cyclists. A big eighteen-wheeler was heading their way; as it neared, Sally gripped the handlebars and held on. A blast of air threw her off balance and she nearly dropped her bicycle.

"Let's go," Mark said. "Be careful, though."

"What?" Sally yelled back over the vehicular roar. "What do you mean, 'Let's go'? No way am I cycling next to those trucks!"

"Sally, you don't have a choice. If you just keep riding, it's not so bad. I just showed you so you'd be careful. I'm taking off."

While Mark pedaled away, Sally sat pouting for several minutes wondering what to do. She thought, "I've come eight thousand miles to do what? Turn around and go home? But there is absolutely no shoulder to ride on, and I still am not able to cycle in a straight line." For a moment, she saw herself added to the ignominious ranks of roadkill, but then the image passed. She inhaled deeply and patted the handlebars. "Oh well, here we go," she said.

Back on the bike, she watched for trucks in her mirror and jumped off every time one passed. That went on for at least thirty minutes before she summoned the courage to follow Mark's advice. Actually, she discovered, sitting on Buddy (her nickname for her bike) was less traumatic than standing beside the road. She just had to hold a line and not veer toward the trucks.

"I later realized that my fear and dislike of truckers made the highway encounters harder than necessary. I knew I had to change my attitude. So the next time I saw a truck approaching, I smiled and waved. After a while, the truckers were cheering me on with their own friendly smiles and waves."

When Sally Vantress set off in January 1988 to bicycle around the world, she was a stone-cold novice bicyclist. She was candid about her deficiencies, which no doubt contributed to the numbers of people who tried to talk her out of doing it. To Sally, a derailleur was a train wreck and toe clips were pedicures. "You can't bicycle around the world," her friends and family said. "You're not a bike rider. You don't speak the languages."

Her father was incapable of talking to Sally at all about her trip. Her mother was more fatalistic. An astrologer, she had done Sally's charts and knew her daughter was in for some big changes; she ac-

Vantress pedaled more than 20,000 miles during her journey.

cepted that a twenty-thousand-mile bike ride was one of them. Never-theless, on the day before Sally's departure her mother took her aside and said, "Dear, have you really thought about what you're doing?"

"Mom, the way I see it, the world is like a pie, and New Zealand is just the first piece. Who knows how much of the pie I'll get to? Right now, I'm just going to New Zealand to ride my bike."

Despite the soothing words, she fully intended to go around the world. "I was saying it to myself, but I had no idea what it meant. 'Bicycle around the world'—it had a nice ring, but did that mean I would pedal every single mile of land? If Mark had his way it did; but I really had no idea what I was getting into. Why, I didn't even know where most countries were; if you'd given me a map, I couldn't have filled it in."

The Hague
York
Belfast
London
Lisbon
Barcelona
Moscow
East Berlin
Munich
Rome
Beijing
Canton
Singapore
Cairns
Brisbane
Sydney
Auckland
Christchurch

───── bike
- - - - other transportation

Her ignorance was partly by design. She didn't want to learn things that might convince her not to go. So in preparation she did only what was absolutely necessary: shots, visas, passport, and a plane ticket to New Zealand.

Outside Wellington, New Zealand. It was late in the day and storming miserably when Sally left Mark. She had never cycled in such bad weather, but she just had to get away. "It was time for Mark and me to split up," she says. "We both knew it wasn't forever."

Now it was just Buddy and Sally. She found herself talking aloud a lot, first to Buddy ("Will it be safe? Will I be all right?"), then to God ("Will it be safe? Will I be all right?"). Even though she was nominally raised a Catholic, prolonged monologues with the deity were new for her. "I guess I was looking for companionship. And someone to look up to and hold on to. He was also the first one I apologized to after I had a temper tantrum."

On the one hand, she knew her journey was the best thing she could be doing for herself; on the other hand, she was frightened as hell. It was an adjustment being alone. She found it reassuring to sing. Her summer favorites were Christmas songs: "Deck the halls with boughs of holly . . ."

About four in the afternoon it cleared up, followed by powerful winds that pushed Vantress around like a cork. After enduring it for a while, she came upon the same river that she and Mark had camped by several weeks before. She figured it was a safe place to pitch her tent. She could wash up in the river, get some sleep, and start fresh in the morning.

"The wind was blowing so hard, it took me an hour to put up the tent. While I held the wet tent material with my teeth and pounded in the stakes, I thought back to the first time I put up the tent with Mark. It was windy then, too, and I accidentally let go of the tent, and it nearly toppled over the edge of a cliff. Mark went crazy thinking that I almost lost the tent. Well, at least I didn't have to deal with that anymore."

She took a swim in the river, but it was different this time. It was murky and gritty, and she felt dirtier coming out than going in. The wind was still a gale, so she crawled under a picnic table to try to light her stove and cook dinner, another project of monumental proportions. She eventually succeeded, then took her vegetable/noodle soup into the tent so she didn't have to share it with the sand flies. She was just about to take the first bite when the unmistakable glare of headlights bore down on her. Frightened, she peeked outside the tent. It was a tall man in a uniform. A cop. Be still, jackhammering heart.

"Are you in there alone," he said.

Still trying to catch her breath, she exhaled a yes.

"How did you get here?"

"My bike. It's parked behind my tent."

For the next ten minutes, the cop ragged on Sally, telling her how that area was not a safe place, how it was a beer-drinking hangout, how it was not wise for a woman to travel alone. The more he talked, the worse she felt.

Finally he told her that he had seen some people nearby in a

Sally Vantress's four favorite places to bike

1. New Zealand
2. Western Germany
3. The Netherlands
4. Northern England

camper and that he was going to go ask them to come over. The people did move over, but they parked their camper right next to Sally; so close, in fact, that with the high winds, she feared their camper would blow over on top of her. "Thanks to the cop and the other people trying to help me, I hardly slept all night."

Searching for clues in Sally's past for her aberrant wanderlust, one is forced to give greater weight to heredity than environment, though one might have trouble making a strong case for either. "My family didn't do anything outdoors," she said. "And we hardly ever took vacations. As a kid, my only exercise was riding my horse – and riding my bike to get to my horse. I remember daydreaming that I'd get on my horse and never stop. I pictured myself riding all the way across the country."

She was an adventurous but not athletic teenager. "My brothers were competent in sports. I was competent in hanging out in the parking lot and smoking. I was very much the rebel."

It was an attitude that spilled over into the classroom. She cold-shouldered school, with one exception: She loved the agriculture program. "I got into Future Farmers of America, participating in everything from soil judging to raising livestock. It gave me direction. It also might have kept me out of jail."

At college – Cal Poly at San Luis Obispo – she expanded her athletic boundaries. She threw away her cigarettes and began jogging with a girlfriend. She clicked with the sport and stayed with it, becoming a daily jogger and eventually running three marathons and a triathlon. With the added muscle on her stocky five-foot-one-inch frame, she leveled out at 120 pounds.

After college she took an office job but still stayed in shape. She became a regular at a health club and on weekends occasionally took a leisurely bike ride. "I didn't know anything about cycling technique," she says, "and until I met Mark I never rode with anybody who knew more than I did."

She preferred pedaling one way, then hitchhiking back. "It made me feel like I'd gone somewhere that day. As long as I can remember, I've hated going in circles. I can't stand running track or swimming laps. I'd rather swim across a lake than swim even two laps."

Perhaps it is the structure, the clamping down on her freedom, that she rejects. As circumstantial evidence, consider her description of a rare family vacation in Hawaii. "Everyone was going to see Pearl Harbor, but I didn't want to go. Even though I was interested in Pearl Harbor, I didn't want to go. It was too organized. So I stayed at the hotel and did something else I hate doing: laid on the beach and got sunburned."

For someone yearning to be free, what better sport than flying, the next sport Sally took up. "It wasn't that I was so interested in planes or instrumentation or any of that. I just wanted to soar like a bird."

She took to flying like, well, a bird. But back on earth she was expected to read flight manuals and technical journals and pass tests. "I'm not an academic person," she said. "I learn by doing things. I couldn't follow the books, but I got my pilot's license in six months and became a really good pilot."

It's clear that Vantress's aerial accomplishments lifted her spirits in a big way. One senses that without flying there would have been no around-the-world bicycling. "Flying definitely pushed me to the edge – a place I'd never been before. In flight school, they send you up solo before you know much of anything. One time as a student pilot, I got lost and had to call the local air force base for assistance. Another time I lost my engine at nine thousand feet. And then I spent an unforgettable night trying to outsmart the fog, finally flying forty-five minutes to another airport. You don't know how you're going to handle the pressure until it happens. It's nice to know that you can."

Outside Auckland, New Zealand. After three thousand miles of cycling in New Zealand, Sally was heading back to Auckland in a driving rain storm. Everything was gray and cold and wet.

She had signed up for a 'mind-relaxation' course that started in a

Sally Vantress's six most dangerous places to bike

1. Rome ("chaotic traffic and clouds of black smoke")
2. Barcelona ("snarls of traffic")
3. Wyoming ("rednecks who believe bicycles don't belong in the same world with cars")
4. China ("people jams")
5. Florida (" 'snowbirds': retirees in mobile homes on narrow roads")
6. Kentucky ("I got shot at there")

few hours. "I hoped it would help me learn more about myself. I also hoped it would help me cope with the episodes on the trip that challenged me physically and mentally – like pedaling into Auckland in a driving rainstorm."

A cyclone had recently passed, but it was still raining absurdly hard. Visibility was poor as she started down Route 2, the same road she and Mark had traveled down the first day. It seemed so long ago.

She had considered leaving Buddy behind at the family farm where she was staying. She could have taken the bus. But Mark's words haunted her: "Buses are for wimps. If you can't ride there, you don't deserve to go." Besides Buddy was her friend, and at 110 pounds loaded, he was also her home. How could she leave him behind?

While she rode into a severe headwind, trucks sprayed her with mud. She was so caked, she looked like the Pillsbury Mud Girl. She was a shivering, miserable mess, but she kept moving until suddenly – six miles from her destination – she felt the bike sink and wobble. She stopped and got off. Damn, a flat tire. Her first in three thousand miles of cycling.

"The problem – besides the rain, the trucks, the mud – was that I'd never changed a bicycle tire before. Back in the United States, Mark gave me a quickie lesson in changing the front tire, but this was the rear. And besides I'd forgotten most of what he taught me."

Suddenly through the curtain of rain she spotted a Shell gas station. "Come on, Buddy," she said. "Someone will help us."

She pushed her bike into the station and greeted the attendant, a friendly Kiwi. "Not a good day to be cycling," he said, with that adorable accent. "And a flat tire to boot."

"Yeah, and I've never changed a flat before. Can I use your garage? I think this might take the rest of the afternoon."

"I'm sorry we don't have any bicycle tools."

"Oh, I've got everything. I don't know what they are or how to use them, but I know I have every tool I could possibly need."

"Ah, no worries then. We'll get you good as gold."

The man's partner walked up. "You all alone in this horrible weather, dear?"

The first man brought her a hot cup of tea and another jacket to keep her warm. Then they unloaded Buddy, removed the tire and began looking for the cause of the flat. It turned out to be a huge piece of glass.

Vantress pulled out a new tube and tire, and the three of them struggled to put Buddy back on the road. Sally even recalled some of Mark's advice – like pinching the tube. "I was glad that I could contribute," she says. "But mostly I watched like a hawk. I figured the next flat might not happen in front of a gas station."

When Vantress looks back on the various crossroads of her life – both literal and figurative – one especially stands out as a major intersection: In 1980 she graduated from college and took a job. A recession loomed, threatening to drag the economy down a notch or two, and this had the class of 1980 in a tizzy. So when companies sent recruiters to look for talent, Sally listened intently.

"I had the urge to travel then," she said. "But I knew that it was easier to take a job offer immediately than to try to come back later. Actually, that was just an excuse. I was afraid. Afraid of not having a job but also afraid of myself. Traveling meant being alone with myself, and I wasn't sure I could stand that."

Besides banks and insurance companies, the Peace Corps was on campus, too. "I thought a lot about the Peace Corps," she said. "I really wanted to go to Ethiopia. I figured I could use my agriculture background. But again I didn't have the guts."

Guts or money? She had been taught early the value of a dollar – and fraction thereof. "My father used to put dimes under our armpits to keep our elbows off the dinner table. Well, I didn't care about the

Sally Vantress's seven most confidence-building (or destroying) mountain climbs

1. The Appalachians
2. Northern England
3. The Ozarks
4. New Zealand – Haast Pass
5. USA – Logans Pass
6. Northern Italy
7. The Pyrenees

elbows – I wanted the dimes." Possibly fueling her interest in hard currency, young Sally and her siblings were not allowed to possess money. They could earn it all right – that was encouraged – but they couldn't keep it in their piggy banks. "We were always stealing it from each other, so Dad took over and became our accountant. Any money brought into the house was immediately turned over to him, and he recorded it in a ledger, doling it out for those big purchases – like when I bought my horse.

"My dad taught me to be very organized," she added. "In the eighth grade I started keeping my own records, and I've always earned my own money. When I was nineteen, I bought a house."

She continued to toe the line through college, accepting a job with Crocker Bank upon graduation. "Two days after finishing school, I'm working in a bank," she said incredulously, as if speaking of someone else. "I didn't even take a week off. It was ridiculous."

Cut to Sally Vantress, five years later, assistant vice president, possessor of a beautiful home, closets full of clothes – in short, all the requisite accoutrements of the upper-middle-class lifestyle. She wears suits to work, has her curly reddish brown hair cut just so, and applies ample amounts of makeup to her fair, freckled skin. She is bright, attractive, successful – and miserable. "I was a frustrated achiever," she said, "going after one goal, then another, then another. I thought I was excelling when I'd set a short-term goal, achieve it, then go on to another. But I discovered they were like quick sugar fixes for me –

ultimately unsatisfying. I'd cross the finish line of a marathon and think, 'Oh God, I did it!' then immediately think, 'Oh no, what's my next goal?' "

By this time, work had ceased to be an inspiration. "I liked my job and I didn't like my job," she said. "I loved working with people. But I hated the structure. I hated having people tell me when to come to work, what to do, etc." So she quit the world of banking and went to work for her mother's company, Vantress (Interior) Design Associates.

She bought an airplane and began taking vacations. On one memorable jaunt to the Northwest, her first trip alone, she flew her plane to Washington's San Juan Islands, then roughed it for ten days with bicycle and backpack. She met Mark while boarding the ferry to Orcas Island. He was tall, dark, handsome, and mad for cycling. They stayed together for Sally's entire trip, bonded by a heartfelt infatuation. Sally liked listening to Mark talk about his adventures. He had just bicycled across America and said he had plans to do the same in China.

As Sally wrote in her book *Seeing Myself Seeing the World*, "Although I wasn't a cyclist, Mark encouraged me, and I began to feel a whole new sense of rhythm and freedom as we pedaled along the undulating terrain. I was completely taken with the outdoors and the beauty that surrounded me. There were no barriers; no windows; no car doors."

Back at work, Sally had trouble focusing on her job. She spent most of her time immersed in another time zone: either the past (the San Juan Islands) or the fanciful future (bicycling China with Mark).

Mark cycled down the Pacific Coast, then stayed with Sally on and off during his forays around California. "Being around him just accentuated the restlessness I was beginning to feel," she said.

After New Zealand, Sally bicycled Australia, then flew to China.

Canton, China. It was raining lightly as Sally and Michelle (an Aussie friend traveling with her for three weeks) began pedaling out of Canton. They were on their way to Wuzhou, two days away. They had a map, but they still couldn't figure out which way to go. So they followed the heaviest flow of traffic, hoping it would lead them out of town. The streets were packed with trucks and bike riders: Chinese people on black, single-geared bikes going very s-l-o-w-l-y. Some of the

With her bike fully loaded, Sally Vantress is ready to hit the road. (Courtesy of Sally Vantress)

older men pedaled so close to zero, it looked like they were going to fall over. The sound of horns honking and bicycle bells ringing was deafening.

At the first major junction, the traffic split evenly. The women stopped, pulled out their map, and began comparing the characters on the road signs to the characters on their map. Nothing matched. "As always, when we stopped everyone else did, too. We were immediately surrounded by at least a hundred people, poking, prodding, jabbering in Chinese, saying hello in their sing-song English. They were fascinated by my red panniers. One guy took one of my books and walked away. 'Is he coming back?' I wondered. Another started playing with the gears on my bike. They pointed and stared and laughed at the freckles on our faces. Even though most were adults, their innocence and curiosity made them seem like children.

In desperation, Sally finally pointed to their destination on the map and shrugged her shoulders to communicate that she didn't know which way to go. The Chinese benefactors immediately began to yell and point in all directions. Sally and Michelle had no choice but to go with the majority and head southwest.

At the next intersection it was more of the same. And the next . . . and the next after that. Finally, the crowd pointed them over a bridge. Their hearts sank. The bridge was totally jammed up with trucks and bicycles. By this time it had stopped raining, and it was just hot and incredibly humid. "Sitting on that bridge in stopped-up traffic, sweltering, exhausted, my clothes stuck to me, with black soot packed into the creases of my arms – it was probably the low point of the trip."

In the evening, feeling more dead than alive, Sally and Michelle searched for a hotel. By now the cast had changed, but the routine was, well, the routine. They stopped and pulled out a sheet of paper displaying the characters for *hotel* and began trying to match them with those on the buildings. No luck. Like ants drawn to picnic remains, a crowd began to form. Sally tried to communicate to the growing assembly with a phrase book; they just pointed at her helmet and giggled.

When she finally did show them the symbol for hotel, several hands reached out and grabbed her book. As they passed it around, she pulled out one of her maps. More hands reached out and grabbed that, too. "What if we don't get that map back?" she wondered.

Finally, after two hours of search and struggle, they settled into a simple hotel. That night, lying in bed, Sally reviewed the day. She calculated that they had traveled twenty-one miles in eight hours.

Listening to Mark, Sally realized how much she ached for adventure. She was increasingly aware of another part of her – a second self? – that had been suppressed, stunted, as though chained its whole life in the basement of her soul. And when Mark announced that he was considering not just cycling across China but going all the way around the world, she heard that other self pounding on the cellar door. "I knew my life was going to change," she said. "How could I watch Mark go off like that while I continued to live such a structured, regimented life?" Not that she thought Mark was forever – and she was sure he felt the same way. But on some level they connected, and maybe they could be good for each other for a while.

But she vacillated. "I knew I needed to make a life change," she said, "but I also believed that I had to work to support my home, airplane, and high cost of living." Then the realization hit her as a revelation: Dump the possessions. Having heard the voice, she heeded it. She sold it all then called Mark and told him everything was gone — car, house, airplane, major household appliances. "What?" he said.

"I hadn't even told him I was doing it," she said, chuckling. "I think it freaked him out a bit. He probably thought I'd done it for him. It didn't matter — I knew it was for me."

The next challenge was how to ask Mark if she could go with him without it appearing that she was asking for permission. After weeks of mulling over complex strategies, she finally found her courage while standing in a Disneyland ride line: "How do you feel about me going with you?" she said.

They debated the matter for weeks, leaving it still unresolved as they traveled to Lake Tahoe to bicycle around the lake. "We rode the seventy-five miles," she said, "and it was November and cold. I was dead at the end, but I did it! And after it was over, Mark said, 'Yeah, okay, let's travel together.'"

After cycling more than eight hundred miles through China — all that was legally possible for an American — Sally took the Trans-Siberian Railway across the Soviet Union. She then bicycled through northern Europe before arriving in the British Isles.

Ireland. It seemed to Vantress that all she saw anymore was rain, rain, and rain. She went to sleep each night to the sound of rain falling on her tent; she awoke each morning to the same. Fortunately, few cars competed with her for space on the slippery Irish roads.

She decided to pedal to the southeast coast of Ireland and take a ferry to Wales. Maybe the weather there would be better. She left in early morning in between rain storms — it was actually hot! — and started jamming. She was not intending to make the ferry that night, but by noon it was beginning to look like she could.

She arrived at the dock at 8:00 P.M., an hour before the ferry was scheduled to leave. She had pedaled 102 miles — her best effort so far. She was so jazzed by her performance that she gave no real thought to what she would do when the ferry dropped her in Wales at 2:00 in the morning. "Oh well, I'll find a campground" was as far as her thinking went. "What's a little rain?"

The ferry departed late, so it was closer to 3:00 in the morning when it docked in Wales. As the cars fired up and the ramp dropped, the full impact of what she was about to face hit her like a wet dish rag. It was pitch dark, of course, and bucketing rain. It was, in fact, one of the hardest rains she had ever seen. "Oh my God," was all she could say, over and over again.

She was reminded of the night in Sydney, Australia, when she was kicked out of the airport and had to sleep in a mosquito-infested swamp. Well, she wasn't going to try to stay in the ferry building and have the same thing happen. She made it then, and she'd make it now. There was always a campground around. She'd find it, then sleep in tomorrow.

It was her belief, thanks to Mark, that she had to stay tough all the time, or she wouldn't make it. "I couldn't stay in B and Bs or eat out, or I'd get soft," she says. "And even though I have to bathe every day, I refused to pay for a hot shower. It wasn't the fifty cents, though that was the excuse I used. I really didn't want to get into needing a hot shower and then not be able to get one. Instead, I used fountains, hoses . . ."

As she pedaled away from the lights of the ferry building, it became so dark that she couldn't see her hand in front of her face. And it was raining so hard that she had to close her eyes, which was no great loss since she couldn't see anyway. It took what seemed like forever to go about a mile but still no campground. She had no idea whether she was even on the right road, and she couldn't pull out her map in the downpour because it would have been ruined in seconds.

She came upon what appeared to be an empty field and decided to try to pitch her tent. Not surprisingly, it was a muddy field, and she had to move slowly to keep from slipping down.

She got the tent out, but before she could get it up, there were puddles everywhere. She finally pitched it and put her gear inside, but now there was a layer of mud everywhere. She was crying like a child and cursing like a seaman. "What the hell am I doing here?" was one of the more socially acceptable things that exploded from her lips.

She began to worry that she might freeze to death. It was a cold rain, and she no longer had anything dry to wear. Finally, in weary desperation, she crawled into the tent and wrapped her soaked sleeping bag around her like a shawl. There she sat – shoes on, rain pelting

Sally Vantress's six things to do before bicycling around the world

1. Prepare a checklist.
2. Learn a foreign language or two.
3. Learn how to change a bicycle tire.
4. Practice riding with your bike loaded.
5. Study geography.
6. Obtain maps.

Sally confesses that she did none of these things before starting around the world – that's why she knows they're important.

the tent like machine-gun fire – until daylight. Apparently she fell asleep, at least briefly, because she was jolted awake by morning traffic sounds.

She could tell from the pitter-patter on the tent that it was still raining, though not as hard as before. When she peeked out, she was shocked to see that she was camped in the middle of a tremendous mud pond. She was a tiny island in a huge brown lake. Buddy was parked outside all covered with mud, and when she saw that pathetic sight, something in her snapped. She started yelling and screaming. "I've had it! I've really had it! What am I trying to prove?! Am I trying to prove that I can keep going, that I can rough it, without Mark? Well, who needs it!"

By now she was packing up, just flinging things into her packs. She stomped around, with no regard for how muddy she was. "I was cursing the gods," she says. "I can have a pretty filthy mouth sometimes, and this was one of those times."

Back on her bike, carrying an extra ten pounds of water-and-mud weight, she took a deep breath and tried to use some of her mind-relaxation techniques. It took a while, but eventually she brought herself back to sanity and perspective.

After Britain, Sally cycled extensively through central and southern Europe, including Germany, Italy, Spain, and Portugal. In her six and a half months in Europe, she covered six thousand miles, all of it by bike except for the short ride she accepted during a blizzard in the Alps. From Lisbon, she flew to Florida.

Southern Florida. In Florida, camping in the state parks cost twenty-five dollars, whether you were a bicyclist with a tent or a huge motor home. It wasn't in the Vantress budget to pay twenty-five dollars a night for camping, so she made deals. She negotiated—that was what she was good at. She had done it all over the world and was always able to hammer the price down. Typically, she asked people at campgrounds if she could share their site. She would pay a couple dollars guest fee and pitch her tent next to friendly strangers.

But at one particular campground in southern Florida, she began asking people in line and some guy went crazy. "He was a complete asshole about it, screaming at me to pay the fee or go somewhere else. On top of that, he reported me to the ranger." When she got to the gate to ask to cycle through to "look for a friend," the ranger told her she'd been reported. He said the guy was real ugly about it, too, adding that he had no choice but to enforce the rules.

Vantress knew that southern Florida was largely mangrove swamps. There wasn't a lot of dry land, which meant not a lot of places to pitch a tent.

"Why don't you go back to the last rest stop?" the ranger suggested.

"That doesn't seem too safe to me. Besides it's illegal."

"The cops won't hassle you there," he said.

Vantress was skeptical but short on choices. She rode to the nearest rest stop. Alas, it was horseshoe-shaped, offering no ideal hiding place. So she set up behind a picnic table, cooked dinner on her stove, and waited. "At dusk the mosquitos come in droves to have their dinner—me. After dark I pitched my tent, crawled in, and waited. For an hour or more, I lay in my sleeping bag peering out at the people walking to and from the bathrooms, trying to determine whether they could see me or not. Finally I fell asleep."

Sally's travels across North America took her from Florida up the eastern seaboard, then west from New York City, through the Ozarks, the

Midwest, Yellowstone and Glacier national parks, into Canada, then back down through Idaho, Oregon, and California: 8,200 miles in all.

California Coast. Riding the home stretch down narrow, winding Route 1, which hugged the glorious Pacific Ocean, Vantress ruminated on the past nineteen months, twenty-one thousand miles, twenty countries, twelve flat tires. It was no overstatement to say that the trip had profoundly changed her life. But how? She needed to know. Well, for one thing, it had given her an opportunity to see who she was. It had been the best darn education thirteen thousand dollars could buy. For example, she had learned about all of the following:

- Unconditional love. Her address book was full of people she'd met who welcomed her into their homes, fed her, even though they hardly knew her. "My life before the trip had mostly been full of the conditional type of love, as in 'You do this for me, I'll do that for you.'"
- Fear. She had confronted every fear she'd ever known—from rape to spiders, snakes, leeches, and the huge, slimy frogs that liked to hang out on the toilets in Australia.
- Rain. Everywhere she went, she had brought rain. "Kansas was in a drought until I went through; it hasn't stopped raining since."
- Exercise. She had bicycled more than twenty thousand miles— maybe seven million pedal revolutions—and gained weight. She had left at 118 pounds and was returning at about 133. Bicycling, she'd decided, was not the greatest exercise—at least not the way she was doing it. "At home I ran and worked out at the health spa and did different things. Now all I did most days was pedal Buddy for ten hours. And I'd gotten so efficient at what I did that I didn't burn up as many calories as I used to. To top it off, at the end of most days I pulled into a campground, ate a heavy meal, and went to sleep."
- People. She had met all kinds: friendly farmers in New Zealand . . . that guy on the Trans-Siberian . . . his mom, whom she stayed with in Ireland . . . Italian men who hassled her . . . the bartender in Monte Carlo . . . the guy in Spain who she was sure had a hypodermic needle and was going to kidnap her but didn't . . . the ex-con in Georgia who date-raped her . . . the people who shot at her in Kentucky . . . the ones who ran her off the road in Wyoming.

Yes, the only violent incidents had occurred in the United States, and she knew why: All the bad stuff in her was working itself out.

"When I left the States, I had a very negative attitude about my country – politics, race relations. But time and traveling had given me a different perspective. Everywhere I'd gone – the United States included – I'd met wonderful, giving people. And I'd learned that I have the power to turn a frown into a smile – both in me and in others."

As she weaved her way down the California coast, she found herself growing timid again. She had ventured out boldly in all sorts of suicidal traffic – cities like Auckland, Canton, Barcelona, Rome. But now, haunted by the knowledge that most accidents happen near home, she was getting conservative again. "I was diving into ditches at the mere sight of a car."

"In some ways," she thought, "I feel like a lost child returning home, like a war vet being dropped back into society. The unsettled feelings that I hoped this trip would resolve are still there. I have tangible questions that cry out for tangible answers: What kind of a career will I have? Where will I live? Will I be married and have kids? There are still way more questions than answers.

"Some things are certain: I'm a different person than before this trip – and for the better. But now what? I've learned a lot about myself, the world, but so what? What does it all mean? So I'm smarter – when do I get happier?

"I've sold all my possessions, everything I own, thinking that when I came back I'd have all the answers. But I have nothing and it's scary.

"Not only am I scared of getting trapped into nine-to-five, of being unhappy in my work, but I'm scared of having to stash my Buddy bike in the garage. Our time together is almost over.

"Maybe I won't stay. Maybe I'll come back for just a month or so. I'll see people, get acclimated, then decide where to go, what to do. Maybe I'll join a convent . . . or a rock band."

The next morning Sally awoke on the beach to crashing surf and pungent salt smells. The sky and sea were decorated in blue, with a misty white overlay, as in a dream. Her body felt gritty, but her spirit was cleansed; she felt emboldened by nature. Before she crawled out of her sleeping bag, she gave quiet thanks "to God or whoever" for the opportunity afforded her – the opportunity to see the world, to step back and see her life from a distance, so much distance.

While she had slept, her doubts and fears had continued south.

Maybe they would be waiting for her when she got home, maybe not, but for now she simply couldn't see failure; it wasn't even on the chart. "Nothing is going to stop me," she thought, punching the air with her fist.

She searched her pack, found her Walkman, and picked out the Bette Midler tape she wanted. She put the tape in, the headset on, and cranked up the volume. Facing the ocean, she breathed deeply, seeming to draw from nature's raw power. With renewed vigor, she sang at the top of her lungs: "I can fly higher than an eagle; You are the wind beneath my wings . . ."

GREG LeMOND
Wheels of Fortune

Versailles, June 1989, final stage of the Tour de France. Win one Tour de France and you are a world-class cyclist. Win two and the pyramid of excellence narrows to a razor edge. Win three and you join the sport's true elite. Only five cyclists have ever won three or more Tours. And only three have ever won five Tours.

Such thoughts flashed quickly through the mind of the American preparing for the final stage of the world's most prestigious bicycle race – quickly, because there was so much else to think about.

By midafternoon, the morning clouds had given way to a white-washed blue sky. The temperature was in the mideighties, hot for France, but a light breeze made it bearable. With only a final fifteen-mile time trial remaining, the race was a showdown between two riders of different temperaments, styles, and nationalities.

The American was Gregory James LeMond, twenty-eight years old, just now hitting his rhythm on the comeback trail. LeMond was feeling strong and loose, and it showed in his face. He was upbeat, chatty, quick to smile. It was a boyish smile that sent dimples rippling across his face like rings upon a lake. Added to his striking pale blue eyes and wind-blown haircut, the impression was friendly youth.

He contrasted sharply with his main adversary, a severe-looking Frenchman named Laurent Fignon who, despite wearing the yellow jersey reserved for the Tour leader, did not have on his happy face. One of Europe's top road racers, Fignon was by nature cranky and

138

arrogant. From the point of view of journalists, he was an unpleasant mope. He had recently won – in a near-unanimous vote – the *Prix Citron* (Lemon Prize) awarded by the press to the least courteous rider. Discourteous was a mild epithet for Fignon: French TV had recently captured him spitting at a camera and snarling at a cameraman, "You want a punch in the mouth?"

With a fifty-second lead, one might have expected Fignon to loosen up a bit, wave to a fan, or sign an autograph. But *au contraire*. Although the consensus was that nobody – not even a rejuvenated Greg LeMond – could possibly make up two seconds per kilometer (three seconds per mile), Fignon looked tight, like a trap waiting to spring closed on itself.

It certainly made sense that LeMond was the more upbeat. After all, he had nothing to lose; he had already come back farther than anyone – including Greg himself – had thought possible. And now he had a chance, albeit a remote one, to put the clamps on one of the most dramatic, improbable comebacks in sports history, a prospect that made him tingle all over.

In 1968, when Greg was seven, the LeMond family moved from southern California to Lake Tahoe, and Greg became interested in hunting, fishing, backpacking, and skiing. "When we moved to Lake Tahoe it really opened my eyes to the outdoors. I was impressed by the mountains and the snow and the sense of freedom. It introduced me to a whole new way of living."

When Greg was ten, the family moved to Nevada, the Washoe Valley, midway between Carson City and Reno, forty-five hundred feet above sea level. Bob LeMond started a real estate business, and Greg grew ever more passionate about skiing. "Skiing became an important part of my life. My dad (who was an active skier) and I drove all around the Sierra Nevada to find the best slopes. As I became better at the mechanics of skiing, I inevitably wanted something more challenging than riding up a ski lift and whizzing right back down again. Although I liked racing, I was more impressed with freestyle skiing. To me acrobatic skiing was the best brand of the sport, a mix of competition and incredible skill, of showmanship and derring-do."

He worked odd jobs in the summer of 1974 to earn money to buy a ten-speed bicycle, using it strictly for transportation. He was still faithful to freestyle skiing, longing to be a champion hotdogger who could do the aerial flips he saw on TV. To learn how, he traveled to Vancouver to enroll in Wayne Wong's hotdog training camp. Although he hurt his back and couldn't do flips, the camp was a major turning point in LeMond's life. It was Wayne Wong who first recommended bicycling as the ideal off-season exercise.

LeMond took note of a coincidence: Days before he had left for ski camp, the Nevada State Cycling Championships went right by his house. He and his dad watched the race, captivated by the speed, the action, the effort. "Those guys have to be soooo fit," thought LeMond.

He returned from Vancouver with half-hearted resolve to start cycling. "At first, cycling seemed like hard work to me. But I was dedicated to freestyle skiing, and if cycling was going to make me a better skier, I thought a little drudgery couldn't hurt."

He had the support, even the participation, of his father, who decided that bicycling was the ideal way for him to lose twenty pounds. He and Greg began riding about twenty miles a day, and soon they were climbing mountain passes around Washoe. "I was lucky that my dad was so involved and loved the sport so much," Greg has said.

They entered races – intermediates for Greg, seniors for Bob – and little by little, skiing became background. Actually, LeMond has admitted, everything became background. "After I got into cycling, for the first five or six years I worked so hard at it that I never did anything else. I was so hooked that I didn't ski, hunt, or fish anymore. Not until I turned professional at nineteen and cycling became a real job did I go back to those sports as a release."

As a teenager, he hung around bike shops, one of which was owned by Roland Della Santa, a master frame builder who befriended LeMond. Once or twice a week, the youngster would show up at his shop. "As he worked," LeMond remembers, "he often told me stories of the great European stars, the thousands of screaming fans, and the legendary races such as the Tour de France and the *Giro d'Italia*. Although it was as popular there as football and baseball in the United States, on this side of the Atlantic bicycling as a sport was almost unknown."

When he wasn't listening to Della Santa spin yarns, LeMond would rifle through his racing magazines, catching glimpses of his own future. He studied the training tips and admired the photos of European cyclists laboring up mountain passes. He even acquired his own hero: Eddy Merckx, a Belgian rider who won the Tour de France five times. "Sometimes I wondered what it would be like to ride at the same level as Eddy Merckx, climbing up the narrow goat paths they called mountain passes, with millions of frenetic fans cheering, tugging at my sides. Although I probably didn't yet admit it to myself, somewhere in the back of my mind I believed that I could do it, too."

He went at it with the focus of a survivalist rubbing two sticks together, winning the first four races he entered, thirty in the first year. He simply ate up age-group competition, creating mismatches wherever he competed. At fifteen, having beaten up on intermediate racers at will, he petitioned for and received permission to ride with the juniors, the sixteen- to nineteen-year-olds. He was now racing with riders who were stronger and more mature, and that meant "I would just have to work twice as hard to be competitive."

Still fifteen, LeMond entered the Tour of Fresno, where he went wheel to wheel with an idol of sorts, America's top road racer, John Howard. LeMond and his dad had watched Howard win a sixty-mile road race in Nevada two years before, and now LeMond found himself a little awed by his presence. So awed, in fact, that LeMond wouldn't let Howard out of his sight, dogging him to the end of the race. He finished second, only ten seconds behind Howard after three days of racing.

"It was a feat that suddenly turned a lot of heads in the world of bicycling," LeMond says. "Nobody had ever heard of any junior beating John Howard, let alone a fifteen-year-old high school sophomore who wasn't shaving yet. For the first time in my career, I was being heralded as 'that phenom from Nevada.'"

One fateful night soon after that race, LeMond sat down and wrote out, on three sheets of paper, his goals in bicycling. "First of all, I wanted to be Junior National champion that year—in 1977. My goal for 1978 was to place well in the Junior World Championship. In 1979 I intended to win the Junior World Championship. In 1980 I wanted to be Olympic cycling champion, and by 1981 I was going to turn professional.

As a pro, he planned to win the world championship and the Tour de France by the time he was twenty-five. "I made those goals because I knew that a bike racer's career can be short, and I wanted to be focused."

Satellite photography should be so focused. LeMond did, in fact, win the Junior National Championship in 1977. He placed well— ninth—in the Junior Worlds the next year, and in 1979 at the Junior Worlds in Buenos Aires, he won not only the gold medal for the road race but the silver medal in the individual pursuit and the bronze in the team time trial. It was the first time any bicycle rider had ever won three medals in any world championship competition. People in bicycling were beginning to notice Greg LeMond.

The only amateur goal that didn't get a check mark was winning the 1980 Olympics, but he could hang that one on the U.S. government and its Olympic boycott. So instead of going to Moscow, he traveled to Europe to race with the U.S. national team. He felt pressure to prove himself, for despite his reign as Junior World champion, no pro team had yet approached him. (It wasn't surprising: There was no U.S. team, and only one American, Jonathon Boyer, had ever raced on a European pro team.)

One of the races on the 1980 program was the Circuit de la Sarthe, one of the few European events open to both professionals and amateurs. LeMond shocked the bicycling world by winning the race, thereby becoming the first American and the youngest rider (nineteen) ever to win a major stage race, professional or amateur, in the history of the sport.

The publicity that LeMond received for that victory caught the eye of French cycling coach Cyrille Guimard, who went to see LeMond race in the next event: the Ruban Granitier Breton, a stage race in the French province of Brittany. LeMond describes it:

"I was chasing three Russians on a breakaway, ten seconds behind and moving up fast, when I punctured. The French mechanic who was supposed to be looking out for our team had apparently been sleeping in his car. Then, when he finally reached me, he fumbled with the wheel, costing me more precious time. Then he told me I should hurry and ride by myself – for the good name of the team – that I could get at least fifth or sixth place. He must not have realized that the main pack was only thirty seconds behind. Of course I would be caught and lose everything. I was so mad I couldn't see straight. I took my bike and flung it at the car and quit the race."

Such intemperance might have cost him a job, but Coach Guimard struck a "boys-will-be-boys" pose, telling LeMond that he admired his spirit. "You have the fire to be a great champion," he said.

Then he offered him a spot on his Renault team for the following 1981 season.

During the winter, Greg married Kathy Morris, whom he'd met at the National Bicycle Championships in Milwaukee. He was so happy that he cut back on his training and gained a quick fifteen pounds.

In January 1981, the LeMonds, still teenagers, jetted off to Europe to join the exotic, mysterious world of bicycle racing. To Kathy's family and friends in Lacrosse, Wisconsin, it must have seemed like a dream come true—except, that is, when that nagging thought intruded, How is he going to support Kathy by riding a bicycle?

Quite well, actually, though not at first. Greg's contract with Renault called for $100,000 a year, a furnished house, and a car. When the couple arrived in France, however, the car was a lemon and the house wasn't ready. They were temporarily booked into a tiny hotel room in Nantes that had "pretty good food, except that Kathy got food poisoning." Toilet and shower were down the hall—and it was a mighty cold hall. France in January is not often confused with Acapulco. LeMond described it this way: "It rained every day. Four or five times a week, I trained a hundred kilometers (about sixty miles, as opposed to his usual seventy-nine miles), and it rained, rained, rained. I simply couldn't get in shape. Plus we had no car. Something was wrong with it, and they took it away."

In February, just before Greg left for his first race, Guimard found the couple a three-bedroom house. So while Greg was on the road, racing, being the odd man out at team meals because he didn't speak French, Kathy was back on the home front occupying a house lacking basic amenities she had come to take for granted—like heat, hot water, furniture. "We hadn't been paid our salary yet," said LeMond. "We spent all our wedding money waiting for a check. It was a disaster. Kathy and I came from nice homes, with nice families and lots of friends. In Europe we had no friends, no house, no furniture, no money—nothing. We didn't speak French, and there were no American movies. There wasn't even a McDonald's or a Burger King."

In his first professional race in southern France, an eighty-three miler with three kick-ass hills, LeMond received a rude welcome to the sport. "Right from the start I was off the back, dying. I just couldn't believe how fast they were going. I was in shock."

He was also in a bit of a depression, but then what athlete hasn't been there? It comes with the competition. But what's revealing is how LeMond dealt with his emotional decline. Some would have gotten drunk; others would have pigged out on animal fats; still others would have simply quit. *Mais non*, LeMond did none of those things. Instead, after the race and before dinner, he got back on his bike and rode hard into the lengthening shadows for thirty more miles.

The next day he raced again and was dropped twice more. That evening he increased his supplemental training to forty miles.

LeMond was ill much of that first season, but he continued to race criteriums – short exhibition races through town or city streets – for three or four hundred dollars a pop. "It was freezing cold, and I was burning up inside. I didn't want to do them, but I stuck it out because I wanted to make it in cycling. I trained hard, doing nine-hour rides around Nantes once or twice a week to get rid of my fat. I was dedicated, all right."

Mix dedication and talent, and the precipitate is usually success. LeMond's first pro victory came in the Tour d'Oise only three months after his debut. The finale came down to a six-man sprint, with LeMond inching out his Aussie friend Phil Anderson for the win. "That first victory really boosted my confidence and helped me relax a little. After that I raced with more aggressiveness and daring. I realized the great cycling heroes were human. I knew I could compete."

In 1981 LeMond returned to America and won the Coors Classic. It was an especially sweet win for him because (1) although he could conjugate some French verbs, he was still, heart and soul, an American boy; and (2) he beat Soviet star Sergei Soukhorouchenkov, the gold medal winner in the 1980 Olympics. That allowed him to check off that last amateur goal, albeit with an asterisk.

Versailles, 1989. An optimistic Greg LeMond tinkered with his bike and considered his advantages; he was bucking public opinion that this year's Tour de France was all over except for a lot of French people shouting. On a normal day, when both he and Fignon were in top form, he was the better time trialist. On a normal day, he figured he could beat Fignon in this final fifteen-mile time trial by at least a second and a half per mile. And, unlike Fignon, he was using tri-bars and an aerodynamic helmet – how many seconds would they subtract? In addition, he felt marvelous – fully recovered from the mountains – and he had absolutely nothing to lose.

LeMond, having already ridden the course that morning, was dismayed by how easy it was: two-hundred- to three-hundred-foot drop

Greg LeMond takes his turns at full speed. (Courtesy of David Nelson)

in the beginning, no significant climbs. With so little to work with, LeMond seized upon the only strategy that had any chance of leading him to victory: full-bore, guts-out sprint to the finish. Do or bonk. For a half-hour or less his mind would play chicken with his body. He told his aides that he didn't want to hear split times – nothing to distract him, nothing to get between him and pure, unadulterated speed.

Everything he had ever done on a bicycle funneled into this moment. It was the ultimate challenge: take a class-ten cardiovascular system, hone it to perfection with hours of bike time, and take on the best in a sprint to the finish. It was bicycle racing in its elemental form: head to head, head down, head home, first one there wins.

Except that LeMond, to make it sporting, had spotted his competition fifty seconds. "Too great a deficit," said the experts. "Can't be done," they declared. And even LeMond was not without his doubts. Still, he had to love his underdog position.

LeMond entered his first Tour de France in 1984 a few days after his twenty-third birthday. Besides inexperience in three-week stage races, he was hampered by bronchitis and a foot so sore he often couldn't pedal without pain. But then pain was what the Tour de France was all about.

His teammate Laurent Fignon, at the top of his game, had fewer problems, winning that 1984 Tour by more than ten minutes over Bernard Hinault, with LeMond finishing third, 1:44 behind Hinault. It was a wonderful showing for a rookie, and LeMond easily won the white jersey as the Tour's best young rider. Though he was the first North American in history to finish in the top three, he was disappointed. Any hopes he had of being co-leader of the Renault team were shattered by Fignon's second straight Tour victory. Accordingly, LeMond signed a month later with Bernard Hinault's team, La Vie Claire. With Hinault there, LeMond still wasn't top banana. But the Frenchman promised, while wooing LeMond to sign, that he would retire in two years, on his thirty-second birthday. LeMond, of course, would be heir to the throne.

Not incidentally, the contract with La Vie Claire shook up the world of big-time bicycling. At a time when the average rider earned about fifteen thousand dollars and Hinault was making two hundred thousand, LeMond signed for one million dollars over three years.

Hinault and LeMond agreed that La Vie Claire would not have a predetermined leader. Whoever was stronger would take the lead, and the team would work to defend that man – whoever he was.

It was, of course, not that simple. There may be no sport that intertwines individual and team goals quite like European road racing. It is a difficult concept to grasp – sometimes even for LeMond. Because of the importance of drafting and blocking, a race like the Tour de France cannot be simply "every man for himself." The team leaders need the aid of the *domestiques*. Unless a rider is indisputably number one on his team, he cannot always ride as fast as he wishes.

A case in point from the 1985 Tour de France: On the seventeenth stage, as LeMond climbed a mountain into a thick mist, he learned that Hinault, the overall leader, was weakening. LeMond, who was second overall, continued to ride strongly, staying with the stage leaders, intent on taking the yellow jersey for La vie Claire and himself. If Hinault couldn't claim it, LeMond reasoned, it should stay within the team. It seemed to him to be a time when the interests of LeMond and La Vie Claire were one and the same.

But as soon as he started to pull the pace, Maurice Le Guilloux, the assistant coach of the La Vie Claire team, drove to his side to tell him that he could stay with the leaders but he must not break away. The coaches, he said, wanted to preserve La Vie Claire's one-two position. LeMond, who felt he was in the best shape of his life, was confused and hurt. Why wouldn't Guilloux want him to take the yellow jersey and keep it within La Vie Claire? To the American mind it was like asking Babe Ruth to strike out on purpose so teammate Lou Gehrig could win the batting crown.

LeMond had harsh words with Guilloux but eventually relented. He held back and the pace slowed. Bitterly frustrated, he convinced himself that he was throwing away what might be the only chance in his life to win the Tour de France. He was even more certain when Hinault finished 1:13 behind him that day; he could have easily gained another minute, maybe two. In an outpouring of grief, LeMond sat behind a scaffolding and cried while his coach tried to explain why it had happened.

In the end, Hinault won the 1985 Tour, with LeMond finishing second. LeMond's remarks allow us to plumb the depths of his bitterness: "The 1985 Tour de France ended in frustration for me. Although I might not have won the Tour, Hinault wouldn't have won without my help either. When Hinault needed help in the mountains, I was always there. And after he crashed at Saint-Etienne, I didn't leave his side for two days. I think that if I had been allowed to play my hand fully on the terrain that best suited me – the mountains – I could have shown myself to be the equal of Hinault."

Oh well, there was always next year – wasn't there? "Greg knows he can ride for victory next year in the Tour," Hinault proclaimed in the sweet flush of victory. "I'm just planning to have fun and make some trouble in the next Tour. All I want to do is help one of my teammates win. If all goes well, that should be Greg LeMond."

It would be safe to say that LeMond was skeptical and with good reason. Bernard was unpredictable. Perhaps, to give Hinault the benefit of the doubt, the problem was merely that he and LeMond, both world-class competitors, were so alike. "The real conflict was between Hinault and me," LeMond has said. "He wanted to win the Tour and so did I. It was a delicate situation."

That remark is positively altruistic, as it overlooks the fact that Hinault had promised LeMond his support in the 1986 Tour. And from stage one, Bernard had an odd way of showing that support; mostly he showed LeMond and everybody else his backside. Out of the gate, Hinault went for the win (what would be his sixth Tour de France victory), executing one bold breakaway after another.

LeMond felt betrayed and, at least once, openly said so. Hinault played the innocent, as though his stratagem was actually designed to help LeMond. For a time, this open schism divided the entire La Vie Claire team. But LeMond held tough, Hinault eventually faded, and overt rapprochement finally occurred with three days left in the twenty-five-day race. Hinault ceased his challenges and openly supported LeMond, who became the first non-European in history to win the Tour de France.

And thus he hammered in that final nail. Or was it the final nail?

Northern California, 1987. As a country boy, LeMond grew up around guns. He took hunters' safety courses, entered competitions, even won the Nevada Junior Championship in trap-shooting, a sport in which both his mom and dad excelled. He felt comfortable and safe around guns.

In April 1987 he was home with a broken bone in his left hand suffered during a fall in a race in Italy. He usually didn't hunt during the bicycling season — February to October — but for the past six weeks his only outdoor activity had been riding his bike through the Sierra foothills. So when his uncle urged him for the umpteenth time to join him on his property to hunt wild turkeys, he finally accepted.

Three days before he was supposed to return to Europe, Greg, his uncle Rod, and his brother-in-law Pat, who was an inexperienced hunter, donned army camouflage and trekked up a hill covered in berry bushes. They split up, Uncle Rod going left, brother Pat going right, LeMond staying put. They were supposed to walk a bit, then sit and wait for the birds to make their move.

After awhile, LeMond heard Pat whistle. He was trying to determine the whereabouts of the others, but LeMond decided not to respond. After all, if he could identify the human whistle, so could the turkeys. He decided instead to stand and thus quietly communicate his position. He had reached a crouch when a shot rang out, cutting the silence and dropping LeMond back to earth like a stone. Pat was about thirty yards away, but the noise was so loud that for a moment Greg thought his own gun had discharged.

Blood appeared on his left ring finger, the first clue that he'd been hit. Then a numbness washed over him. He tried to stand but almost passed out – he was in shock. He tried to call out but couldn't breathe – his right lung had collapsed.

When Pat realized he had shot the world's most famous bicyclist, he too went into shock. That left it to Uncle Rod to run back and call 911. By pure chance, a helicopter hovered nearby. The pilot, hearing the emergency call, briefly debated whether to attend the shooting accident or a nearby auto crash. Deciding on the shooting, he swooped down, picked up LeMond and dropped him at the U.C. Davis hospital less than a quarter-hour later. If LeMond had relied on an ambulance, it would have meant a longer wait and then a thirty-minute ride on bumpy roads; at least one doctor told LeMond that he came within twenty minutes of bleeding to death.

Doctors performed five hours of surgery to remove about half of the sixty pellets that had penetrated the slender young man's liver, kidneys, intestines, and arm. They inserted a tube into his chest – without anesthesia – to draw blood from his collapsed lung. It was a procedure that served to redefine pain for LeMond, who thought he knew a thing or two about suffering. "I never thought I'd be the type who needed painkillers. You think you're used to pain on your bike, but that's not pain. The suffering you feel on your bike is nothing compared to real pain. I think of that sometimes when I ride."

For those keeping track, the other thirty pellets remain tucked neatly away in his body, including two in the lining of his heart. The medicos say no problem, since the body, in its infinite wisdom, has formed protective scar tissue around them.

"The pain persisted for at least three or four weeks after I came home. I'd sit in a chair at home shaking with pain, sweat running down my face. I'd cry and cry because it hurt so much."

He lost fifteen pounds from his already lean frame in the first week and a half. For the first two weeks he moved gingerly from his bed to a chair – no farther than that. After three weeks he was able to walk a couple of blocks. Five weeks after the accident, he started fly-fishing. But fifteen or twenty minutes of that had his back in a knot. LeMond, who prided himself on his recuperative powers, had to wonder whether he would ever again be a stronger bicyclist than his son, Geoffrey, who was three.

He indeed faced a formidable physical battle: At the time of the accident, LeMond weighed 151 pounds with a body-fat content of 4 percent; when he began training again, those numbers were 137 and 17 percent. His thigh muscle had lost almost an inch. In its survival mode, his body had gobbled up vast quantities of muscle.

He described one phase of his attempted return: "I came back from nothing. I'd been training about three weeks, riding with a guy who kept dropping me all the time. I was becoming demoralized. Here I had won the Tour de France, and now I was being left behind by some guy riding back roads in California! Then one day I dropped *him*. I started feeling like a normal racer, an out-of-shape racer, but not one with a disability."

It was a temporary feeling. He developed a stomach ache, and less than three months after the accident went under the knife again, this time to remove an inflamed appendix. The triple whammy – the crash that broke his hand, the shooting, the emergency appendectomy – took him down for the count, ending the 1987 season.

Big-time bicycling regularly separates, in rather brutal fashion, the fit from the superfit. Proving that he rightfully belonged in the former category, LeMond began the 1988 season with a pathetic showing in a Spanish race, the Ruta del Sol. "One day I had to be pushed up some of the hills," he later admitted. But there were witnesses who reported that LeMond finished one stage of the race only because his teammates pushed him along the flats, too. In any case, word spread throughout the European circuit that LeMond was finished. The murmurs of doubt did not escape his own ears.

For psychological support during those hard times, he relied heavily on his family, especially his wife and father, and on that little voice within that kept whispering encouragement. His confidence was also bolstered by his masseur, Otto Jacome, who publicly predicted that LeMond would once again climb the Big Mountain. His injury was not bicycle-related, said Jacome. His tendons and knees are fine. The vital organs would heal themselves. And he's clean. Never takes drugs, not even vitamin shots. And, of course, he was born with the cardiovascular system of a god.

And unfortunately, the connective tissue of an increasingly fragile mortal. Early in the 1988 season, LeMond crashed again. "It happened at fifty kilometers an hour. One guy went down, taking others with him, and I was one of them. All I remember is doing a flip, rolling on the ground, doing another flip, and hitting on my back. I slid about thirty meters and landed on my head and shoulder. Luckily I was wearing a hard-shell helmet."

LeMond is caught in a rare moment of repose. (Courtesy of California Bicyclist)

He thought he had broken his collarbone, but X-rays were negative. Still, he was forced off his bike for two weeks. According to LeMond, "For every week you take off, it's nearly three weeks to get back to where you were."

Despite his wealth of experience and knowledge, he tried to come back too fast. After two weeks of R and R, he started four races in the first week – and didn't finish any of them. Then he fell during a race in Belgium and another rider's pedal bruised his right shin, causing an inflamed tendon. His body had once again thrown up a hurdle that no amount of mental toughness could overcome.

On July 12, 1988, while his colleagues were going wheel-to-wheel in the Tour of France, LeMond was in a hospital in Minnesota, undergoing surgery to repair the injured tendon. The operation itself was minor. LeMond cut his own cast off after a week. But the 1988 season was effectively lost – his second straight incomplete.

He was forced to face the fact that very few world-class athletes had ever regained top form after what his body had been through. For the first prolonged period in his life, doubt assailed him.

Riders in the 1989 Tour de France raced through 2,025 miles of historic French countryside.

Notwithstanding the doubts and his precipitous slide from number 2 to number 345 on the computerized rankings of professional riders, LeMond began the 1989 season characteristically sanguine about his chances. He bubbled to reporters, "I feel strong, the fittest I've ever been this time of year. I've done a lot of cross-country skiing and a lot of power training on my bike. I've only taken a week off all winter. With time, patience and a little luck, good things might come my way. Watch for me in the Tour de France."

First, though, there was the Tour de Trump, a return-to-America event that LeMond always looked forward to. This time, though, he finished an also-ran twenty-seventh, describing the event as probably the low point in his career. "After the second day I wanted to stop," he told his biographer, Samuel Abt. "I thought about having my lungs examined to see if there were some undiscovered pellets in there."

Next on the schedule, in mid-June, was the Tour of Italy – the *Giro d'Italia*. Only a month before the Tour de France, it was high time for LeMond to start feeling strong, but it wasn't happening for him. "Even on the first climb, I had no strength at all," he said. He lost eight minutes on that climb. Eight minutes! He couldn't believe it. He was used to being the one doing the dropping.

He considered quitting – not just the race but cycling altogether. "He was very depressed," reported Kathy. "It had never happened to him before, dropping to the back of the pack, riding with people who finish forty minutes down."

Otto Jacome, his masseur, came to the rescue. He noticed at the beginning of the Tour of Italy that LeMond's pallor had deteriorated to a whitish gray. He recommended iron, and LeMond put aside his drug bias long enough to take an iron injection.

But it didn't seem to help. Immediately after the first injection, during a climb in the eleventh stage of the Tour of Italy, LeMond finished seventeen minutes behind the leaders. His confidence was in tatters. Riders he had once dominated were leaving him behind like a schoolboy on a bad bike, and he seemed incapable of response.

"I came back to the room and was ready to cry. I called Kathy that night and told her, 'Get ready to sell everything. I want no obligations. If things don't turn around, I'm quitting at the end of the year.'"

It was another low point. He was in a canyon, and he was beginning to lose sight of the rim. Then he received a second iron injection and – lo! – like a fictional hero, like Superman escaping the debilitating effects of kryptonite, he began to feel invigorated. "I started feeling like I was getting oxygen again," he said.

He went from feeling better to performing better a few days later. The final stage of the Tour of Italy was an individual time trial of about thirty-four miles. Hopelessly far behind in the overall standings, he decided to go all out. If he bonked, so be it; at least he would give it a go. Attitude firmly in place, he put forth his best effort in almost two years, finishing second, a huge sixty-eight seconds faster than Fignon, the overall winner of the Tour. "It changed my entire outlook," LeMond later said. "I knew there wasn't anything wrong with me physically."

Tour de France, 1989. In the eighteenth stage, Fignon nearly doubled his lead to fifty seconds over second-place LeMond. With only three stages to go, it looked bleak for the American. When a dejected Le-Mond saw Kathy afterward, the first thing he said was, "I might have lost the Tour today."

Certainly no one else gave him much chance to win. French newspapers and TV analysts discussed the matter as if Fignon's victory were a *fait accompli*. Oh, they routinely praised LeMond for injecting a little drama into the Tour but always in tones suggestive of a postmortem eulogy: LeMond is dead; long live Fignon!

LeMond didn't gain many converts with the nineteenth stage, the final one in the mountains. He outsprinted Fignon to the finish line but picked up no time. Then before the twentieth and penultimate stage, a short, uneventful ride in which no time was gained or lost, Fignon approached his former teammate. "You raced a great race, Greg," he said. "I have to tell you that coach Guimard predicted that this is the way it would finish, me winning and you second. He said at the Tour of Italy, you'd be the most dangerous rider."

LeMond remained outwardly gracious, thanking Fignon and telling him that he too had ridden a great race. Inwardly, LeMond saw Fignon's gesture for the psyche job it was.

Versailles, 1989. LeMond rolled down the ramp—"I started extremely fast"—and out into the southwestern suburbs of Paris, through Viroflay, Chaville, Sevres, Meudon. Although this stage was a sprint, LeMond could not simply overpower the bicycle; instead, he had to pedal with a rare rhythm, an uncommon fluidity. He had to ride like Rembrandt used to paint.

In the time-trial tradition, Fignon, the race leader, started last, two minutes behind LeMond. With typical hauteur, he disdained the helmet, preferring to let his ponytail drag behind. It seemed that while LeMond was confident, Fignon refused to consider even the possibility that he might lose. Blind faith made him sloppy.

At the five-kilometer mark, Fignon's coach shouted to him that he had already dropped ten seconds to LeMond. *What?* Fignon couldn't believe it! He cranked it up a notch, but after ten kilometers, the difference was nineteen seconds. It was twenty-four seconds after fourteen kilometers, thirty-five seconds after eighteen kilometers, and forty seconds after twenty kilometers. Fignon, fully cognizant that he was in a tight race, tried to crank it up another notch.

LeMond reached the Champs Elysees, about three miles from the finish. Hundreds of thousands of fans lined the wide cobblestone street, some of them waving tiny American flags. Most of them, for the crush of humanity, couldn't see LeMond, and he couldn't see most of them. Heading toward the Arc de Triomphe, he kept his head down, helmet slicing through the wind, his body in an aerodynamic tuck. Every few seconds he raised his head slightly, just long enough to make sure of his line, like a swimmer catching a breath.

LeMond blasted across the finish line in 26:57, thirty-three seconds faster than the second-best time of the day. In averaging thirty-four miles per hour, the fastest time trial ever in the Tour de France, he had nearly caught Delgado who had started two minutes before him. It was a great run – would it be enough? It was all over but the waiting.

Standing in the middle of the Champs Elysees, amid a thicket of race officials and journalists, LeMond watched alternately the ticking digital clock and the straight, wide avenue stretching before him. A moment later he saw the yellow-shirted Fignon coming straight at him. He was bent over his handlebars, pedaling furiously. Loud-speakers boomed his times, the fans cheered, and LeMond watched and waited, sweat rolling down his face. He could tell it was going to be close, which was exciting, but it was frustrating that he couldn't help himself. "How terrible to lose by one second," he thought. "After 2,025 miles, to lose by one second."

Then that second passed – 27:47 . . . 27:48 – with Fignon still about fifty meters from the finish. LeMond had won! With the realization of victory, of completed comeback, his face exploded into a wide, open-mouthed smile, and he punched his gloved fist at the sky. All the joy he had ever known in his life was flooding over him.

All around him was bedlam, people shouting congratulations and clapping him on the back and firing questions. "How do you feel?" "Can you describe this moment?" While politely mouthing platitudes, he pushed his way through the crowd toward Kathy.

Fignon crossed the line, fell from his bike and collapsed in exhaustion, believing that he had won the race. It was left to his masseur, cradling the lanky racer in his arms, to reveal the truth: "Laurent, you lost the race." With that, Fignon's world fell apart like a jigsaw puzzle. He buried his face in his hands and wept – the first time he had cried since childhood.

To give Fignon his due, he did not fold under pressure. His time of 27:55 was the third fastest of the day. It was, however, 58 seconds slower than LeMond and 8 seconds slower than he needed to tie. After more than ninety hours – 324,000 seconds – on his bike, he had lost by a mere 8 seconds. It was the closest Tour in the eighty-six-year history.

Two months later LeMond won, for the second time, the professional road race at the world championships in France. He thus became only the fourth cyclist ever to win both the Tour de France and the worlds in the same year. His main antagonist? Laurent Fignon, whom LeMond chased down three times in the final minutes of the 161-mile race.

The next season, 1990, he began in another valley. He was plagued by a virus all spring, which again kept him back in the pack for most of the early races. He was plagued by saddle sores, swollen feet, and a bad attitude. Then, in what could have been a satisfying return to America, he finished seventy-eighth in the Tour de Trump. Back in Belgium, he was spat upon and heckled during a race for what some took to be a half-hearted effort. Once again, word went out that Greg LeMond was finished. And faintly in the distance, you could hear a cavalry charge.

In the 1990 Tour de France, he still had the saddle sores and the swollen feet, but what an attitude! After being behind for the first twenty of the twenty-one stages, (the first 2,100 of the 2,122 miles), LeMond rallied to win by two minutes and sixteen seconds.

A great comeback – or not? Although some saw LeMond's 1990 win as just that, others regarded his strategy as distastefully conservative. Even Greg's boyhood hero, Eddy Merckx, blasted him for lacking the panache to win a single stage. Granted it was unusual: It had been nearly a quarter-century since a Tour winner failed to win a single stage.

After his 1990 Tour de France win (his third in the last three tries), LeMond announced that he was giving the $360,000 first-prize money to his teammates, as well as the $300,000 bonus that his Z Team had promised him if he won the Tour.

Even for a guy making more than four million dollars a year, that's panache.

RESOURCES

Tips to Improve Your Riding

PREPARATION

- Give yourself time to prepare physically and mentally for your rides. Studies show that nearly half of the "bad" rides were planned less than an hour in advance.
- Look forward to having fun. Riders tend to enjoy themselves more when they ignore the clock.
- Practice visualizing success. See yourself excelling on the bike. See your ride in as much detail as possible – the course, the scenery, the competition. Feel the pain, the exhilaration, the weather. Do this regularly. Most successful athletes use visualization to some degree.
- Stretch regularly. This is one of the best injury preventions, and it improves performance. If you're flexible, your body will recruit the most efficient cycling muscles, thereby conserving energy.
- Sleep regularly and well but don't worry about it. In the short run, the amount of sleep you get affects physical performance very little – the biggest impact is psychological. Lying awake worrying about not sleeping can become a self-fulfilling prophesy.

   In the long run, the average person requires eight hours of sleep every twenty-four, and virtually everyone – except that rare breed, the RAAM rider – needs between four and ten. How much sleep you need is genetically determined, but you can affect the quality of your sleep. Classic bromides are still operative: Drink warm milk; take a warm bath before bedtime; avoid regular use of sleeping pills. Also, getting exercise makes you a better sleeper.
- Leave negative emotions in the locker room. A bad day at home or the office can easily spill over, causing a bad day on the bike. For most people, emotions like guilt and anger interfere with the quality of a ride. Some people, however, thrive on negative emotions, allowing them to fuel their exercise.

159

- Use weights, especially in the off-season. Riding a lot will minimize the need for leg exercises, but balanced weight training will permit you to sprint faster, push bigger gears, and be a more powerful climber.
- Don't tinker with your bike the day before an event. There are oft-told stories of the rider who does a bike overhaul the night before a ride then forgets to tighten something, which begins to loosen during the ride or race.
- Fit your bike properly. Bike fit is an inexact science, open to debate, but the following is a prevailing opinion (for more information on bicycle fit, see *Bicycling* magazine, April 1987).

    Frame size. The measurement along the seat tube from the center of the bottom bracket to the top of the top tube should be ten inches less than your inseam. There should be about one inch of clearance between your crotch and the top tube when you stand over your bike.

    Saddle height. Sitting clearly in the saddle with the crankarm in the six o'clock position, you should have no more than one centimeter clearance between your heel and the pedal. Put another way, your knee should be bent about twenty degrees. Exact seat height, however, will depend on the type of pedal, the thickness of your shoe's sole, the crankarm length, and the saddle tilt.

    Handlebar reach. When you sit on the bike with the crankarm in the three o'clock position, with your hands on the drops, your knee should be just inside your bent elbow.
- Don't eat heaps just before a big ride. Allow two to four hours for digestion before setting off on your bike. Eating just before a ride recruits blood for digestion when it should be available to flush out the lactic acid that builds up in the muscles during a high-intensity workout.
- Use an empty 35mm film cannister to hold small necessities. It's ideal for things like tube patches, aspirin, glue, or emergency money (scientific tests have shown that it will hold $6.75 in quarters).
- While riding at night, use something other than stock reflectors. Reflective tape doesn't weigh much, doesn't rattle, rust, catch wind, or get in the way. It can be artistically cut and placed all over the bike.
- Set goals. Realistic short- and long-term goals will serve as both a motivational tool and a way of measuring progress.

Ex-champ Marion Clignet's four tips for recreational cyclists who want to be competitive cyclists

1. Join a local bicycling club.
2. Get a feel for competition by riding in local fun rides or weekend tours.
3. Watch and ask questions of more experienced riders.
4. Obtain a license from the U.S. Cycling Federation.

TRAINING

- Take your time warming up on the bike. Professional racer Ian Jackson says it may take him thirty to forty-five minutes to start feeling right, "so that I feel like going hard."
- Whenever possible, ride into the wind at the start of a long training ride. With the wind at your back on the way home, you can ride faster even if you're tired; also you won't be as chilled by the wind.
- If you drink, don't ride—at least not right away. Alcohol alters the body's chemical balance, diminishing performance. Your body needs eight ounces of water to metabolize one ounce of alcohol, so ironically when you drink to excess, you risk dehydration. After a binge, it takes more than one good night's sleep to make it right. If you get tanked on Friday night, don't expect to ride well Sunday.
- Work on bike handling. Learn to negotiate in traffic and avoid accidents. Those childhood follow-the-leader games were better training than you realized.
- Learn proper brake position. According to Connie Carpenter Phinney, the first American woman to win an Olympic gold medal in cycling, your dominant hand should control the rear brake; if you're right-handed, that hand should control the rear brake. That's because the rear brake can be used with more force than the front one. If you hit the front brake too hard, you could be catapulted over the handlebars. Use the front brake for fine-tuning.

- Finish strong. No matter how long your training ride, ease up the first three-quarters and go harder the last quarter. If you try to go hard the whole way, you increase the chances that you or your fellow rider will want to cut the ride short because you are tired.
- Learn to spin the pedals quickly for long periods of time. Unless you're on a steep climb, maintaining a cadence of eighty-five to ninety revolutions per minute is the most efficient way to propel a bicycle.
- Alter your hand placement on long rides. That will vary the weight and pressure on your hands and distribute the strain on your upper body.
- Eat during long rides. Bicycling is different from most sports in that you can munch while you exercise, thereby replenishing glycogen supplies and prolonging peak performance.
- Ride to relax. According to at least one study, the best way to ease tension is by exercising. After forty minutes of rest, stress levels remain low for another twenty minutes; but after forty minutes of exercise, stress levels remain low for three hours.
- Use a heart-rate monitor to gauge effort and assure aerobic fitness, suggests Greg LeMond. LeMond trains at 65–80 percent of maximum heart rate for endurance, at 80–90 percent for sustained, intense efforts, and at 90–100 percent for sprints. "Below 65 percent, you might as well stay home," he says.
- Cross railroad tracks near the side of the road, where it's usually less worn. Always cross with your wheels perpendicular to the tracks, and be especially careful if the tracks are wet.
- Never ride with earphones. You must be able to hear trouble as well as see it.
- Try to outrace charging dogs. If you appear to be losing that race, look authoritatively down at said dog, raise your hand threateningly (as if it contains a rock or a small missile), and yell commandingly, "No!" or "Stay!" If you can't outrun or outbluff the outlaw dog, dismount and hold your bicycle between the animal and yourself until help arrives. If it goes that far, report the incident to the local authorities.
- When slowing in a pack of riders, use the brake as little as necessary. Try to anticipate the tiny accelerations and slowdowns, and soft-pedal to maintain your distance from other bicycles. If you must brake, feather the levers lightly.

- Concentrate on pulling back on the pedal as it comes through the bottom of the stroke. Greg LeMond suggests you imagine that you're scraping mud off your shoe.
- Diversify your training. Popularized by triathletes, cross training is useful for stimulating interest and improving overall body strength and endurance.
- Ride with a group—at least some of the time. Other people can provide the push we all sometimes need. It's easier to skip a solo workout than one done with other people.
- Be dedicated but not obsessive; flexibility is good for the soul.
- Monitor your progress. A training diary will allow you to keep regular records of your pulse rate, weight, and length of rides (both time and mileage).
- Build a mileage base, or as five-time Tour de France winner Eddy Merckx suggests, "Ride lots." The general conditioning rule is to accumulate one-third of your mileage at a spinning cadence (eighty-five-plus pedal revolutions per minute) before advancing to hard climbing or big gears.

UP AND DOWN

- Never climb in the drops. Hunching over the handlebar drops is an inefficient position for climbing because it constricts breathing. Always sit up while climbing.
- Maintain a strong cadence on climbs. Good climbers rarely let their revolutions per minute fall below seventy-five seated and sixty-five standing. A slower cadence means pushing a larger amount of resistance on each pedal stroke, risking injury to the patellar tendon and fatigue to the quadriceps.
- Weight your outside leg on descents. By weighting the leg, says Connie Carpenter Phinney, "I mean putting pressure on the outside pedal. This can be taken one step further by weighting the outside arm and gripping the handlebar a bit tighter with the outside hand." Such a technique will increase your stability.
- Think of weight—as in your own. According to Greg LeMond, "If you're carrying an extra ten pounds of fat, you can be five minutes behind at the top of a seven- or eight-mile climb." His suggestion: ride hard up hills.
- On downhill braking, control your speed periodically throughout the descent rather than letting it build to excessive levels and then over-

reacting. Use both the rear and front brakes, but favor the rear. Don't use the front brake on a downhill corner. Avoid continual braking on steep descents; the brake pads can overheat, which is a particular problem with sew-up tires.

WINTER RIDING

- When it's cold, drink, drink, drink. In winter, the causes and dangers of dehydration are somewhat different than in summer but no less real. You actually lose more fluid in winter – by breathing air that must be warmed and moistened before the lungs can absorb it, then exhaling water vapor. Because you are less likely to feel thirsty, however, it's easy to forget to drink.
- Don't overdress. When you're deciding what clothes to wear on your ride, take into account that you'll generate as much as ten times the heat cycling that you would at rest and that you will feel about twenty degrees warmer than the real temperature. Another important consideration is that the burden of heavy clothing can add 5 to 15 percent to your energy requirements.
- After the ride, get out of damp clothes. Heat loss occurs five times faster in wet clothing.
- Eat right. Food is the fuel that provides the energy for warming activities. Although you don't need to add calories to your diet, winter is no time to fast. You should follow the high-carbohydrate diet conducive to good health and optimal performance.
- While braking in the rain, be steady and avoid herky-jerky stops. Anticipate and allow plenty of time to slow down.

RECOVERY

- Cool down after a long ride by riding easily for several extra laps.
- After a ride, make sure you are fully hydrated. Weigh yourself before and after a long ride and compare the two figures. Short-term weight loss is almost certainly fluid loss from perspiration, so drink plenty of fluids until your body weight returns to normal.
- Replenish the calories burned on a long ride as soon as possible. Studies indicate that your exercised and glycogen-depleted muscles are most receptive to repacking with glycogen within two hours after exercising. One effective way to increase the total amount of glycogen stored in the muscles is to consume one of the specially formulated high-carbohydrate drinks.

- Get a massage after a long ride or a hard workout, LeMond suggests. It promotes muscle recovery. If you can't get to a professional, massage yourself – especially your legs. Start at the calf, then move to the knee and thigh, always stroking toward the heart.
- Do at least two quarter-hour stretching sessions a day, one of which should be after training. Concentrate especially on the lower back and leg muscles. Many cyclists and sports medical people are convinced stretching reduces injuries.
- For inflamed tendons and damaged joints, alternate ice and heat, favoring the ice.
- LeMond's advice on crashing: "Get back on your bike and try to forget it."

Special thanks to *Bicycling* magazine

BIKING PAINS AND WHAT TO DO ABOUT THEM

Back pain. Cycling puts an unusual strain on back muscles, especially if your bike doesn't fit properly. With muscles in the tensed positions for hours at a time, the back can stiffen.

Solution. Make sure your bike is sized correctly for you. On a well-fitted road model, you should have a flat back while riding on the drops. (Check yourself with a stationary trainer and mirror or when riding past a glass storefront.) A hunched back can occur if your handlebar is too high or your stem and top tube combo is too short. On a mountain bike, strive for a back angle of 45 degrees, which helps evenly distribute the work load among the arms, legs, and butt. Vary your posture often during a ride.

Tired arms. Riding trails and rough roads sends shock waves into your bike and through your arms. All the while, you're subtly pulling and pushing the handlebar as you complete each pedal stroke. The arm muscles fatigue.

Solution. Set the saddle so that it's level or pointed up slightly. This will keep you from sliding forward and then resisting it with your arms. Ride with your elbows loose and bent to absorb road shock. If it is impossible to do this comfortably, you probably need a shorter stem or top tube.

To increase arm strength, add rowing and/or weight training to your workout.

Numb hands. Gripping the handlebar puts pressure on the ulnar nerve, which runs through the palm. This can result in pain, tingling, or numbness, which in turn can cause weakness or even loss of muscle control in your fingers.

Solution. Wear cycling gloves. They soak up the increased vibration and shock from bumpy terrain. Use thick bar tape to further cushion the impact of hands on bar. Maintain a relaxed grip whenever conditions permit. Periodically change from the hoods to the bar tops to the drops. Flutter your fingers every few minutes. On a mountain bike, avoid overly soft grips that make you squeeze too hard.

Stiff neck/shoulder. Your shoulder and neck muscles must bear the burden of inaction. While your neck supports the combined weight of head and helmet, your shoulders must cope with the accumulated tension of a basically static riding position. With little movement in that area, the shoulder muscles' response is to contract and stay that way. Thus the stiffness you feel on long rides.

Solution. Avoid hunching your shoulders, especially when climbing. On flat, untrafficked sections of road, stretch your muscles. Periodically reach behind you with one arm as if to receive a baton pass. To keep your neck from getting stiff, wear a lightweight helmet and periodically roll your head gently from side to side.

Swollen feet. As your feet heat up, they may swell slightly, making your shoes too tight, which in turn restricts the blood flow to the ball of the foot. This can cause tingling and burning in the nerves.

Solution. Wear cycling shoes that aren't too snug. Make sure your toe straps aren't too tight. Except for sprints or climbs, it's not necessary to cinch them tight.

Butt ache. When you push down on the pedals, much of your power comes from the large buttocks muscle, affectionately known as the gluteus maximus. To perform well for thousands of pedal strokes (about a million if you do RAAM), the "glutes" need energy and correct bike setup. If either is lacking, fatigue will result. Meanwhile, your rear-end tissue is pained by this bicycle seat wedged into it. Butt pain is probably the number one reason would-be cyclists give up the sport.

Solution. Set your saddle high enough so that your knees bend slightly at the bottom of each pedal stroke. Stand occasionally to stretch. To solve the problem of tissue soreness, ride often. The more time you spend in the saddle, the tougher your hide will become. Women may find relief in one of the anatomic saddles on the market.

Or you may try the technique employed briefly by Pax Beale when he rode San Francisco to Ketchikan with Kenneth Crutchlow: He sat on raw steaks.

Sunburn. The incidence of the deadly skin cancer malignant melanoma has risen nearly 100 percent in the past ten years.

Solution. Use a good sunscreen (one that works through perspiration) with a SPF (sun prevention factor) of at least fifteen. Cover exposed skin whenever possible.

Saddle sores. Saddle sores are small boils that form where the tender skin of your buttocks meets the bicycle seat. Bacteria enter this damp and irritated area and cause the sores.

Solution. Wear cycling shorts with chamois (or synthetic equivalent) to cut down on irritation from the saddle. Change bicycle shorts often and wash your crotch area before each ride with a good antibacterial soap. After the ride, shower and again scrub thoroughly. Cleanliness, simple but effective, should prevent the painful boils from ever developing.

Eye strain. Sunshine and fresh air can overwhelm the eyes. Invisible ultraviolet light can damage eyes—even on cloudy days. Glare can cause squinting, which tires the facial muscles and causes headaches. Rushing air dries the lenses. In response, your eyes water. This clouds vision and makes you feel tired.

Solution. Wear shades, particularly the type that blocks ultraviolet light. You were looking for maybe a medical breakthrough?

Source: *Bicycling* magazine

BUILDING BLOCKS OF ATHLETIC SUCCESS

- Competitive and energetic childhood. Competitive, energetic play develops coordination, confidence, self-assertiveness, sociability, and intelligence.
- Family participation and sports instruction. Athletic development is greatly augmented by parental involvement.

- Personality development. The chief psychological factor determining success is positive self-concept, the total package of views the athlete holds to be true about himself or herself.
- Sports achievement and attraction. When athletes excel in sports, they are attracted by the attention they receive and consequently participate with even greater zest.
- Setting constructive goals. Casual participants who do not establish their goals drop out as they fall behind the athletes who know what they want to accomplish.
- Intelligent and inspirational coaching. Great coaching can make the difference between a second-place finish and a championship performance.
- Sports study and understanding. Successful athletes have a complete understanding of their sports.
- Continued conditioning and skill development. Athletes who reach the top and rest on their laurels will soon fall from grace.
- Continued sports experience and success. In short, "success breeds success."

Source: Karl M. Woods, *The Sports Success Book* (Austin, Texas: Copperfield Press, 1985)

NUTRITION QUESTIONS AND ANSWERS

Why eat and drink on the bike?

Food replaces the energy burned while riding. When you eat something, your body stores it as fuel (glycogen) in your muscles. You have enough stored glycogen for short rides, but for longer ones you will need to nibble or your glycogen stores will be depleted.

When should I eat and drink?

While riding you should eat before hungry, drink before thirsty. If you wait for those signals, the energy won't reach your muscles in time to help. One popular strategy is to swig from your water bottle about every fifteen minutes, consuming about twenty ounces of liquid per hour—more if it's hot and humid. Avoid large meals on the bike—digesting gobs of food takes blood away from its main task of supplying your muscles with oxygen.

What should I eat and drink?

It's a matter of opinion, but here are some suggestions. For fluid replacement on short rides, water is best. For longer rides you may want to go with some type of sports drink – such as BodyFuel, Exceed, Max – that replenishes lost liquid and glycogen and that the body can process more easily than solids. According to studies, cyclists can pedal nearly one-third farther when ingesting a sports drink.

The most popular on-bike food is no doubt the banana. Quick, easy, healthful (80 to 120 calories), it replaces the potassium you lose when sweating. Other fruits such as pears and apples are also beneficial. Avoid high-fat foods while cycling, since fat is an inefficient fuel source compared to carbohydrates.

Many long-distance cyclists mix nuts, grains, and raisins into a snack called "gorp" (good ol' raisins and peanuts). This bike-friendly food provides a steady flow of carbohydrates to the body.

Off the bike, your diet should be about 60 to 70 percent carbohydrate, 20 to 30 percent protein, and ideally less than 20 percent fat. High-carbo foods include fruits, vegetables, pasta, and whole-grain bread. Avoid large doses of caffeine – it encourages fluid loss through urination. Besides, with continual use it ceases to be much of an energy boost.

How do I eat while riding?

A good place to store snacks is in the back pocket of your jersey. Before reaching for that banana or apple, grip the handlebar near the stem with the other hand to hold the bike steady. Another strategy is to snack during rest stops. In any event, don't forget that post-ride meal; you have burned hundreds if not thousands of calories while exercising. You deserve it.

Source: *Bicycling* magazine

Safety

- About half of the people riding bikes are children under the age of fifteen.
- In the under-fifteen age group alone, there are 550,000 cycling injuries each year.
- Each year, about 70 percent of the approximately nine hundred bike deaths in this country involve children younger than fifteen. The rate is highest for ages ten to fifteen.
- Bicyclists make up 2 percent of all traffic fatalities.
- At all ages, males are much more involved in bicycle crashes than females. In 1988, males accounted for more than 85 percent of the fatalities.
- Among nine-to-twelve-year-old boys, bike deaths account for about 30 percent of their motor vehicle–related deaths.
- Most fatal bicycle injuries involve collisions with motor vehicles; most nonfatal injuries do not. More than half of all bicycle injuries involve hitting the ground or roadway.
- Deaths of adult bicyclists are increasing. In 1977 only about one in five bicycle deaths involved a rider twenty-one years or older; in 1988, that figure had risen to one in three.
- Most bike deaths result from head injuries.
- Most bicyclists do not wear a helmet.

A FINAL EXAM FOR AN EFFECTIVE CYCLING COURSE

The following questions are typical of those found on final exams for "effective cycling" courses. Students should be able to answer the following questions completely and correctly on the basis of information given in John Forester's book *Effective Cycling* (Cambridge: MIT Press, 1984). Answers follow.

BICYCLIST HIGHWAY-RELATED FATALITIES

Year	Male	Female	Total
1977	730	192	922
1978	714	178	892
1979	759	173	932
1980	782	183	965
1981	748	181	929
1982	720	144	864
1983	700	130	830
1984	684	153	837
1985	732	137	869
1986	789	140	929
1987	826	115	941
1988	781	129	910

BICYCLIST INJURIES TREATED IN EMERGENCY ROOMS

1983	571,000
1984	557,000
1985	582,000
1986	564,000
1987	562,000
1988	525,000

1. Why is it important to stop brake cables from unraveling? How do you do this?

2. In developing your physical capacity for cycling, which should you concentrate on first — muscle strength or breathing and circulatory capacity? Explain your answer.

3. What precautions should you take for cycling in hot weather?

4. What is the difference in technique between using your brakes for quick stops and using them for speed control on a long downhill stretch?

5. What hazards become more significant at night, and what equipment do you need to protect yourself against them?

6. On a two-lane country road with medium traffic, why do you watch groups of cars approaching in the opposite lane?

7. In steering your bike, which do you do first — turn the handlebars in the direction you wish to go or lean in that direction? Why?

8. Bicycle traffic safety has three aspects: prevention, avoidance, and injury reduction. Select and describe a traffic situation that could result in a car-bike collision. What are the appropriate techniques for prevention, avoidance, and injury reduction in this case?

Suggested Answers

1. If the brake cables (inner wires) unravel as far as the anchor bolt that locks them to the brake arm or brake hook, it will be difficult to make a major brake adjustment (the adjustment in which the anchor bolt must be moved up the cable). Also, and equally important, any unraveling will prevent the inner wire from being rethreaded through the cable housing and cable stops. This prevents you from removing the inner wire, greasing and inspecting it, and replacing it. Inner wires that are not greased make brake control more difficult and are more subject to rust damage.

To avoid these problems, check the newly installed inner wires for proper operation. Apply flux and solder to a half-inch length of wire two to three inches from the anchor bolt. When the solder has cooled, inspect it to see that it has coated and penetrated between the individual strands. Then cut the wire through the soldered section. The solder will prevent the strands from unraveling, both as they are cut and with later handling.

2. For most people, muscle strength must be developed before aerobic capacity. This is because without strength you cannot develop the speed that necessitates the aerobic capacity.

3. Carry plenty of water, and drink before you are thirsty. Make sure more water can be obtained en route. Wear clothes that permit a free flow of air near the body; that evaporates the sweat and cools the body. If you tend to suffer from salt deficiency after sweating a lot, you need to replace those salts using either Gatorade-like supplements or a supplement prepared at home according to the recipe in *Effective Cycling*.

4. When you want a quick stop, hit the front brake much harder than the rear, say three times as hard. This provides the maximum safe deceleration. When the rear wheel starts to skid, ease up on the front brake to put more weight on the rear wheel and stop the skid. On a long downhill, the problem is not immediate deceleration but the rising temperature in the wheel rims, which tends to break down the glue that holds tubular tires onto the rim. Therefore, use the brakes equally on long descents, so the rims maintain equal temperatures. That diminishes the chances that either rim will overheat.

5. At night in the country, you can't see the road without an effective headlamp; even in a well-lighted city, you cannot see road surface defects without an effective headlamp. Also, other road users – motorists, cyclists, pedestrians – must be able to see your approach. If they cannot see you approaching because you have no headlamp, they will see no traffic to which they must yield. Result: They drive or step in front of you in perfect confidence. No reflector can perform this function because pedestrians and other cyclists have no strong headlamp to power the reflector and even motorists aren't always pointing their strong headlights at a bicycle's reflector when deciding whether to pull

out or not. Generator-powered headlamps are cheap and easy to use but ineffective at low speeds. If you must travel on dangerous darkened paths, use an expensive, powerful lamp powered by rechargeable NiCad batteries.

You must also alert faster road users that you are on the road ahead of them. A rear reflector will suffice for protection in this direction. But the typical bicycle reflector is poorly designed and inefficient. A better one, about ten times brighter, is the three-inch diameter amber reflector available from auto supply stores. Get and mount the amber reflector.

6. Each group of cars on a two-lane road means that the ones behind want to travel faster than the one in front. When you see such a group approaching, watch for a car at the back moving into your lane to pass. If it does so, look for a place to get off the road, and use it if the car continues in your lane. It is quite possible that the passing motorist, who may be a half-mile away, does not see you at that distance and is prevented from returning to the proper lane by the vehicles that he or she is trying to overtake.

7. You must lean before you steer the handlebars; turning the handlebars before leaning steers the wheels out from under you, and you will fall.

8. Consider the motorist-right-turn type of car-bike collision. Prevention means using good habits to stay out of situations that encourage this type of collision. Don't hug the curb, but ride close beside the straight-through traffic. Never use right-turn-only lanes unless you are going to turn right. Never creep up on the right-hand side of a vehicle that can turn right. When riding in heavy traffic, try to approach intersections or shopping-mall driveways ahead of the nearest vehicle, not just alongside or slightly behind it, where you are in the driver's blind spot. Overtake on the left, not the right.

Avoidance means preventing a collision with a driver who overtakes you and suddenly turns right. If he does so, make an instant right turn (see answer to question 7) into a side street or driveway.

The best way to reduce injuries in any bicycle accident is to wear your helmet. Always. There are some other techniques—such as trying to stay up as long as possible to reduce the chances of getting run over and trying to match speed and direction to reduce impact – but they are much less certain.

Source: John Forester, M.S., Phys Ed., cycling transportation engineer (consulting engineer, expert witness and educator in effective cycling, bicycles, highways and bikeways, and traffic laws).

Pedaling into the Past

NINETEENTH CENTURY: THE VELOCIPEDE

The idea of "riding a wheel" has no doubt been around almost as long as the wheel itself. Although no one knows when or where the first bicycle ride took place, there are depictions of bicyclelike apparatuses in ancient Egyptian art. And Babylonian bas-relief sculptures show human figures riding a pole connecting two wheels. Roman frescoes in Pompeii show men in togas on two-wheelers. And a stained-glass window near Windsor, England, shows a cherub straddling a wheeled vehicle that looks decidedly like a bicycle. The window was installed in 1642.

Nevertheless, if one accepts the definition of a bicycle as a "two-wheeled, *steerable* machine propelled by its rider," its origin should rightfully date to 1816 with the invention of the *draisienne* by Baron Karl von Drais. Like its forerunner the unsteerable *celerifere*, the draisienne weighed about eighty pounds and had to be propelled by the rider paddling his or her feet against the ground. The front wheel of the celerifere had been fixed in place; but the draisienne had a steering bar connected to the front wheel. Humans could not yet pedal, but at least they could point themselves in the right direction.

The draisienne spawned many imitators. By 1819 a London blacksmith, Denis Johnson, was building draisiennelike machines under the name "dandy horse." Johnson's improvement: He replaced the heavy wooden frame with an iron one, which made the vehicle lighter and more rigid.

In the 1820s the dandy horse was imported to the United States. For a time it was all the rage among rich New Yorkers who liked to paddle around the city parks straddling their machines. But the fad soon died and so did the draisienne-dandy.

The problem was that movement on these contraptions was still dependent on the padding of the rider's feet against the ground. Its only real advantage, then, was on downhill slopes. What bicycling needed was pedal power.

That was achieved in 1839 by Kirkpatrick Macmillan, a Scottish blacksmith, who developed the first foot-pedaled bicycle in his workshop in Dumfriesshire, Scotland. It included pedals and primitive cranks and drive rods to turn the rear wheels. Although the Macmillan model still weighed almost eighty pounds, it had a front wheel that could be steered, a brake system fingered from the handlebars, a spring seat to cushion road shock, and even a fender to protect the rider from mud thrown up by the rear wheel. Because he made it possible for bicyclists to pedal and stay continuously out of contact with the ground, some would call Macmillan the inventor of the true bicycle.

To prove that he had a truly rideable bicycle, Macmillan rode his machine the one hundred miles to Glasgow, a remarkable feat given the hilly country and the abominable road conditions. En route, he staged what was likely the first bicycle race, beating a horse-drawn coach to the next town. He also received the first recorded bicycling traffic ticket, a fine of five shillings for knocking down a child who was in one of the curious throngs that surrounded him wherever he stopped.

Despite the local attention he received, Macmillan's model never really caught on. It might have been that the bike was too heavy or that the primitive drivetrain was clumsy and unreliable. In any event, bicycling remained a fringe pursuit.

The next significant development in the evolution of the two-wheeler occurred in 1861 when a man brought his old-style velocipede—no crankarms, no pedals—to the Paris workshop of Pierre Michaux. Michaux, a blacksmith and coach builder, was renowned as a creative thinker. Trying the velocipede, he quickly realized the practical limitations of a contraption requiring constant foot stomping to get anywhere. It was exhausting work. And as soon as he stopped moving his feet on level ground, the beast stopped.

Michaux took the idea of foot propulsion and adapted it. He designed and built pedals for his customer's velocipede. The pedals were attached to crankarms fixed to the front axle. The cranks could be rotated by the rider's feet.

Although Michaux's new velocipede was the first of its ilk that could be a viable form of transportation, the public did not gather at

A proud rider poses with his bicycle in 1868. (Courtesy of the Seaver Center for Western History Research, National History Museum of Los Angeles County)

his door: only two sales in 1861. But business picked up in 1862; the Michaux family sold 142. By 1865 they were turning out 400 a year. In 1866 their mechanic, Pierre Lallement, emigrated to the United States, where with a Connecticut man he took out the first U.S. patent on a pedal bicycle.

In the 1860s, bicycling in the States experienced its first real growth spurt. The first cycling magazine, *The Velocipedist*, was published in New York. In 1869 it ran the following paean to the bicycle: "The two-wheeled velocipede is the animal which is to supercede everything else. It costs but little to produce, and still less to keep. It does not eat cartloads of hay, and does not wax fat and kick. It is easy to handle. It never rears up. It won't bite. It needs no check of rein or halter, or any unnatural restraint. It is little and light, let alone it will lean lovingly against the nearest support."

Because there was no patent taken out in Europe, the Michaux machine was quickly copied by dozens of small manufacturers in France and Germany. Michaux had ignited a flame that became a raging fire throughout Europe. Paris became the unofficial capital of the bicycle industry. At the first bicycle show in Paris in 1869, the ancestors of the chain-driven, freewheel, and gear-shifting models were shown.

The bicycle had a huge impact on society. The average person living in Europe and America couldn't afford a horse. Getting out of town—even for an afternoon frolic—was expensive and impractical. The bicycle changed that. It offered the masses the adventure and romance of travel. It offered them the opportunity to get beyond the city limits.

The bicycle also afforded the opportunity to race. Michaux quickly realized the marketing value of racing. He decided to put together an event—the first organized bike race on record—May 30, 1868, in the Parc de Saint-Cloud on the outskirts of Paris. An Englishman living in Paris, James Moore, won the race and collected the six-hundred-franc first prize.

Months later Moore also won the first endurance race, from Paris to Rouen, eighty-three miles over rough, cobbled roads. He beat more than two hundred cyclists, averaging a torrid eight miles per hour and solidifying his position as bicycle racing's first superstar.

Racing was a great way to spread the word about the new contrivance. Early cycling journals like *Le Velocipede Illustre* helped, too. Partly due to Moore's notoriety, the Michaux bicycle made the leap to England, where an innovative young craftsman named James Starley began trying to improve the still-primitive machines.

Problem number one, he believed, was the heavy, wooden wheels, resembling those found on farmers' carts; they were clumsy things connected to the hubs by fourteen massive wooden spokes. Starley replaced the wooden spokes with iron ones, then came up with the idea for a tension-spoked wheel in which the rim and hub were connected by looped wire spokes.

Another limitation he sought to correct was that one turn of the pedals translated into but one turn of the wheels. So Starley built a bike with a huge front wheel and a small rear wheel, then developed a gear that allowed the wheel to be turned twice for each revolution of the pedals. This evolved into the speedy "ordinary" or "penny-farthing" (the front wheel was large, like a British penny, while the rear wheel was small like a farthing), which was to dominate the cycling scene for the next ten to fifteen years.

Starley became known in England as the father of the bicycle industry. A statue of him stands today in Coventry. Although he was an impact player in the history of the bicycle, he really was but one of many "fathers" in an industry that could use a paternity suit to sort out its lineage.

The evolution of the bicycle continued. Even with Starley's new gear, the diameter of the front wheel still determined the distance one rotation of the pedals took the ordinary. In pursuit of more speed, manufacturers built bikes with bigger and bigger front wheels—some as large as sixty-four inches in diameter. Meanwhile, the rear wheel shrank to less than twelve inches. As the ordinary did indeed go faster, it quickly became the choice of serious racers.

Yet the design had real drawbacks. The high center of gravity meant poor stability, which made it especially treacherous on rough roads and downhill. The seat was above the front wheel, so climbing up onto a perch more than five feet above the ground was an athletic feat in itself—as well as a test of faith. Given the state of the roads at that time, "headers" were common. Clearly, other improvements were needed in order to make the bicycle appealing to the masses.

In 1874 H. J. Lawson gave the industry a shove with his rear-drive machine. It had a chain between the driving sprocket and the rear wheel—and two medium-sized wheels of equal diameter. It went further on one rotation of the pedals than the ordinary.

Called the "safety" bicycle, it was a huge improvement over the ordinary in stability, braking, and mounting. But it had an image problem. It lacked the sexy aura of adventure enjoyed by the ordinary. The safety was, in fact, billed as the bicycle "safe for all the people," assuring, of course, that the ordinary would continue to be favored by the fringe.

The ordinary, or penny-farthing, enjoyed huge popularity during the 1880s despite the difficulties and dangers involved in climbing onto its seat. (Courtesy of the Seaver Center for Western History Research, National History Museum of Los Angeles County)

Bicycle races were wildly popular events in the 1890s. (Courtesy of the Seaver Center for Western History Research, National History Museum of Los Angeles County)

In 1885, James Starley's nephew came out with an improved version of the safety. Called the "Rover," it had a sleek, smooth chaindrive, a sturdy "diamond" frame and two standard-sized wheels. It was a high-performance machine strikingly similar in appearance to today's bicycle.

Next came the pneumatic tire. In 1888 John Boyd Dunlop, an Irish veterinarian, seized upon the idea of making rubber tubes and filling them with air. Until then, riders had jarred their innards on metal rims or rock-hard rubber tires. The Rover and the pneumatic tire combined to kill the ordinary. The diamond-pattern bicycle frame (three triangles and a pair of forks) and the air-filled tire were here to stay.

Bicycling technology again spread to the United States. Small manufacturing companies popped up along the eastern seaboard. Americans caught the fever, developing a love affair with bicycles that foreshadowed the one they would have fifty years later with the automobile. Bicycling clubs took root, sponsoring and organizing "century" rides, awarding medals to any rider who could pedal a hundred miles in less than ten hours. A grueling ultramarathon event, the six-day bicycle race, became all the rage, and the competitors the new superheroes. For many years to come, bicycling would be the biggest sport in the United States.

The 1890s was bicycling's own true decade. A mania for the sport swept the United States, bringing with it a social revolution. As with all revolutions, this one left some people standing at the station. Society polarized into two camps – pro and con. Many denounced the bicycle as an instrument of the devil, the potential ruin of civilization. In Flushing, New York, for example, a school board declared that it was immoral for any young lady to ride a bicycle. Actress Sarah Bernhardt decried the bicycle because "it brought young people together in conditions unfavorable to strict surveillance."

Although some doctors endorsed the bicycle as a means of healthful exercise, others pointed to the contraption as the cause of many new maladies said to be sweeping the land. Many believed, for example, that too much time bent over a bicycle could produce a hump in the back or a funny walk, or that whizzing along on a bike with all that air whooshing through your mouth would cause your teeth to fall out, or that women who rode bicycles risked sterility. Someone was ready to blame that damned two-wheeler for almost any ailment known to humankind.

Others objected to it on aesthetic grounds. Witness this bitter newspaper editorial from 1881: "Undoubtedly the bicyclist is a curious object. His calves are elaborately displayed, and are, in most cases, as grossly improbable as those of the ballet. His flannel clothes, which sometimes emulate the zebraic beauty of the Sing Sing convicts, and at other times approach the simplicity of the most delicate undergarments, may perhaps bring a blush to the cheek of a young person. . . . It has been alleged that the bicycle itself frightens horses . . . it is the bicyclist who inspires the horse with terror."

In Europe, too, the bicycle often faced severe prejudice. In Paris they closed the Bois de Boulogne to velocipedes. In Brussels the police commissioner prohibited bicycling in alleyways, sidewalks, paths, and parks. He further required that all cyclists riding at night had to be equipped with an oil-burning lantern positioned at least three-and-a-half feet above the ground.

The conservative French daily *Le Rappel* railed against bicycling, sparing no hyperbole: "It is time that all concerned governments take serious measures against the velocipedes, as much for their own security as for that of others . . . the two-wheel velocipede resembles a balancing act and its use is nothing short of a dangerous game. This rush of velocipedists against peaceful pedestrians could very well transform France into a country of savages."

The changes wrought by the bicycle were especially dramatic for women. For the first time they could get out of their homes on their own, free of restrictive clothing and chaperones. The *Minneapolis Tribune* reported, "Cycling is fast bringing about a change of feeling regarding woman and her capabilities. A woman awheel is an independent creature, free to go whither she will. This, before the advent of the bicycle, was denied her."

It also loosened the shackles of bulky Victorian garb. At first woman cyclists wore baggy knickerbockers under their long frocks, but the intricacies of riding a bicycle made that costume impractical.

Members of a bicycle club prepare for a Sunday ride (circa 1905). (Courtesy of the Seaver Center for Western History Research, National History Museum of Los Angeles County)

By the 1890s women were into shortened bloomers with knee-length skirts. The bicycle gave women a liberty of dress that reformers had long sought.

Mrs. Reginald de Koven, wife of a famous operatic director, was quoted in *Cosmopolitan Magazine*, August 1895, as saying, "To men rich and poor, the bicycle is an unmixed blessing, but to the woman it is deliverance, revolution, and salvation."

Indeed, the bicycle became the vehicle of choice for a whole armada of semiliberated women. As women's rights advocate Susan B. Anthony said, "I think it [bicycling] has done more to emancipate women than anything else in the world. I stand and rejoice every time I see a woman ride by on a wheel. It gives women a feeling of freedom and self-reliance. It makes her feel as if she were independent. The moment she takes her seat she knows she can't get into harm unless she gets off her bicycle, and away she goes, the picture of free, untrammeled womanhood."

TWENTIETH CENTURY: THE BICYCLE

By 1900 in the United States alone 7,573 patents had been granted for cycles and their parts. Yet the introduction of the derailleur around the turn of the century was the last major advance in bicycle technology until the 1960s. Why such a lengthy period of creative dormancy? The answer, of course, is the automobile. As the public fell in love with the car, it became less interested in the bicycle. As a mode of transportation for the masses, the bicycle hovered just above extinction for the first half of the twentieth century.

As a racing vehicle, however, the bicycle continued to thrive. In 1899 Charles "Mile-A-Minute" Murphy became unofficial world sprint champion when he bicycled a measured mile in 57.8 seconds, using the slipstream of a locomotive. That record survived for forty-two years, until May 17, 1941, when Alfred Letourner used a midget-racing-car windbreak on a Bakersfield expressway to cover a measured mile in a time of 33:05, or 108.92 miles per hour (174.27 kilometers per hour). Then in 1973 Dr. Alan Abbott improved the record to 138.67 miles per hour (221.87 kilometers per hour) on the Bonneville Salt Flats, Utah, behind a specially designed pace car. That left it to John Howard to set the present-day record of 152 miles per hour. Will it ever be broken?

Meanwhile, on the endurance level, the new heroes were the six-day cyclists, incredible athletes who captured the imagination of the public. The six-day races were 144-hour endurance wars, and the winners were those who could withstand the incredible physical and mental punishment of prolonged sleep deprivation. Around the turn of the century a man named Charlie Miller bicycled 2,088 miles in 144 hours. At one stretch, he didn't get off his bike for nearly 50 hours.

The most famous international cycling event, the Tour de France, originated in 1903. Today it is bigger than ever, a grueling three-week stage race that attracts the world's foremost cyclists to compete over a course of more than twenty-five hundred miles (four thousand kilometers).

Cycling in the past seventy years has undergone an uneven growth. It was retarded by World War I and the passion heaped upon Ford's Model T and Model A. It made a partial comeback during the Great Depression of the 1930s, when for many the bicycle was the only affordable alternative to walking. It hit the skids again during World War II and the automobile-crazed fifties. But in the alternative-seeking sixties and the fitness-starved seventies, bicycling made huge gains. In 1971, about 6.9 million bicycles were produced in the United States. In the same year, according to the Bicycle Institute of America (BIA), there were 55 million bicycles in use in the United States.

Today the BIA estimates that there are about 90 million bicycles in the United States. "Of course," a BIA spokesperson says, "that includes all those clunkers collecting dust in garages."

It's still a hell of a lot of bicycles.

THE DAZZLING DECADE

So pervasive was bicycling in the 1890s that the period has been called bicycling's "dazzling decade." Indeed, the two-wheeled image adorned everything from playing cards to drinking cups to decorative pottery.

Here are some highlights:

1890: In manufacturers' catalogs "safety" bicycles with two equal-sized wheels replace high-wheeled "ordinary" bicycles.

1891: The *Literary Digest* announces the publication of Luther H. Porter's *Cycling for Health and Pleasure.*

1891: The first continuous six-day bicycle races at Madison Square Garden begin an endurance craze that lasts for decades.

1891: "Cushion" semipneumatic tires are introduced. Their brief but important reign over solid tires paves the way for true pneumatic tires.

1891: The League of American Wheelmen's "Good Roads Campaign," credited with many road improvements in the United States, commences in New Jersey.

1892: Dunlop Detachables, the first pneumatic tires, make their debut on a Raleigh "Roadster." Developed by Scottish veterinary surgeon John B. Dunlop, the pneumatic tire is the single most dramatic bicycle-inspired device, a real impact invention.

1892: The song "Daisy Bell" (a.k.a. "A Bicycle Built for Two"; a.k.a. "Daisy, Daisy") is written by Harry Dacre (a.k.a. Frank Dean; a.k.a. Henry Decker).

1892: The Dayton Bicycle is introduced by Davis Sewing Machine Company, forerunner of the Huffy Corporation, the largest bicycle manufacturer in the United States.

1893: Wood rims are patented. Bicycles become lighter, cycling more comfortable.

1893: Willie Windle rides three miles in 6.43 minutes against the clock in Springfield, Massachusetts.

1893: Margaret Gast buys a bicycle and within three years wins a string of medals. By 1900 she sets many national and world records.

1894: Mrs. E. E. Witchie becomes the first woman in the Midwest to ride a hundred miles in one day.

1894: Amateur racer J. S. Johnson rides one mile in one minute, four seconds, in Buffalo, New York.

1894: First introduced by Amelia Bloomer in 1851, divided skirts— bloomers—become the practical choice of women cyclists in the 1890s.

1895: Livery stable owners complain that the bike craze is killing the demand for buggies.

1895: Arnold, Schwinn, and Company begins business.

1895: Streetcars in New York are equipped with hooks for bicycles.

1895: New York City police commissioner Avery D. Andrews starts the bicycle police with four patrolmen.

1895: A racing cyclist pedals the mile in one minute, thirty-five seconds, and beats the fastest horse for the first time.

1895: The Michaux Cycle Club is organized in New York City and becomes the social gathering place for high society's elite.

1896: More than 350 exhibits are featured at the New York Bicycle Exposition.

1896: Leon Flameng wins the first cycling event at the first modern Olympics held in Athens, Greece. His time of 3 hours, 8 minutes, 19.2 seconds, wins the one-hundred-kilometer race.

1896: At a rural debate in Rooks County, Kansas, the issue is whether the bicycle is of more use than the telephone. The affirmative wins.

1896: More than four hundred companies in the United States are building bicycles. Piano sales decline by 50 percent and book sales plummet.

1897: New York City's Ninth Avenue "L" begins carrying bicycles on its trains.

1898: Over-saturation of the market causes the price of bicycles to drop from one hundred dollars to fifty dollars. Two years later, the price is less than fifteen dollars.

1898: Moral decay is predicted for America as men and women begin taking cycling outings together.

1898: American W. W. Hamilton becomes the first person to ride twenty-five miles in one hour in Denver.

1898: The coaster brake is introduced by Eclipse Bicycle Company, ancestor of Bendix.

1898: The Troxel Manufacturing Company is started; the "Troxel" bicycle saddle makes its appearance.

1898: Clipless pedals are introduced. A twist of the foot interlocks prongs on a shoe plate with lugs on a pedal.

1899: Charles "Mile-a-Minute" Murphy rides one mile in 57.8 seconds behind a Long Island Railroad train.

1899: James C. Anderson, Highland Park, Illinois, patents a bicycle designed from the outset for military use. The only one of its kind ends up in the Smithsonian collection.

1899: The derailleur system is developed.

1899: The "Black Wonder," American cyclist (Marshall Walter) "Major" Taylor, becomes USA World Sprint Champion.

1899: Nineteen principal bicycle manufacturers, collectively producing more than seven hundred thousand bicycles, form the American Bicycle Company, a trust headed by A. G. Spaulding.

1900: *Outing* magazine announces that the automobile is the "machine of the future."

Special thanks to the Bicycle Institute of America.

Oddities

- Leonardo da Vinci (1452–1519) is credited with the first design of a machine propelled by cranks and pedals with connecting rods, circa 1493. But the earliest foot-pedaled machine to get off the drawing board was invented by Kirkpatrick Macmillan of Dumfries, Scotland, in 1839, nearly 350 years later.
- David Steed balanced on his bicycle for twenty-four hours and six minutes nonstop in 1986 at the NYC Coliseum. Steed remained upright without a break, without touching either foot to the floor, and without either of his bike wheels ever making a complete revolution forward or backward.
- Six-day bicycle champion Bobby Walthour broke his left collarbone eighteen times and his more injury-prone right collarbone twenty-eight times. During his career, he took forty-six stitches on his legs and sixty-nine stitches on his face and head. Walthour also suffered eight broken fingers and thirty-two fractured ribs. He was considered fatally injured six times and twice pronounced dead, but he lived on.
- The longest true tandem bicycle ever built (without a third stabilizing wheel) was just under sixty-seven feet long and weighed 2,425 pounds. With seats for thirty-five riders, it was first ridden in 1979 by the Pedaalstompers Westmalle of Belgium.
- Measured by front-wheel diameter, the biggest bike was the "Frankencycle," built by Dave Moore of Rosemead, California. First ridden in 1979, the wheel diameter was ten feet, with a total height of eleven feet, two inches.
- The tallest unicycle ever mastered was 101 feet, 9 inches tall, ridden by Steve McPeak for a distance of 376 feet in 1980.
- The world's smallest rideable bicycle was one with three-quarter-inch wheels (.76 in.) built and ridden by Neville Patten of Australia in 1988.

- The smallest unicycle, with a wheel diameter of five inches, was ridden in 1990 by Peter Rosendahl.
- The record for most riders in a bicycle tour is 27,220 in the fifty-six-mile London to Brighton Bike Ride on June 15, 1986.
- The longest cycle tour on record is the more than 402,000 miles amassed by Walter Stolle (b. Sudetenland, 1926), an itinerant lecturer. From January 24, 1959, to December 12, 1976, Stolle's personal book of lists looked like this: 159 countries cycled; 5 bicycles stolen; 231 other robberies; and 1,000 flat tires, more or less.
- From February 25, 1974, to August 27, 1975, Veronica and Colin Scargill of Bedford, England, traveled 18,020 miles around the world on a tandem, setting a world's record for the most tandem miles.
- Colonel Royal Page Davidson organized the military bicycle corps in 1894. It was composed of cadets from the Northwestern Military Academy at Lake Geneva, Wisconsin, riding on sixteen bicycles, each equipped with special clips for carrying rifles. Their best feat was a maneuver in which the riders put themselves and their bikes (which with all their military equipment weighed fifty-four pounds each) over a sixteen-foot wall in two minutes, forty-eight seconds.

BEST ENDURANCE NUTS

- Pakistani ultramarathon cyclist Khaled Javed routinely rides for up to 216 hours nonstop on his single-speed coaster model bicycle, all the while entertaining incredulous onlookers with grueling bicycle stunts, such as being driven over by a tractor, having two motorcycles pull in opposite directions on ropes tied to his hair, and having a stack of bricks crushed while stacked upon his chest.
- Carlos Vieira cycled for 191 hours "nonstop" at Leiria, Portugal, June 8–16, 1983. He covered 1,496.04 miles and was moving 98.7 percent of the time.
- Nicholas Mark Sanders (b. Nov. 26, 1957) of Glossop, England, circumnavigated the globe (13,035 road miles) in seventy-eight days, three hours, and thirty minutes from July 5 to September 21, 1985.
- Tommy Godwin (1912–75, UK) in the 365 days of 1939 covered 75,065 miles, an incredible average of 205.65 miles a day. Soon thereafter he biked 100,000 miles in a stretch of 500 days.
- The fastest bicycling without the aid of drafting was 65.484 miles per hour (flying start), attained by Fred Markham at Mono Lake, Califor-

nia, in 1986. From a standing start, Markham also set the one-hour mark of 45.366 miles per hour at the Michigan International Speedway in 1989.

- An underwater team of thirty-two divers pedaled 116.66 miles in 1980 in a little more than seventy-five hours on a standard tricycle. There was meaning to their madness: The stunt raised money for the Muscular Distrophy Association.

Glossary

adjustable cone A hub cone that can be removed from the axle (in contrast to a "fixed" cone).

adjusting screw (alignment screw) A screw threaded into the rear dropouts to control the positioning of the rear axle. Adjustment insures alignment of the rear wheel.

aero-bars A new generation of handlebars that allow the rider to ride in a more aerodynamic position with the elbows resting on the tops of the handlebars and the hands positioned together out in front of the rider.

aerobic An intense exercise level but one at which the body's oxygen needs are still being met; literally, "with oxygen." A conditioned athlete can carry on aerobic exercise for a long time (in contrast to anaerobic exercise).

aerodynamic Having to do with air in motion – specifically, the movement of air over, under, and around a cyclist and bike. Better aerodynamic efficiency – in the bike, helmet, rider positioning – means less wind drag, less energy expenditure, and greater speed.

alignment screw (adjusting screw) A screw threaded into the rear dropouts to control the alignment of the rear axle. Adjustment insures proper positioning of the rear wheel.

allen wrench A six-sided, often L-shaped wrench that fits into the recessed head of allen bolts. Sometimes called hex key or hex wrench.

alloy A mixture of two or more metals. In bicycle parts, the alloy is typically duralumin.

all-rounder A bike with conventional, old-style handlebars that rake back and don't curve under.

alpine gears Very low gears designed for mountain cycling. Gear ratios typically have lows in the low twenties to low thirties.

amino acids A group of organic nitrogen compounds found in protein and necessary for metabolism; called the building blocks of life. Of the twenty amino acids, eleven are called "essential," meaning that they are not produced by the body. They are obtained through foods such as meat, cheese, and soy.

anabolic steroid Any of a group of synthetic drugs that stimulate protein-building functions in the body. Steroids are used by athletes to build muscular strength, power, and size exceeding the range of a natural training program. Illegal in cycling.

anaerobic Exercise at an intensity level that exceeds the ability of the body to dispose of the lactic acid produced by the muscles. As a result, this exercise can only be sustained for a short time.

anaerobic threshold The point in an exercise at which further increase in effort will cause more lactic acid to accumulate than can be readily eliminated. Past this point, the body is working so hard that it is unable to supply enough oxygen for the muscle cells to work efficiently.

ankling A pedal motion that utilizes a maximum number of muscles in the foot, ankle, and leg, resulting in increased efficiency and power. By dropping and raising the heels, the rider applies constant pedal pressure throughout the full 360-degree revolution of the cranks (unlike the 180-degree, up-and-down motion favored by novices).

ANSI American National Standards Institute, one of two organizations responsible for testing and certifying cycling equipment and helmets. The other is SNELL.

apron The optional flat surface just inside and below the banked racing part of the track. This area can be used as a running track.

ATB All-terrain bicycle, also known as a fat-tire bike. The preferred term now is mountain bike.

atmosphere A measure of air pressure. One atmosphere (14.69 lbs. per sq. in.) is the normal air pressure at sea level.

ATP Adenosine triphosphate, a chemical compound produced in the transformation of food to muscular energy. Food is broken down into ATP,

which is then stored in muscle cells until needed.

attack To accelerate suddenly, pulling away from another rider or group of riders.

Australian pursuit A track event in which three or more riders start at the same time evenly spaced around the track. Riders who are caught are removed from the race, which continues until only one rider is left.

axle The bar, shaft, or pin around which something turns; wheel axle, pedal axle.

baffle A wall of fabric inside of a sleeping bag shell used to limit the shifting of the down fill.

balancing The act of maintaining the bike motionless on the track with the feet still in the pedals. Ironically, this technique is most often used by sprinters.

balloon tire Low-pressure, wide-tread tire found on many coaster-brake bikes.

banking The main surface of a track, the incline of which is expressed in degrees. The banking going into a turn is a little less steep than the banking coming out of a turn. The smaller the track, the steeper the banking needs to be.

bar-end shifter (fingertip shifter) A gear-shift lever located at the end of the handlebar.

bar plug A stopper used to close the end of a handlebar.

bead A wire—either fiberglass, steel, or nylon—on the inner edge of wired-on (clincher) tires that seats in the rim to hold the tire in place.

biathlon A two-sport event featuring

bicycling and running.

bicycle A vehicle having two wheels and no motor; more specifically, a lightweight, two-wheeled, nonmotorized, steerable machine propelled by its rider, who pedals the bicycle to make it move. The bicycle is said to be the most efficient means yet devised of converting human energy into propulsion. In its modern form, it dates to the nineteenth century. Today, it is used worldwide and is an important mode of transportation, playing a huge role in both commerce and sports. (See also touring bike, track bike).

bicycle-friendly Designed to accommodate bicycles and facilitate their use; especially, artificially constructed environments. More broadly, a nice place to cycle.

bike-a-thon An event usually held to raise money for a cause. Teams or individuals collect contributions based on the distance they ride.

bike-hiking A new, fast-growing sport in which the participant uses a mountain bike for "hiking," usually on dirt trails and fire roads.

bivouac sack A hooded sleeping bag cover; also known as a bivvy sack.

block (cluster) A freewheel.

blocking The act of legally getting in the way of riders in a pack so as to allow one's teammates in a breakaway a better chance to stay away.

blood doping Generally, a natural ergogenic aid that is illegal for most competition. Specifically, the act of increasing blood volume – and thus oxygen-carrying capacity – by drawing blood from an athlete well in advance of competition (blood that is replaced by the body's natural processes) and then returning the drawn blood to the athlete's system just before competition.

blow up To overexert and sap oneself of energy.

BMX Bicycle motocross. BMX racing is a sport for young riders on short dirt tracks using small, sturdy, single-speed bikes. These bikes are great for stunts, not so great for distance.

bonk, bonks, bonking, getting the bonks The feeling of total physical collapse that accompanies depletion of glycogen in the muscles. It is the point of "no quick return."

bottle cage A bracket for carrying a water bottle.

bottom bracket The short cylinder through which the pedal crank assembly fits. The seat tube, down tube, and chainstays are brazed on or welded to the bottom bracket.

bracket height The measurement from the ground to the center of the bottom bracket with the bicycle vertical.

brake block The rubber part of a rim brake that is pressed against the rim of the wheel; also sometimes, the combined brake pad and brake shoe.

brake block holder (brake shoe) The metal part of a rim brake that holds the brake pad in place.

brake boss A brazed-on fitting, usually on the forks, seatstays, or brake bridge, to which rim brakes are mounted.

brake bridge A short tube between the seatstays to which the rear brakes are attached.

brake hanger A metal bracket that hangs down from the top of the headset; also, a seatpost binder bolt to hold the brake casing of centerpull and cantilever brakes.

brake lever A squeeze control on the handlebars for activating the brakes.

brake pad The rubber part of a rim brake that is pressed against the rim of the wheel.

brake shoe (brake block holder) The metal part of the brake that holds the brake pad in place.

break, breakaway The act of escaping the main pack in a race; also, one or more riders who have escaped the main pack.

breathability A fabric's capacity to allow water vapor to pass through it.

bridge, bridge a gap To catch a rider or group that has opened a lead.

bunch The main group of riders, also known as the pack, field, and peloton.

butted spoke A spoke that is thicker at one or both ends.

butted tubing A type of tubing in which the thickness of the walls increases at the end – to provide strength at the points of intersection – though the outer diameter remains the same. Double-butted tubing is thicker at both ends. Butted tubing is found in high-quality bike frames.

cable The wound or braided wire that regulates the movement of the derailleurs and brakes.

cable guide A clamped or brazed fitting on the frame that holds the casing and guides the brake and derailleur wires.

cadence The rate of pedaling, measured in revolutions per minute (RPM).

cage The portion of the derailleur through which the chain passes.

caliper brake A rim brake with opposing-arm construction. Both side-pulls and centerpulls are caliper brakes.

calorie Technically, the amount of heat needed to raise one kilogram of water one degree centigrade; practically, a measure of energy – either how much a certain food provides or how much the body burns when exercising. For example, one apple equals approximately one hundred calories equals approximately one mile of running.

cantilever brake The type of brake found on mountain bikes and some touring bikes. It consists of rim brakes mounted on the fork and seatstays that pivot independently, but in unison, via a yoke (transverse) cable.

carbohydrates The sugars and starches in food that provide a valuable source of muscle energy. In their most healthful state, carbohydrates are found in fruits, grains, potatoes, beans, bread, and pasta. "Carbs" are stored as glycogen in the liver. In contemporary athletic circles, carbohydrates are "in"; fat and protein are "out."

carbo loading A complicated dietary technique developed by Swedish scientists in the 1970s. Over a period of about a week, a cyclist depletes the body's glycogen stores, limits intake of carbohydrates, then, three days before competition, loads up on carbohydrates. The technique has been shown to increase muscle energy but not without a price. The process puts stress on the body and can cause excess water retention in the muscles.

cardiovascular Pertaining to the heart, lungs, and circulatory system.

carrier A bicycle-mounted rack for

carrying luggage; also, a car-mounted rack for carrying bicycles.

casing The outer covering or housing through which the brake and derailleur cables pass; also, the outer covering of a tire (in contrast to the tube).

centerpull A type of caliper brake in which the two arms pivot from two different points.

CAT I, II, III, IV The racing categories designated by the U.S. Cycling Federation. They are based on a rider's ability and/or experience, with CAT I having the most ability and CAT IV the least.

century A one-hundred-mile (one-hundred-sixty-kilometer) bicycle ride. The term is also used in shorter rides of twenty-five miles (quarter century), fifty miles (half century), and one hundred kilometers (metric century). Most recreational bicycle clubs sponsor at least one century a year. September is National Century Month, sponsored by the League of American Wheelmen.

chain Articulated drive unit that transmits power from the chainwheel to the rear wheel.

chain angle, chain deflection The angle between the plane of the chainwheel and the line of the chain, seen when looking down on a bicycle. More chain angle means more friction. Therefore, when changing gears, the choice between moving the front or rear derailleur should be based on minimizing chain angle.

chainring (chainwheel) The toothed wheel or sprocket attached to the crankarm, over which the chain passes. Through the chain, it delivers power from the crank to the rear wheel.

Chainwheels can be single, double, or triple wheel. The number of wheels on the chainring times the number of gears on the freewheel determines the number of available gear ratios or speeds.

chain rivet One of the pins that hold the links together in a chain.

chain rivet extractor (chain tool) A tool used to remove the chain rivets so that the chain can be taken apart.

chainstays One of two tubes extending from the frame's bottom bracket to the rear dropouts. The rear wheel rides between two chainstays.

chain tool (chain rivet extractor) A tool used to remove the chain rivets so that the chain can be taken apart.

chainwheel (chainring) The toothed wheel or sprocket attached to the crankarm, over which the chain passes. Through the chain, it delivers power from the crank to the rear wheel. Chainwheels can be single, double, or triple wheel.

changer Derailleur.

chase The act of riding to catch a breakaway.

chasers Those riding to catch a breakaway.

chondromalacia A knee injury involving disintegration of cartilage due to improper tracking of the kneecap. It is aggravated by overuse. Symptoms include deep knee pain and a crunching sensation during bending. Chondromalacia patella is a roughening of the inner surface of the kneecap.

chrome-molybdenum A high-strength steel alloy used in the construction of quality bicycle frames.

chucker (jamming tool) In team racing, an object put in the left hip pocket to be grabbed by a partner so as to relay a rider into a race.

circuit A road course that is ridden at least twice to comprise a race.

class A division of U.S. Cycling Federation racers based on sex and age.

cleat Slotted, wedge-shaped fittings on the bottom of cycling shoes. Made of metal, leather, or plastic, they keep the shoe clamped to the pedal during riding.

clincher, clincher tire A conventional tire with a separate, detachable inner tube. Used in the vast majority of production bicycles, it mounts on a rim in the same way as an automobile tire.

cluster (block) A group of cogs fastened together and mounted on the rear wheel; also, a multispeed freewheel.

coaster brake Foot-activated, internal-hub rear brake.

coccyx The tailbone; the part of the anatomy that meets the bike seat, sometimes painfully.

cog A gear of a freewheel, usually one of five, six, or seven gears; also, the toothed wheel or sprocket that attaches to the rear wheel and over which the chain passes.

complete protein A protein food (such as meat, milk, eggs, or cheese) that contains all eleven essential amino acids.

component A part of a bicycle that is attached to the frame.

cone A threaded part usually found next to a bearing and used for adjusting.

cone nut A thin nut that is screwed onto the axle shaft to adjust and lock the wheel bearings.

cone wrench A thin, open-ended

wrench used to adjust the bearings on hubs.

corn A callus that often occurs between or on top of the toes.

cottered crank A crankset in which the crankarms are fastened to the axle via threaded cotter pins and nuts.

cotterless crank A crankset in which the crankarms are fastened to the axle via a bolt or nut instead of cotter pins.

cotter pin A wedge-shaped pin with a nut on one end to hold the crankarms on the bottom bracket axle of cottered cranks.

cramping Painful contraction of muscles due to the loss of potassium and other minerals during the excessive sweating of exercise.

crank The entire assembly that includes the crankarms, spindle, and chainwheel.

crankarm One of the arms extending from the spindle axle of the bottom bracket assembly to the pedals.

crank axle The axle that passes through the bottom bracket and holds the crankarms.

crank bolt In cotterless cranks, the bolt that holds the crankarms onto the axle.

crank extractor (crank tool) For cotterless cranks, a tool to remove crankarms from the axle.

crankset The group of components fitted to a bicycle's bottom bracket, consisting of one to three chainwheels, two crankarms, and the spindle. Sometimes called the chainset.

criterium A multilap bicycling event held on a short road course, generally one mile or less per lap. These short-to-medium races are fan favorites because they get to see the racers up close and often. The pace is fast and excitement is further increased with sprints for special lap prizes called primes.

criterium bicycle A racing bike used in criteriums that is particularly rigid and responsive.

cross The number of times a spoke crosses another spoke on the same side of the wheel.

cross three A spoke pattern in which each spoke passes over two and under a third spoke before being attached to the rim.

crown The lug where the fork blades and steering tube attach at the top of the fork.

cup The bearing race that curves around the outside of a ring of ball bearings to hold them in position.

cyclocross An off-road bicycling event involving obstacles, steps, and steep hills that force the riders to dismount and carry their bikes.

cyclometer (odometer) Bicycle gauge for measuring distance traveled and speed. Some models also measure cadence and changes in altitude.

cyclo-puter A bicycle-mounted electronic accessory used to measure distance, elapsed time, pace, and sometimes elevation.

dehydration A depletion of body fluids that can hinder the body's ability to regulate its own temperature. During exercise, one can become dehydrated if the fluids lost through perspiration are not replaced by drinking water.

depression insomnia A sleep disorder brought on by overtraining. It is characterized by ease in falling asleep followed by a period of wakefulness in the early morning hours.

derailleur The mechanism for shifting gears; French, meaning "to derail." By moving a lever, the rider can guide the chain off one sprocket and onto another, thus changing the gear ratio. There are both front and rear derailleur units.

derailleur cage The mechanism that holds the rear derailleur idler wheels.

derailleur hanger The part of the bicycle frame (or an attachment to the frame) from which the derailleur hangs.

diamond frame A bicycle frame with a high cross bar (top tube), so called because when viewed from the side it is shaped approximately like a diamond. Also called a "men's" frame.

dish, dishing, dishing a wheel The offset of the hub of the rear wheel to accommodate the width of the freewheel and still allow the wheel to run centered within the frame. The wider the freewheel, the more the rear wheel needs to be dished.

domestique A rider who sacrifices individual performance to work for the team leaders.

downstroke The act of pushing down on the pedal with the rider's foot.

down tube The frame member that runs from the steering head to the bottom bracket. It is one part of the main triangle of a bicycle frame.

drafting The act of riding in the slipstream (quiet air) of a rider ahead, which can dramatically cut wind resistance and reduce the effort needed to pedal a particular speed. Ideal distances for drafting vary, but generally the closer the better. Drafting is central to the strategy of winning in road and track races but is not usually allowed in ultramarathon racing or triathlons.

drive train The components involved in making a bicycle's rear wheel turn, namely, the crankset, chain, pedals, derailleur, and freewheel.

drop To fail to keep pace with a group of riders.

drop bars The curved, turned-down handlebars found on racing bikes, touring bikes, and the traditional ten-speed. These allow for riding in various hand and body positions, including a relatively aerodynamic body position when the rider is "down on the drops."

dropout One of the slots in the frame into which the wheel axles fit.

drops (hooks) On a road bicycle, the sections of the handlebars below the brake hoods that turn down and run nearly parallel to the ground.

dural, duralumin An alloy commonly used in bicycle parts.

dust cap A metal cup that fits into a hub shell to keep dirt and moisture out of hub bearings; also, a plastic or metal cover for a spindle in a pedal or cotterless crankset.

echelon A staggered line of riders, each positioned slightly downwind of the rider ahead in order to get the maximum draft protection from a sidewind.

ergogenic aid Any stimulant or artificial aid used to improve athletic performance. Just about all are illegal for competition. An exception is the caffeine in coffee.

ergometer A stationary, bicyclelike device with variable pedal resistance used as an indoor training aid and for physiological testing.

extension The distance from the center of the handlebar clamp to the center of the vertical part of the stem.

facility A capital improvement designed to accommodate bicycles, such as a bike path or lane, a bikeway, a shared roadway (when designed for such use), or bicycle parking.

fairing Anything designed to lower wind resistance when attached to a bike.

fartlek A Swedish word (meaning speed play) that refers to a type of interval training in which the rider alternates sprinting with relaxed riding. A clock is not used. Instead the rider sprints for a telephone pole, city-limit sign, sleeping dog, etc. The technique lacks structure in pace and intensity but can be a useful training aid for the disciplined rider.

fast-twitch muscle fiber Muscle fiber with two to three times the contraction speed of slow-twitch muscle fiber. A rider strong in fast-twitch muscle fiber is likely to be a strong sprinter.

feeding The act of passing food to riders during a road race, either from a moving vehicle or from the side of the road. Liquids are passed via water bottles; food, via cloth musette bags. In ultramarathon races, feeding occurs at the rider's request. Shorter road races usually have designated feed zones or times.

fender A mudguard.

ferrule A metal cap put around a slender shaft to strengthen it.

field The main group of riders. Also known as the bunch, pack, and peloton.

field sprint The last dash for the finish line by the main group of lead riders.

fill Sleeping bag insulation, usually either down or polyester.

fingertip shifter (bar-end shifter) Gearshift lever located at the end of the handlebars where it is "at your fingertips."

fit kit A kit that includes instructions and equipment to assure a proper bicycle fit.

fixed gear, fixed wheel A cog attached to a hub without a freewheel, making coasting impossible. The cog always turns as fast as the wheel, and when the rear wheel turns so does the chain and crank. Essentially, when the rider stops pedaling, the bicycle will stop moving. Fixed gear is the standard for single-gear bicycles used in track-racing events.

flange The part of the wheel hub shell to which spokes are attached; also, the piece of metal inside the teeth on a chainring.

force the pace To increase the speed of the race to test the competition.

fork The piece of the frame that fits inside the head tube and holds the front wheel. The front wheel rides between two forks. Also, the point where seatstays and chainstays join to hold the rear axle.

fork blade One of two curved, parallel tubes that hold the front wheel.

fork crown The small horizontal piece of metal that serves to attach the steering tube to the fork blades.

fork end dropout The slotted tip of a fork blade into which the front wheel axle fits.

fork rake The degree of bend put into the forks in the frame-building process. The fork rake, along with head tube angle, affects steering responsiveness and stability.

fork stem (steerer tube) Attached to the fork crown, it fits inside the head tube.

frame The main structural element of a bicycle, consisting of three main tubes (top, seat, and down), a head tube, a fork, seatstays, and chainstays.

frame geometry A property of the bicycle frame determined by its specific dimensions, including the tubing lengths and the angles at which the tubing is joined. Frame geometry largely determines a bike's handling qualities.

frameset The bicycle frame plus the bottom bracket and headset parts.

Fred Pejorative term used by cycling snobs to describe beginning riders or tourists.

freestyle A type of bicycling favored by young riders that involves cycling acrobatics on modified BMX-style bicycles.

freewheel The cluster of cogs (usually five, six, or seven) on the rear of the bicycle. The number of cogs times the number of wheels on the chain ring determines the number of available gear ratios or speeds. The freewheel has a ratchet mechanism that allows the wheel to spin forward even though the pedals and chain have stopped turning. This permits the rider to coast without pedaling.

full tuck An extremely crouched riding position used mainly to reduce wind resistance on descents.

G.A.B.R. The Great American Bike

Race, the original name for what is now known as the Race Across AMerica (RAAM).

gear hanger (derailleur hanger) The part of the bicycle frame (or attachment to the frame) from which the derailleur is hung.

gear range The difference between the high and low gear ratios.

gear ratio The mechanical advantage of a bicycle expressed as a number, with one number for each "speed" on a bicycle. To determine the gear ratio for any particular setting, multiply the diameter of the rear wheel by the number of teeth in the chainwheel being used, and then divide that number by the number of teeth in the freewheel cog being used. Low gear ratios (for climbing) combine small chainwheels with large freewheel cogs. High gear ratios (for speed) combine large chainwheels with small freewheel cogs.

general classification A rider's overall standing in a stage race (e.g., the Tour de France); also called g.c.

glucose The sugar that results when carbohydrates are converted to glycogen for storage. Because drinks made of glucose solutions require relatively little work to digest, they are commonly used by professional cyclists.

glycogen The glucoselike chemical that is the principal carbohydrate storage material in the body.

glycolysis The process of breaking down glucose into ATP.

gooseneck (handlebar stem) The component that fits into the steering tube and holds the handlebars in place.

Gore-Tex The trademark of a material for clothing or tents that allows

water vapor from the body to escape but will not allow liquid water droplets (rain) to enter. It has high breathability.

gorp A high-carbohydrate snack food made primarily from nuts and dried fruit.

hammer (jam) To ride hard.

handicap In road races, an event in which groups of riders start at different times, with the slower ones starting earlier. On a track, this is usually done by starting the riders on different lines rather than at different times.

handlebar(s) The lateral bar attached to the stem used to steer the bicycle.

handlebar stem (gooseneck) The component that fits into the steering tube and holds the handlebars in place (top part to handlebars; bottom part to top of fork).

handsling A handclasp that is a method of changing partners in a team race.

hang in To barely keep contact at the rear of a group of riders.

hang on To ride in the draft of the rider in front without taking a turn; to barely maintain contact with the back of the pack.

hard-shell helmet A cycling helmet usually constructed of a hard plastic shell with a compressed polystyrene or Styrofoam liner. Hard-shell helmets provide greater protection against puncture by sharp objects in the event of a crash and are more likely to pass both the SNELL and ANSI Z90.4 crash tests.

head The flat, hooked end of a spoke; also, what a rider can damage if he or she doesn't wear a helmet.

headset, headset bearings The

bearing mechanism (cups, cones, ball bearings, locknuts) responsible for holding the steering tube in place in the head tube. This allows the fork column to rotate inside the head tube and is responsible for the smooth turning of the steering mechanism.

head tube The vertical frame member to which the top and down tubes are attached and through which the steering tube passes. It is the shortest of the four tubes in the main triangle.

head tube angle The acute angle between the centerline of the top tube (extended in front of the head tube) and the centerline of the head tube. It usually measures between sixty-eight and seventy-five degrees. The head tube angle is important in determining a bike's steering characteristics.

helmet Protective head covering for bicycle riders. Helmets meeting the standards set by the American National Standards Institute (ANSI) or the Snell Memorial Foundation (SNELL) provide proven protection for bicyclists of all ages. Helmets are legally required in progressive states.

hemoglobin The coloring pigment of the red blood cells that contains iron. It enables the cells to carry oxygen from the lungs to the tissues of the body.

honking The act of standing with one's hands on the brake lever hoods while climbing.

hood The rubber covering for a brake lever on drop handlebars, which provides improved grip and comfort.

hook A collision in which two riders lock handlebars or wheels; also, to deliberately move one's back wheel into the front wheel of a pursuing rider.

hooks The curved, "dropped" sections of a set of turned-down handlebars.

hub The center portion of a wheel to which spokes attach and through which the axle runs. It consists of two sets of bearings, bearing cones, lockwashers, locknuts, and parts for attaching the wheel to the frame.

hub brake A type of brake – whether disc, drum, or coaster – that operates on the wheel hub rather than on the rim.

hypothermia A dangerous drop in body temperature. A cyclist is at greatest risk when continuously out in very cold weather, especially if wet and/or injured.

idler pulley The pulley in a rear derailleur that stays farthest away from the freewheel cogs and serves to keep tension on the chain.

incomplete protein The protein found in grains and vegetables, lacking one or more of the essential amino acids necessary for good health. Strict vegetarians sometimes have trouble obtaining all eleven essential amino acids and must rely on dietary supplements.

index shifting A precise method of shifting gears in which moving the shift lever for the rear derailleur is accompanied by an audible click that can also be felt. This results in the precise movement of the chain to the next larger or smaller freewheel cog.

intervals A training method used in bicycling and other sports that alternates short periods of near maximum effort with rest periods of minimum effort.

invitational ride A recreational cycling event – often a century ride or a multiday tour – promoted by a club, business, or organization that invites other riders to participate.

italian pursuit A race event in which two teams of four or more riders start on opposite sides of the track. Each rider drops out after sprinting a lap. The race ends with single riders from each team, and the winning team is the one whose rider crosses the team's finish line first.

jam (hammer) To ride hard.

jamming tool (chucker) In team racing, an object put in the left hip pocket to be grasped by a partner so as to throw or relay the rider into the race.

JMO John Marino Open; the qualifying race for the three-thousand-mile Race Across AMerica. It is named for the founder of ultramarathon racing, John Marino.

jockey pulley (jockey sprocket, jockey wheel) The top wheel or "roller" in the rear derailleur that derails the chain from one rear sprocket to another.

jump To rise out of the saddle and accelerate. Also called the kick, it is a sudden burst of speed that constitutes the change of velocity for the sprint.

kickstand A prop for holding a bicycle in an upright position while it is parked. Most quality bicycles have eliminated the kickstand to save weight.

kilocalorie One thousand calories.

kilometer One thousand meters; also, a time-trial event that covers that distance on the track.

knobby tire The heavy-duty tire used on off-road bikes, so called because of the large rubber knobs that

provide traction in muddy terrain.

lactic acid A byproduct of anaerobic exercise that accumulates in the muscles, causing pain and fatigue.

ladies' frame A type of frame in which the top tube is replaced by a second down tube to make mounting and dismounting in a skirt easier. This is not to be confused with a women's bike, a standard diamond-framed bike proportioned to fit a woman's body.

lay-back The amount that the seat is positioned behind the center of the cranks.

leadout A race tactic in which a rider accelerates to maximum speed so that a teammate can draft and then sprint past to the finish.

left-hand threads Threads on a screw or bolt that need to be turned clockwise to loosen, which runs counter to the norm.

limit rider Any of the cyclists who have the shortest distance to ride in a handicap event.

loaded tourer A bicycle whose structure and geometry allow the rider to carry forty to fifty pounds of gear; also, a rider carrying such gear, whether or not he or she has been drinking.

loft A sleeping bag's thickness or height when it is fully fluffed and lying flat.

LSD Long, steady distance; a training technique calling for continuous rides of at least two hours at a steady aerobic rate, usually at about 75 percent of maximum heart rate.

lug An external metal sleeve into which the frame tubes are fitted, making the bicycle frame into a single unit.

madison A team event on the track

in which riders relay their partners into the race (via a chucker) and take turns being in contention.

main triangle (front triangle) The section of the bike frame composed of the head tube, the seat tube, the down tube, and the top tube. (Because the top tube and down tube join the head tube in slightly different places, this triangle is actually a quadrangle.)

manganese-molybdenum A high-strength steel alloy used in the construction of quality bicycle frames.

mass start The beginning of a race in which the competitors leave the starting line at the same time, as in events such as road races and criteriums.

master link A single link on some bicycle chains that can be opened without a rivet tool, allowing the chain to be removed easily.

match sprint A track event involving two to four riders who start at once. The winner is the one who crosses the finish line first. Time is taken on the last two hundred meters but is not used for any judging purposes.

maximal oxygen consumption (VO$_2$ Max) A measurement of the maximum amount of oxygen a person can transfer from the lungs to the cardiovascular system in one minute. Though generally predetermined by heredity, improvements can be made by engaging in a serious exercise program. It is a strong indicator of potential performance in aerobic sports.

metric century A hundred-kilometer (sixty-two-mile) ride.

metric wrenches Wrenches to be used with metric nuts and bolts — that is, those measured in millimeters (mm).

microadjust seatpost A mechanism — usually attached to the seatpost — that allows the tilt of the saddle to be adjusted in tiny increments.

miniclips Toe clips that only partially cover the toe and are used without straps.

minuteman In a time trial, the rider who is one place ahead of another in the starting order, so called because in most time trials riders start at one-minute intervals.

miss-and-out A track event in which the last rider over the line on each lap — or certain number of laps — is eliminated from the race. It is also known as **devil-take-the-hindmost**.

mixte frame A frame that replaces the top tube with twin parallel tubes that run from the top of the head tube all the way back to the rear dropouts.

motorpace A team event in which a bicyclist races in the slipstream of a motorcyclist to achieve speeds in excess of fifty miles an hour. The cyclist uses a special bike with a small front wheel and a big gear; the motorcycle has a bar behind its rear wheel that rolls easily if the bicycle should happen to touch it.

mountain bike A bike characterized by upright handlebars, heavy-duty brakes, wide tires, and low gearing and used for both on-road and off-road biking, as well as bike hiking. Also called all-terrain bike, city bike, or fat-tire bike.

mudguard A fender.

mudguard stay A fender brace.

multispeed hub The multiple-speed gear mechanism located in the rear hub.

musette bag A cloth bag packed with

food used in feeding cyclists on long road races.

myoglobin The muscle's version of hemoglobin, myoglobin engages in oxygen transport and storage in muscle tissue.

National Bike Ride An annual, noncompetitive national event designed to encourage bike riders everywhere to ride their bikes.

nipple A small threaded piece of metal that fits through a wheel rim to receive the end of a spoke.

odometer (cyclometer) A bicycle gauge for measuring distance traveled.

off the back Having fallen behind the main pack, as in "The slow riders are now off the back."

orthotic A custom-made, hard-plastic support worn inside the shoes to compensate for arch defects and other biomechanical imbalances in the feet and legs.

out-and-back A course, usually used in time trials, that goes to a certain point, makes a 180-degree turn, and returns the same way.

overgear To use a gear that is too big for the cyclist's fitness level or for the particular terrain or wind conditions.

overtraining Any intense training to which the body cannot adapt and that results in physical and mental fatigue not easily overcome.

oxygen debt The quantity of oxygen a rider needs to consume during exercise to "pay back" the deficit incurred by the muscles during anaerobic work.

paceline A single-file line of riders in which each rider takes a turn leading (and therefore breaking the wind) before dropping back to the rear posi-

tion and riding in the others' draft until at the front again.

pacer (stayer) A rider with the ability to pedal at a relatively high speed for a long time.

pack The main group of riders. Also known as bunch, field, and peloton.

pannier (saddlebag) A bag for toting gear, used in pairs, that attaches to a rack and hangs alongside the front and/or rear wheel; literally, "bread basket."

pawl A pivoted arm that catches on the teeth of a ratchet mechanism so that the mechanism can spin in only one direction. On bicycles, pawls are found in the freewheel units.

peak A period of time when the mind and body are operating at maximum performance level. Some athletes have "peak seasons"; others peak moments; most are left with the plateaus.

pedal action The freedom and ease with which the pedals turn.

pedal wrench A long, thin wrench for removing pedals from crankarms.

peloton The main group of riders, also known as bunch, field, and pack; French, meaning "pack."

pick-up Changing partners in a team race.

pizza elbow The cuts and abrasions received when a tumbling rider meets the ground.

point race On both track and road, an event in which the winner is determined not by finishing first but by garnering the most points. Points are determined by placings in several primes during the race.

point-to-point A road race that is run from point A to point B and that covers the course only once.

pole The area on the track between the pole line and the sprinters' line.

pole line The innermost line of the track, around which it is measured. Starting from the lowest line nearest the infield, the markings are called the pole line, the sprinters' line, and the stayers' line.

porosity A fabric's capacity to allow air to pass through it.

presta valve A bicycle tube valve whose stem has a small nut on top. The nut must be loosened during inflation. The presta valve is held closed by air pressure, rather than by a spring as on the more traditional Schrader valve.

prime (pronounced "preem") A prize or award given to the leader on selected laps of a criterium or to the first rider to reach certain landmarks in a road race. Used to increase the excitement.

pro-am A competitive event in which professional and amateur cyclists compete in the same race.

pull To ride at the front of the pack, where there is no protection from wind resistance.

pull off To move over after riding lead to let another rider move to the front.

pull through To take a turn at the front of a paceline after the leader has pulled off.

pursuit A cycling race in which riders start on opposite sides of the track and try to catch each other.

pusher A rider who pedals in a large gear at a slower cadence, relying on the gearing for speed.

quadriceps The four large muscles on the front of the thigh, the strength of which go a long way in determining a cyclist's ability to pedal with power. Arguably the strongest muscles in the body (though Trivial Pursuit says the tongue muscle is strongest), they are often exceptionally well developed in cyclists. Since they attach to the patella tendon, the "quads" play an important role in recovery from knee injuries. Therapy often centers around quad-strengthening exercises.

quick-release A spring-loaded hand lever that releases a bike part, such as a wheel, with a flick of the finger rather than turning a nut.

quick-release brake A button or switch located on the brake lever, brake, or brake hanger that temporarily allows slack in the brake cable so the wheel can be removed without the tire binding on the brake pads.

quick-release skewer A thin rod running through the center of a wheel axle with a quick-release lever attached to one end. It allows for speedy removal of front or rear wheel without use of a tool.

RAAM The Race Across AMerica, the longest ultramarathon cycling event in the world. Started in 1982 as the Great American Bike Race, it is a three-thousand-or-so-mile race from the Pacific Ocean to the Atlantic Ocean. Besides being an amazing endurance event, it is an exercise in sleep deprivation. When Pete Penseyres set what was then the RAAM record in 1986 (8 days, 9 hours, 47 minutes), he averaged 22.1 hours per day on the bike.

race The groove or track in which ball bearings run.

randonneur handlebars Specially shaped handlebars developed in France for the needs of touring cyclists. They are flat on the top section, rising slightly and flaring outward near the hooks. The design allows the rider a more upright position; this is practical because touring speeds lack the bent-over-the-bars intensity of sprints and many road races.

rattrap A type of pedal with thin metal plates with serrated edges running parallel on both sides of the pedal spindle. The thin cage plates means that pedaling in, say, tennis shoes will cause pressure to be transmitted unevenly to the soles of a rider's feet. The result is tender spots on rides longer than five to ten miles.

reach The distance from the front to the back of the handlebar tops when viewing a bicycle from above.

rear dropout One of two rear axle holders, located near the confluence of the seatstays and chainstays.

rear triangle The frame triangle formed by the seatstays, seat tube, and chainstays.

recumbent A two-wheeled bicycle that allows the rider to pedal from a prone or reclining position. These bikes typically have long wheel bases and sit close to the ground.

repetition Each hard effort in an interval workout.

rim A circular band of aluminum alloy attached by spokes to a hub and upon which is mounted a tire and tube. It equals the wheel minus the hub and spokes.

rim brakes The type of brake in which pads press against the side of the wheel rim (e.g., caliper brake, cantilever brake).

rim strip Rubber, plastic, or cloth strip around the inside of a clincher rim to protect the tube from the spoke ends.

road bike The type of bike used for touring and road races. It has several gears and at least one handbrake.

road race The general term for all road events – including criteriums, stage races, time trials – but usually in reference to a race of twenty-five to a hundred miles over a large course.

road rash The cuts and abrasions received when a tumbling rider meets the ground.

roller racing Indoor events in which the rear wheel of the bike is placed on a stationary roller so that the bike can be pedaled without moving. A distance recorder is attached to rollers for the purposes of competition.

roller An indoor training device upon which the bicycle balances. It has rotating cylinders for the rear wheel, which allow the cyclist to ride in place. Besides training, it is used for racing and warming up before a race.

roll a tire To accidentally separate a tire from a rim. This usually happens when a tubular tire has been improperly glued to the rim and the rider puts the tire under pressure, as when turning a corner.

runner A dished section of a track between the apron and the banking.

saddle The seat; also, the metal piece that connects the brake cable to the transverse cable on a centerpull or cantilever brake.

saddlebag (pannier) A bag for toting gear, used in pairs, that attaches to a rack and hangs alongside the front and/ or rear wheel.

saddle time The time spent cycling.

sag wagon A support vehicle accompanying a rider, race, or tour to carry gear, provide mechanical and nutritional aid, and troubleshoot. Also called a "broom wagon" because such vehicles usually follow, or sweep, a race or tour.

sanctioned event A recreational or racing event conforming to the rules of the appropriate governing organization.

Schrader valve The most common bicycle tire valve, similar to the type found on automobile tires.

scratch The full distance in a handicap race.

scratch man Every rider in a handicap race who goes the full distance. They are said to have started "on scratch."

scratch race A racing event in which every rider goes the same distance (in contrast to a handicap event).

seat cluster A three-way lug into which is welded or brazed the top tube, seat tube, and seatstays.

seatpost, seat pillar A hollow cylinder that fits inside the seat tube to which the saddle is attached.

seatstay Either of two parallel frame tubes running from the top of the seat tube back to the rear axle.

seat tube The bicycle frame member that runs from the bottom bracket to just below the saddle. Into it fits the seat post. A bike's size is measured (in inches or centimeters) along the seat tube from the center of the bottom bracket to the center or top of the top tube. Sometimes called the center tube.

seat tube angle The acute angle measured between the seat tube and the top tube. Seat tube angle, to some degree, determines the fore-aft position of the rider in relation to the axle. It affects the rider's pedaling motion and weight distribution.

set In interval training, a specific number of repetitions of an exercise.

sew-up tire (tubular tire) A type of lightweight racing tire that has an inner tube sewn inside the casing. Sew-ups are glued to the rim.

shim A spacer to insure a better fit.

shin splints An all-purpose category describing pain in the lower leg, usually about coffee-table height.

side-by-side A bicycle built for two in which the riders sit next to each other instead of front and back.

sidepull A caliper brake having both arms pivoting from the same bolt.

silk A sew-up tire constructed with silk thread in the casing. The result is a very light, very expensive tire.

sitting in, sitting on a wheel The act of drafting, or staying tight behind a rider to take advantage of the slipstream, sometimes as a tactic to try to exhaust an opponent; also, a pejorative term to describe a teammate not taking his or her turn at the front.

six-day (short for six-day bicycle race) An indoor track race that was the rage in the nineteenth century. Run by teams of two or three riders, mostly in madison-style racing, it is to the track what a stage race is to the road.

skewer The tension rod extending through a quick-release hub.

sleigh riding (wheel sucking) The act of sitting in without doing any work at the front.

slick A tire with no tread, used in racing.

slingshot To sprint around a rider after taking advantage of his or her slipstream.

slipstream The area of least wind resistance, tight behind another rider. Unless sprinting for the finish line, it is the place to be.

slow-twitch muscle fiber Muscle fiber that contracts one-half to one-third as fast as fast-twitch muscle fiber. Cyclists strong in slow-twitch muscle fiber are likely to be better endurance riders than sprinters.

snap The ability to accelerate quickly.

SNELL One of two organizations responsible for testing and certifying cycling equipment and helmets. The other is ANSI.

soft-pedal To rotate the pedals without actually applying power.

soft-shell helmet Head protector without a hard plastic outer covering. Lighter than a hard-shell helmet, it provides less protection in a crash. [Always look for both SNELL and ANSI ratings on any helmet you buy.]

solo/unpaced An Ultra-Marathon Cycling Association category—single cyclist, conventional bicycle, no drafting—that applies to most ultramarathon events.

specificity A theory in athletic training that says athletes become proficient at the specific tasks they practice.

speed work Training that emphasizes sprinting; it includes fartleks, intervals, and motorpacing.

spider The star-shaped (with three or five arms) part of the crankset to which chainwheels are attached.

spin To pedal at high cadence.

spindle The shaft in the bottom bracket upon which bearings are mounted and to which the crankarms are attached; also refers to the axles themselves.

spinner A cyclist who pedals in a low gear with a high cadence.

spinning The act of high-RPM pedaling in low to medium gears. Spinning is primarily used on recovery rides after races and for developing fluidity on the bike.

spoke One of several wires used to maintain the hub at the center of a wheel rim. It also serves to transfer the load from the perimeter of the wheel to the hub and then to the frame.

sprint A short burst of speed by rider(s) vying for the finish line of a road race or a long track race; also, a competitive track event matching two to four riders over one thousand meters.

sprinters' hill A steep hill that is short enough to be climbed quickly, out of the saddle, without hindrance from muscular bulk.

sprinters' line A line on a track that is seventy centimeters to the outside of, and parallel to, the pole line. In the final two hundred meters of some races, once the lead rider moves inside the sprinters' line, he or she must stay inside that line for the remainder of the race.

sprint rim An English term for a rim to which a sew-up tire is glued.

sprocket A disc with teeth for driving a chain; also, a general term for cogs and chainwheels.

squirrel A nervous or unstable rider.

stage race A series of different types

of individual races – such as criteriums, point-to-point, circuit road races, and time trials – combined into one event that lasts several days. The winner is the rider with the lowest elapsed time for the entire event. It is possible for a cyclist to win the overall race without winning any of the individual stages – as Greg LeMond did in the 1990 Tour de France.

stayer (pacer) A rider with the ability to pedal at a relatively high speed for a long time.

stayer bike A bicycle specially designed for the motorpace event, with a small front wheel, special fork, and other novel features.

stayers' line On a track, the line farthest from the infield, circling the track about halfway up. It is used for motorpace events and team racing.

steerer tube (fork stem) The frame tube that forms the top of the fork, rotates inside the head tube, and attaches to the handlebar stem.

stem The aluminum alloy part that holds the handlebars; the bottom of it fits into the steerer tube.

stirrup cable (straddle cable, transverse cable, yoke cable) On centerpull brakes, the short cable, each end of which attaches to a brake arm and which is pulled up at the center to work the brakes.

straddle height The distance from the top of the top tube to the ground.

straight block A freewheel with cogs that increase in one-tooth increments, used primarily for racing.

straight-gauge tubing (plain-gauge tubing) Frame tubes that have uniform inside diameters throughout their entire lengths (in contrast to butted tubes).

streamlined A term used to describe bicycles designed with full fairings to minimize wind resistance.

string A line of riders at the front of the pack, often on the attack.

stuff bag A water-repellent or waterproof nylon bag with a drawstring, used for compact storage of sleeping bag, down jacket, etc.

supple muscles The loose, highly conditioned leg muscles that permit a rider to pedal at a high cadence with a smooth power.

support crew The staff of people who bring aid and comfort to a cyclist. Depending on the length and nature of a race, the crew may supply food, water, clothing, medical aid, moral support, and/or psychological counseling – anything short of physically helping the cyclist propel the bicycle.

support vehicle The motorcycle, car, van, truck, motor home – or combination thereof – that is staffed by the support crew. [In the 1986 RAAM, Elaine Mariolle had twelve people on her support crew in three vehicles.]

take a flier To ride away suddenly from the pack by oneself.

tandem The classic bicycle built for two (or, occasionally, more), one seated behind the other. The rider in front is the driver or captain; the rider in the rear is the stoker.

tandem sprint A track race over the number of laps closest to fifteen hundred meters for two riders on one bicycle.

team pursuit A track race in which two teams of four riders each start on opposite sides of the track. Each team covers four thousand meters; time is taken on the third rider.

team time trial A race held on highways in which two or more riders working together compete against the clock; usually fifty kilometers long for women's teams and one hundred kilometers long for men's teams.

tear strength A fabric's capacity to resist further tearing once it has been ripped.

tempo riding Fast-paced training.

tendinitis An inflammation of a tendon.

tension roller The lower of the two rear derailleur wheels, which keeps proper tension on the chain.

third hand A brake tool that compresses the brakes against the rims for easier adjustment.

thread count The number of threads in one inch of material. The higher the thread count, the lighter the fabric will be.

three-piece crank A bicycle crank system in which the crankarms can be detached from the crank axle.

throw the bike A racing technique in which a rider pushes the bike ahead of his or her body at the finish, hoping to edge another sprinting rider.

thumb-shifter A gear-shift lever located on top of the handlebars of mountain bikes and worked with the thumb.

time bonus In a stage race, the number of minutes/seconds subtracted from the rider's overall time as an award for winning a prime.

time trial (TT) A race in which the individuals or teams start at different times and race the clock over a fixed course. Drafting is not allowed.

tire booting A cloth or rubber piece glued inside the tire casing to repair a damaged tire.

tire iron A leverlike tool for removing clincher tires from their rims.

toe clip A flexible metal strip that attaches to the pedal and bends around the toe and over the top of the forefoot. Used with a toe strap, it secures a rider's foot to the pedal.

toe in A way of positioning the brake shoe so that the front of the pad strikes the rim first.

toe strap A leather or nylon strap that passes through the cage of the pedal and attaches to the toe clip. It works with the toe clip to secure a rider's foot and permits pulling up on the pedal as well as pushing down.

tops The portion of the handlebar between the stem and the brake levers.

top tube The horizontal frame tube that connects the top of the seat tube and the top of the head tube. Its length affects a rider's torso and arm position. On a ladies' frame the top tube is replaced by a second down tube; on a mixte frame, by twin lateral tubes.

tour A general term for a long recreational ride or vacation by bicycle.

touring bike A bicycle designed for comfort and easy handling. It has a drop-handlebar design with a wide-range derailleur.

track bike A fixed-gear bicycle with no brakes, derailleur, or shifting mechanism. It is built for speed. Because of the often extreme banking on tracks, track bikes have a higher-than-normal bottom bracket. In many large American cities, bicycle messengers use track bikes modified with a front brake.

track race Any event held on a track or a velodrome.

training effect The positive physiological changes that can be brought on by intense, continuous exercise. These include increased number and size of blood vessels, increased lung capacity, increased maximal oxygen consumption (VO₂ Max), reduction of body fat, improved muscle tone, increased blood volume, and lowered resting pulse.

transverse cable (cantilever cable, stirrup cable, straddle cable, yoke cable) On centerpull brakes, the short cable, each end of which attaches to a brake arm, that is pulled up at the center to work the brakes.

triathlon A three-sport event featuring swimming, bicycling, and running. The Ironman [Dave Scott's specialty] includes 2.4 miles of ocean swimming, followed by 112 miles of biking, finishing with a marathon of running.

tri-bars Handlebars that place the rider in a flattened, more aerodynamic position; named for triathletes for whom the bars were designed.

tricycle A three-wheeled cycle with two of the wheels in the rear. Although in the United States it is associated solely with children, Europe holds tricycle events in road racing and ultramarathon racing.

true To straighten or align a wheel in both radial and lateral directions by tightening and loosening spokes. The point of consummate straightness with minimal tension is called ground zero.

tubular tire (sew-up tire) A type of lightweight racing tire that has an inner tube stitched inside the casing. It requires a special type of rim, to which it is glued.

turkey An unskilled cyclist.

turnaround On an out-and-back course, the point at which the riders reverse themselves.

two-by-two method/formation A ride pattern commonly used for training in Europe, with pairs of riders forming a double line.

ultramarathon cycling Riding a bicycle for distances in excess of common human limits in the shortest time possible. The exact distances will vary. Besides RAAM, other major ultramarathon events include the Seattle to San Diego course, the Miami to Maine course, the Spenco 500, the British Land's End to John O'Groat course, the Bicycle Across Missouri, and the Paris–Brest–Paris race in France.

unship the chain To remove the chain.

upstroke The act of pulling up on the pedal, made possible by the toe clips and straps.

valve core On Schrader valves, the skinny, removable inner portion of the valve stem.

valve stem The part of the tube through which air is pumped.

velodrome A bicycle racing track with banked turns. The United States has nineteen permanent velodromes.

vital capacity A measurement of the total volume of air expelled after full inspiration. The subject blows into a machine that measures the amount of air intake, output, and residual. Vital capacity and VO₂ Max together indicate how much of the athlete's oxygen is being utilized and how much is residual.

vitamin Any one of several biochemical substances essential to good health and that help regulate metabolic processes. Contrary to popular belief, vitamins are not sources of energy, but rather they play a role in "energy transformation." Contemporary opinion is that athletic performance is not enhanced by megavitamin supplements; a well-balanced diet is enough.

VO_2 Max (maximal oxygen consumption) A measurement of the maximum amount of oxygen a person can transfer from the lungs to the cardiovascular system in one minute. Though generally predetermined by heredity, improvement can be made by engaging in a serious exercise program. It is a strong indicator of potential performance in aerobic sports.

wheelbase The distance on a bicycle from the center of the rear axle to the center of the front axle. The length of the wheelbase affects a bike's handling properties, especially its turning ability.

wheel sucking A pejorative term for drafting too much and refusing to take a turn at the front of the pack.

windchill The cooling of the body that results from wind passing over its surface – especially dramatic if the surface is wet. It is a more useful measurement of meteorological discomfort than is temperature alone.

wind drag (wind resistance) The force a cyclist encounters trying to propel his or her bike and body through wind. See *drafting*.

wind foil An object attached to the bike to lower wind resistance.

wind resistance (wind drag) The force a cyclist encounters trying to propel his or her bike and body through wind. See *drafting*.

wind up To accelerate toward top speed.

wired-on tire A tire with a wire-bead edge that fits inside a trough-shaped rim.

yoke cable (transverse cable, stirrup cable, straddle cable) On centerpull brakes, the short cable, each end of which attaches to a brake arm, that is pulled up at the center to work the brakes.

Z–90.4 The test used by ANSI to determine bicycle helmet safety.

Organizations

The National Association of Velocipedists, founded in England in 1869, is recognized as the world's first bicycle touring organization. Nine years later the Bicycle Touring Club of England was established; in 1879 women were admitted to membership.

In the United States, the League of American Wheelmen (LAW) was founded at Newport, Rhode Island, in 1880. Since then, cycling organizations with a variety of agendas have cropped up. The following is a wide sampling.

American Association of State Highway and Transportation Officials
444 N. Capitol St. NW, Suite 225
Washington, DC 20001
202-624-5800
Publishes the *Guide for the Development of New Bicycle Facilities* ($3.75 postage paid), with important information on planning and designing wide curb lanes, bicycle lanes, and off-road paths.

American Bicycle Association
Box 718
Chandler, AZ 85244
602-961-1903
FAX: 602-961-1842
Organizes BMX races.

American Youth Hostels, Inc. (AYH)
National Offices
Box 37613
Washington, DC 20013-7613
202-783-6161
Organizes bike tours, provides hostel accommodations, publishes directory.

Bicycle Federation of America (BFA)
1818 R St. NW
Washington, DC 20009
202-332-6986
FAX: 202-332-6989
A nonprofit corporation established in 1977 to promote the safe use of bicycles for all purposes. A clearinghouse for information on all aspects of bicycling. Works with government agencies to ensure proper facility design. Publishes a monthly newsletter and educational literature; organizes a biennial conference and conducts research on bicycling topics. Questions about who works in bicycling in your state or city? Contact the BFA.

Bicycle Forum
Box 1776
Missoula, MT 59807
406-721-1776
The advocacy and education arm of Bikecentennial. It promotes cycling via technical papers, safety literature, and a quarterly publication.

214

Bicycle Institute of America
1818 R St. NW
Washington, DC 20009
202-332-6986
FAX: 202-332-6989
An international association of bicycle businesses and interests working together for the expressed purpose of increasing participation in bicycling and getting "more people on bikes more often."

Bicycle Manufacturers Association of America
1055 Thomas Jefferson St. NW, Suite 316
Washington, DC 20007
202-333-4052
A trade association.

Bicycle Market Research Institute (BMRI)
1443 Beacon St., Suite 517
Boston, MA 02146
617-277-5660
FAX: 617-566-4937
An independent, for-profit research group, with 150 clients in twenty countries.

Bicycle Parking Foundation
Box 7342
Philadelphia, PA 19101
215-222-1253
A nonprofit foundation that designs and installs bicycle racks. Also offers workshops, promotional literature, and a quarterly newsletter.

Bicycle Path League of America (BPLA)
An organization chartered for the express purpose of promoting bicycle paths across America. Membership dues are $10.

Bicycle Ride Directors Association of America
12200 E. Washington Blvd., Suite 0
Whittier, CA 90606
213-945-6366
An association of public ride organizers.

Bicycle Wholesale Distributors Association (BWDA)
1900 Arch St.
Philadelphia, PA 19103
215-564-3484
A trade association.

Bikecentennial
Bicycle Travel Association
Box 8308
Missoula, MT 59807
406-721-1776
A membership organization that provides information on bicycle touring, conducts tours, maps long-distance routes, publishes a membership magazine (*BikeReport*), and supports advocacy efforts.

The Bike Farm
Rt. 1, Box 99
Cushing, WI 54006
715-648-5519
Publishes a catalog featuring numerous safety materials and devices and conducts seminars on ways to improve cycling in your community through the four E's: engineering, education, encouragement, and enforcement.

Canadian Bicycle Hall of Fame
Exposition Grounds
Canadian National Exposition
Toronto, Ontario
Canada

Canadian Cycling Association (CCA)
1600 James Naismith Dr.
Glouchester, Ontario K1B 5N4
Canada
613-748-5629
Governs amateur and professional racing in Canada. Offers information
on touring, safety, maps, and provincial
cycling associations.

Collegiate Cycling
Kathy Volski
11300 Regency Green Dr., No. 3108
Cypress, TX 77429
The USCF's liaison for information on
collegiate cycling in the U.S. Aids in
starting local cycling clubs.

**Concerned Off-Road Bicyclists
Association (CORBA)**
15236 Victory Blvd.
Box 149
Van Nuys, CA 91411
818-991-6626
Focuses on trail patrol and education
about mountain bike trail use.

Cycle America
Box 547
Capitola, CA 95010
408-476-7773
FAX: 408-476-0473
A clearinghouse for bicycling informa-
tion. This organization works closely
with the Bicycle Path League of
America toward the establishment of a
coast-to-coast bicycle path.

**Cycle Parts and Accessories
Association (CPAA)**
181 Salem Rd.
East Hills, NY 11577
516-484-7194
A trade association.

Effective Cycling League
726 Madrone
Sunnyvale, CA 94086
408-734-9426
Devotes itself to pursuing the goals
implicit in its motto: Cyclists fare best
when they act and are treated as drivers
of vehicles. It teaches cyclists how
to ride in traffic and persuades government and society to accept them as
serious drivers.

Green Pedalers
Box 31099
San Francisco, CA 94131
415-334-6908
An environmental bicycle organization.

**International Human-Powered
Vehicle Association (IHPVA)**
Box 51255
Indianapolis, IN 46251-0255
317-876-9478
Promotes human-powered vehicle
(HPV) development and sponsors HPV
rallies and races.

**International Mountain Bicycling
Association (IMBA)**
Rt. 2, Box 303
Bishop, CA 93514
619-387-2757
An advocacy organization concerned
with off-road access for cyclists and
with educating the public on trail use
by mountain bikes. Offers support and

advice for groups involved in land access issues. Publishes a newsletter, *Land Access Alert*.

International Randonneurs
Old Engine House No. 2
727 N. Salina St.
Syracuse, NY 13208
315-471-2105
Promotes long-distance bicycling with an emphasis on self-sufficiency. Sponsors events in which everyone who finishes within the prescribed time limit is a winner.

International Unicycling Federation (IUF)
16152 Kinloch
Redford, MI 48240
313-537-8175
A nonprofit organization founded in 1982 that helps to heighten awareness of unicycling. The IUF is striving to attain Olympic status for the sport of unicycling. It sponsors an annual World Unicycling Convention, which includes the unicycling championships for that year. Membership is $15 per year in the United States, Puerto Rico, and the Virgin Islands; $20 for the rest of the world. Members receive cards, newsletters, and a subscription to *Unicycling* magazine.

League of American Wheelmen
6707 Whitestone Rd., Suite 209
Baltimore, MD 21207
301-944-3399
A national organization of bicyclists established in 1880 to advocate for the access right of bicyclists to public roads. Sponsors annual rallies and publishes a member magazine (*Bicycle USA*) and an

annual almanac, both of which include an events calendar. Twenty-two thousand members in all fifty states and Canada.

National Association of Bicycle Commuters
2904 Westmoreland Dr.
Nashville, TN 37212
Advocates for bicycle commuting; publishes newsletter.

National Bicycle Dealers Association
129 Cabrillo St., Suite 201
Costa Mesa, CA 92627
714-722-6909
FAX: 714-722-6975
A trade group.

National Bicycle League (NBL)
211 Bradenton Ave., Suite 100
Box 729
Dublin, OH 43017
614-766-1625
A nonprofit membership organization that sanctions bicycle motocross races and rides in North America. Established in 1975 by George E. Esser, it has 20,000 members.

National Cycling Organizers Association
Box 1961
Nevada City, CA 95959
916-265-9444
A trade group.

National Off-Road Bicycle Association (NORBA)

c/o U.S. Cycling Federation
1750 East Boulder St.
Colorado Springs, CO 80909
719-578-4717
Plans off-road events and governs off-road racing in the United States.

Race Across AMerica (RAAM)

c/o Ultra-Marathon Cycling Association
4790 Irvine Blvd., No. 105–111
Irvine, CA 92720
714-544-1701
An ad-hoc organization dedicated to putting together the annual Race Across AMerica bike race.

Rails to Trails Conservancy

1400 16th St. NW
Washington, DC 20036
202-797-5400
A national membership organization dedicated to the conversion of abandoned rail lines to recreational bike paths.

Recumbent Bicycle Club of America

427 Amherst St., Suite 305
Nashua, NH 03063
Provides all you ever wanted to know about recumbent bikes.

Tandem Club of America

19 Lakeside Dr. NW
Medford, NJ 08055
An organization that keeps its members abreast of rides, rallies, races, and technical innovations in the tandems.
Fifteen hundred members. Publishes a bimonthly magazine, *Doubletalk*.

Triathlon Federation USA

Box 1010
Colorado Springs, CO 80901-1010
719-630-2255
The national governing body for triathlons.

Ultra-Marathon Cycling Association (UMCA)

4790 Irvine Blvd., No. 105–111
Irvine, CA 92720
714-836-7856 or 544-1701
Sanctions long-distance record attempts (for example, city-to-city, point-to-point, twenty-four-hour road and track). Organizes and provides information on the Race Across AMerica and other long-distance events. Fifteen hundred members; six newsletters per year.

Unicycling Society of America (USA)

20 Turn Ln.
Levittown, NY 11756
516-796-8762
An organization founded in 1973 to foster social and athletic interest in and promote the sport of unicycling among youth and adults and to disseminate information on all phases of the sport.

U.S. Association of Blind Athletes

33 N. Institute St.
Brown Hall, Suite 15
Colorado Springs, CO 80903
Or call Simon Rose at 719-687-3833
Provides information on tandem races with sight-impaired stokers.

U.S. Bicycle Polo Association

Box 565
FDR Station
New York, NY 10150
An affiliate of the U.S. Polo Association, organized in 1942. Through its chapters, it governs and regulates bicycle polo tournaments.

U.S. Bicycling Hall of Fame

34 E. Main St.
Box 8535
Somerville, NJ 08876
800-BICYCLE or 201-722-3620
FAX: 201-722-5411
Honors the great individual and organizational contributors to the sport of bicycling. Publishes a quarterly newsletter.

U.S. Cycling Federation (USCF)

1750 E. Boulder St., No. 4
Colorado Springs, CO 80909
719-578-4581
Governs amateur bicycle racing in the United States.

U.S. Environmental Protection Agency (EPA)

Ross Ruske, Bicycle Coordinator
Office of Air and Radiation, EN397F
401 M St. SW
Washington, DC 20460
202-382-2671
Supplies free bicycling information in several areas, for example (1) *Bicycling to Work*, a sixteen-minute video in which real bike commuters explain equipment, security, and how to find a route; (2) *How to Organize a Bike Day*, a brochure on how to put together a community bike event; (3) *Bicycling to Work Seminar Information*, a booklet outlining the necessary steps.

U.S. Professional Cycling Federation

Rt. 1, Box 1650
New Tripoli, PA 18066
215-298-3262
FAX: 215-298-3199
Governs professional racing in the United States.

Velo Promo

414½ Soquel Ave.
Santa Cruz, CA 95062
408-425-8688
Promotes USCF racing; provides support materials for club-promoted races.

Wandering Wheels

Box 207
Upland, IN 46989
317-998-7490
A no-dues, nonprofit Christian touring organization. International and domestic (including coast-to-coast) tours of varying degrees of difficulty.

The Wheelmen

c/o Michael Spillane
307 Mulberry Point Rd.
Guilford, CT 06437
A national membership organization dedicated to the preservation and restoration of antique (pre-1918) bicycles.

Women's Cycling Network

Box 73
Harvard, IL 60033
A membership organization offering seminars, workshops, rides, and a quarterly newsletter for women cyclists.

Women's Mountain Bike and Tea Society (WOMBATS)

Box 757
Fairfax, CA 94930
A membership organization founded by NORBA champion Jacquie Phelan in 1984 to perpetuate the philosophy that the essence of a good ride is good company and good food. Five hundred members. Publishes a quarterly newsletter (*WOMBAT News*).

Women's Sports Foundation

342 Madison Ave., Suite 728
New York, NY 10173
800-227-3988 (except NYC)
212-972-9170
FAX: 212-949-8024
A nonprofit educational organization established by Billy Jean King in 1974 to promote and enhance the sports experience of all girls and women. Provides educational services, opportunity, advocacy; also sponsors the Women's Sports Hall of Fame.

World Bicycle Polo Federation (WBPF)

Box 1039
Bailey, CO 80421
303-892-8801
An organization dedicated to bringing "polo to the people." WBPF sets up and sanctions tournaments and acts as a clearinghouse for bike polo information. Publishes a newsletter (*Chukkar Times*).

Worldwatch Institute

1776 Massachusetts Ave. NW
Washington, DC 20036
202-452-1999
A nonprofit research organization that recently published *The Bicycle: Vehicle for a Small Planet*, which describes the role of bicycles in the world today and discusses the possibilities for the future.

Bibliography

PERIODICALS

American BMXer
6501 W. Frye Rd.
Chandler, AZ 85226
602-961-1903
Bicycle motocross news.

Bicycle Business Journal
1904 Weneca St.
Fort Worth, TX 76102
817-870-0341
FAX: 817-332-1619
Trade publication for independent
bicycle dealers who service what they
sell. Circulation 10,000.

Bicycle Dealer Showcase
1700 E. Dyer Rd., Suite 250
Santa Ana, CA 92705
714-250-8060
800-854-3112
Provides dealers with practical product
and business information. Circulation
10,600.

Bicycle Forum
Box 8308
Missoula, MT 59807
406-721-1776
For activists, educators, and bicycle
program specialists.

Bicycle Guide
711 Boylston St.
Boston, MA 02116
617-236-1885
FAX: 617-267-1849
Published nine times a year (plus
annual buyer's guide), covering "the
world of high-performance cycling" –
racing, touring, and mountain biking.
Challenges readers to pursue their
personal best. Circulation 200,000.

The Bicycle Paper
Box 842
Seattle, WA 98111

Bicycles Today
211 Bradenton Ave., Suite 100
Box 729
Dublin, OH 43017
614-766-1625
FAX: 614-766-5302
Official monthly publication of the
National Bicycle League. Focuses on
bicycle motocross. Circulation 30,000.

Bicycle USA
6707 Whitestone Rd., Suite 209
Baltimore, MD 21207
301-944-3399
Association publication of the League of
American Wheelmen. Includes articles

about touring club activities, legislative successes, equipment, and other cycling topics.

Bicycling Magazine
33 E. Minor St.
Emmaus, PA 18098
215-967-3044
Published ten times a year, providing how-to information on cycling for adults with an emphasis on fitness, adventure, touring, mechanics, and racing. Circulation 266,000.

BikeReport
Bicycle Travel Association
Box 8308
Missoula, MT 59807
Bimonthly bicycle touring magazine for Bikecentennial members. Circulation 18,000.

BMX Action/Freestylin'
3882 Del Amo Blvd., No. 603
Torrance, CA 90503–2119
213-539-9213
Monthly magazine for BMX enthusiasts, with emphasis on equipment and competition. Includes tests of latest equipment, coverage of major races, tips and tricks, profiles of stars. Circulation 200,000.

BMX Plus
10600 Sepulveda Blvd.
Mission Hills, CA 91345
818-365-6831
FAX: 818-361-4512
All you ever wanted to know about BMX racing.

California Bicyclist (North)
490 Second St., Suite 304
San Francisco, CA 94107
415-546-7291
Covers all aspects of cycling in northern California.

California Bicyclist (South)
Box 25697
Los Angeles, CA 90025
213-478-7954
Covers all aspects of cycling in southern California.

College Cycling
Box 4083
Newport Beach, CA 92661
714-631-4106
Covers college bicycle racing.

Cycle World
1499 Monrovia Ave.
Newport Beach, CA 92663
714-720-5300
FAX: 714-631-2374
Published nine times annually for the consumer. Emphasizes stories and articles about equipment, apparel, and events. Circulation 350,000.

Cycling U.S.A.
1750 E. Boulder St.
Colorado Springs, CO 80909
303-578-4581
Monthly publication of the U.S. Cycling Federation. Communicates federation information to the membership and provides a commentary on American bicycle racing. Circulation 17,000 (all of whom are federation members.)

Fitness Cycling
7950 Deering Ave.
Canoga Park, CA 91304
818-887-0550
Bimonthly magazine "designed for recreational cyclists who don't necessarily think of themselves as cyclists."

Mountain and City Biking Magazine
7950 Deering Ave.
Canoga Park, CA 91304
818-887-0550
Monthly magazine for the fat-tire biker, the largest such bicycling magazine in the world.

Mountain Bike
33 E. Minor St.
Emmaus, PA 18098
215-967-5171
FAX: 215-967-3044
Published ten times a year, primarily for the consumer. Features profiles, adventure, equipment, competition, and environmental issues.

Mountain Bike Action
10600 Sepulveda Blvd.
Mission Hills, CA 91345
818-365-6831
FAX: 818-361-4512
Monthly publication for mountain bike enthusiasts.

Network News
Box 8194
Philadelphia, PA 19101
215-222-1253
Press clippings about bicycling around the world.

Northwest Cyclist
Box 9272
Seattle, WA 98109
206-286-8566
Covers cycling in Washington State.

Oregon Cycling
12200 N. Jantzen, Suite 300
Portland, OR 97217
503-283-1999
Covers all aspects of cycling in Oregon.

Pro Bike News
1818 R. St. NW
Washington, DC 20009
202-332-6986
Publication of the Bicycle Federation of America. Reports on new developments in the sport – products, races, legislation.

Rocky Mountain Sports & Fitness
1919 14th St., Suite 421
Boulder, CO 80302
303-440-5111
Covers cycling in Colorado.

Southwest Cycling
301 W. California, Suite 201
Glendale, CA 91203
818-247-9384
Covers cycling news in California, Arizona, and New Mexico.

Super BMX Freestyle
7950 Deering Ave.
Canoga Park, CA 91304
818-887-0550
FAX: 818-883-3019
Features and articles geared for the freestylers.

Super/Moto Cross
8300 Santa Monica Blvd.
Los Angeles, CA 90069
213-854-2222
FAX: 213-854-2865
Bimonthly publication geared to the motocross enthusiast. Includes stories and features about motocross racing, products, and people. Circulation 177,000.

Texas Bicyclist
3600 Jeanetta Dr., Suite 1604
Houston, TX 77063
713-782-1661
FAX: 713-782-7666
Monthly consumer-oriented publication focusing on the Texas bicycling experience. Circulation 50,000.

Triathlete
1415 3d St., No. 303
Santa Monica, CA 90401
213-394-1321
Publication for triathletes.

Velo News
1830 N. 55th St.
Boulder, CO 80301
303-440-0601
800-888-6087
FAX: 303-444-6788
Journal of competitive racing.

Winning/Bicycle Racing Illustrated
1127 Hamilton St.
Allentown, PA 18102
215-821-6864
FAX: 215-821-1321
Monthly publication for the consumer and bicycle racing aficionado. Provides comprehensive coverage of the highest level of bicycle racing in the United

States and Europe, with racer profiles, features, and previews of the world's major races.

Women's Sports & Fitness Magazine
1919 14th Street, Suite 421
Boulder, CO 80302
303-440-5111
Covers information pertinent to women and cycling.

BOOKS
Anybody's Bike Book
Tom Cuthbertson
Berkeley, CA: Ten Speed Press, 1984
Basic information about fixing your bike – and much more. Humorous prose and drawings. The classic repair manual.

Back Country Bikepacking
William Sanders
Harrisburg, PA: Stackpole Books, 1982
Complete guide to bikepacking by a knowledgeable veteran of the sport.

Bicycle Mechanics
Steve Snowling and Ken Evans
Champaign, IL: Leisure Press, 1989
Deals comprehensively with the care, preparation, and repair of the racing bicycle. Coauthored by top international team mechanic Steve Snowling.

Bicycle Technology
Jim Langley
Mill Valley, CA: Bicycle Books, 1990
Great source of technical information on today's bicycle. Superbly illustrated with seven hundred drawings and photographs.

Bicycling Fuel
Richard Rafoth, M.D.
Mill Valley, CA: Bicycle Books, 1989
Discusses nutrition theory and basic
physiology, including the unique diet
needs of competitive and touring
cyclists.

*Bicycling Magazine's Complete Guide to
Bicycle Maintenance and Repair*
Editors of *Bicycling* magazine
Emmaus, PA: Rodale Press, 1990
The usual impressive job by the editors
of *Bicycling* magazine: clear, elucidating
how-to book, with hundreds of black-
and-white photos.

*Bicycling Magazine's Complete Guide to
Riding and Racing Techniques*
Fred Matheny
Emmaus, PA: Rodale Press, 1989
Provides both the novice and the expert
the information needed to enjoy bicycling to the maximum. Well organized,
with plenty of black-and-white photos
and diagrams.

The Book of the Bicycle
Roger St. Pierre
London: Triune Books, 1973
Short volume with a little information
on just about every aspect of cycling.
The best part, though, is the 120 photos,
including some great historical shots.

The Complete Cycle Sport Guide
Peter Konopka
England: EP Publishing, 1982
Brief but informative book on riding
technique and training to race.

*The Complete Guide to Choosing a
Performance Bicycle*
John Lehrer
Philadelphia: Running Press, 1988
Everything from how to buy a bicycle
to bike maintenance, with a rich display
of color photographs.

Cycling, Endurance, and Speed
Michael Shermer
Chicago: Contemporary Books, 1987
Authored by a man who should know
about both speed and endurance.

Cycling for Women
Editors of *Bicycling* magazine
Emmaus, PA: Rodale Press, 1989
Little handbook that provides valuable
information on a wide range of subjects
of interest to women cyclists.

Cycling Is My Life
Tom Simpson
London: Stanley Paul, 1966
Autobiography of Tom Simpson, Brit-
ain's world champion cyclist who died
tragically in the 1967 Tour de France.

The Cyclist's Companion
John Howard
Brattleboro, VT: Stephen Green Press,
1984
Compendium of cycling information
that allowed Howard to set many speed
and endurance records.

Effective Cycling
John Forester
Cambridge: MIT Press, 1984
Most authoritative manual on how to
ride safely in traffic.

Endurance
Albert Gross
New York: Dodd, Mead, 1986
All about, yes, endurance.

The Fabulous World of Cycling
Eddy Merckx
Belgium: Andre Grisard, 1982
All about cycling by the man Greg
LeMond calls the greatest cyclist ever.

Glenn's New Complete Bicycle Manual
Harold Glenn and C. W. Coles
New York: Crown, 1987
The favorite word in bicycle books is
complete, but this one almost lives up to
its name. Detailed instructions come to
life with nearly one thousand photos.
Covers removing, disassembling, cleaning, inspecting, installing, and adjusting
components.

*Greg LeMond's Complete Book of
Bicycling*
Greg LeMond and Kent Gordis
New York: Putnam, 1987
The usual how-to information, as well
as a short bio of the Great One himself.

Hearts of Lions
Peter Nye
New York: W. W. Norton, 1988
The story of American bicycle racing.
Thoroughly researched if not always
brilliantly written; a significant contri-
bution to American sports history.
Also includes some great old photos.

John Marino's Bicycling Book
John Marino
Los Angeles: J. P. Tarcher, 1981
All about bicycling, from history to
techniques, by one of the founders of
the Race Across AMerica.

*LeMond: The Incredible Comeback of an
American Hero*
Samuel Abt
New York: Random House, 1990
Hastily done and rushed to print to beat
the Tour de France; not well written.
Does, however, contain heaps of fasci-
nating information about America's –
and Europe's – number-one bicyclist.

Living on Two Wheels
Dennis Coello
Berkeley, CA: Ross Books, 1983
Covers the process of buying a bike,
bike safety, and bike mechanics. Most
valuable as a source of information
and advice on commuting and touring.

*Major Taylor: The Extraordinary Career
of a Champion Bicycle Racer*
Andrew Ritchie
Mill Valley, CA: Bicycle Books, 1987
Biography of Marshall W. "Major" Taylor, the first black world champion in
any sport, who dominated sprint
cycling for a dozen years at the turn of
the century.

The Mountain Bike Book
Rob Van der Plas
Mill Valley, CA: Bicycle Books, 1989
(Revised)
Choosing, riding, and maintaining the
off-road bicycle. Detailed table of
contents; generous use of diagrams.

Mountain Bike Repair Handbook
Dennis Coello
New York: Lyons & Burford, 1990
Title says it all. Coello competent, as
always.

Multi-Fitness
John Howard, Albert Gross, and
Christian Paul
New York: Macmillan, 1985
Experience the joys of cross-training
without breaking a sweat.

Pedaling the Ends of the Earth
David Duncan
New York: Simon & Schuster, 1985
Four young men come of age in an
around-the-world bicycling adventure.

*The Physiology and Biomechanics
of Cycling*
Peter Cavanagh
New York: John Wiley & Sons, 1978
Title says it all.

Richard's Bicycle Book
Richard Ballantine
New York: Ballantine Books, 1982
Plenty of general information,
but mostly a maintenance book. Good
diagrams.

RISK!
Steve Boga
Berkeley, CA: North Atlantic Books,
1988
Profiles of ten world-class adventure
athletes by the author of *Cyclists*.
Includes cyclists John Howard and
Dave Scott but also a rock climber,
speed skier, whitewater canoeist, and
others.

A Rough Ride
Paul Kimmage
London: Stanley Paul, 1990
Insider's look at professional bicycle
racing in Europe. Cuts below the
surface, allowing us to see the illegal
and the unpleasant.

Science of Cycling
Edmund R. Burke
Champaign, IL: Human Kinetics, 1988
Practical information on the physiological, biomechanical, psychological, and
medical aspects of cycling. Topics such
as training principles, nutrition, equipment selections, pedaling mechanics,
and speed improvements – all of aid to
the competitive cyclist.

Seeing Myself Seeing the World
Sally Vantress
Capitola, CA: Cycle America, 1990
Story of the author's nineteen-month
bicycle journey around the world.

A Social History of the Bicycle
Robert A. Smith
New York: American Heritage Press,
1972
Detailed account of the history of the
bicycle.

The Sports Success Book
Karl M. Woods
Austin, TX: Copperfield Press, 1985
Cogent endeavor to answer the
question, What are the ingredients of
athletic success?

The Ten Speed Commandments
Mike Keefe
New York: Doubleday, 1987
Subtitled "An Irreverent Guide to the
Complete Sport of Cycling." Possibly the
funniest book written on the sport.
Includes fifty cartoons in the 132 pages.

Tour de France
Peter Clifford
London: Stanley Paul, 1963
Detailed history of the Tour de France
from its inception in 1903, including
results and analysis.

Touring on Two Wheels
Dennis Coello
New York: Nick Lyons Books, 1988
Bicycle traveler's handbook. Everything
you always wanted to know about
how to bicycle long distances.

The Tour of the Forest Bike Race
H. E. Thomson
Mill Valley, CA: Bicycle Books, 1990
Entertaining and informative for kids
and adults alike. Beautifully illustrated.

Visions of Cycling
Graham Watson
Boulder, CO: VeloNewsBooks, 1990
Unique view of life inside the European
pro peloton by a top bicycle racing
photographer.

Winning Bicycle Racing
Jack Simes
Chicago: Contemporary Books, 1976
Broad, sweeping look at every type of
road and track racing event.

The Woman Cyclist
Elaine Mariolle and Michael Shermer
Chicago: Contemporary Books, 1988
Definitive how-to book for female
cyclists. Includes interviews and
questions-and-answers on all phases
of the sport.